CONFESSIONS OF A CATASTROPHIST

CONFESSIONS
OF A CATASTROPHIST

CARLO GÉBLER

edited by
Hazel Orme

LAGAN PRESS

Published by
Lagan Press
A Verbal Group Company

Stable Lane & Mall Wall
Bishop Street Within
Derry-Londonderry
BT48 6PU

www.laganpress.co

The moral rights of the author have been asserted.

ISBN: 978 1 904652 37 3

Author: Gébler, Carlo
Title: Confessions of a Catastrophist
2015

This is for Dermot Bolger

Catastrophist, A person who regards historical or political events as progressively disastrous; a pessimist.

- Oxford English Dictionary

AUTHOR'S NOTE

I have changed some names and places but not events or dates. All errors are my own.

I would like to thank Jason Thompson for his good advice and careful winnowing.

Contents

Adolf

My grandfather, Adolf, was an Austro-Hungarian musician. He came to Dublin in 1910 and married a girl from Glasnevin.

In August 1914, when the Great War started, my grandmother was pregnant: it was my father she carried: Adolf, now an enemy alien, was interned almost immediately at Oldcastle Camp, County Meath: for this reason he missed the birth of his first son, my father, on 1 January 1915. Of his father's time in the POW camp my father told me very little: one of the few crumbs of family lore he threw me was that while in Oldcastle Adolf became a prolific butter blackmarketeer.

Post-Armistice, the Géblers relocated to Berlin. Another crumb from my father: as a child of six or seven he regularly stole tins of herring from a cannery and, taking the boiling cans to his family (the fish was steamed before sealing), burned his fingers.

Back in Ireland, in July 1921, the IRA and the British Army, who'd been at war with one another, agreed to a truce.

Negotiations between the Irish and the British followed, which concluded with the Anglo-Irish Treaty (6 December 1921) and the establishment of the Free State in the southern part of Ireland. (Northern Ireland had already been established in six of the nine counties comprising Ulster). At some point following these momentous political changes, the Géblers returned to Ireland, first to Dublin, later to Waterford where Adolf worked as an accompanist to silent films, later still they went to Wolverhampton in the English Midlands; and then finally they came back to Dublin again.

Adolf was unhappy throughout. No one appreciated him. No one recognised his talent. He grew bitter. He drank. His tongue was sharp, his manners harsh, and his judgements fierce and inflexible. He taught his several daughters how to play the piano and other instruments but my father, a dim Caliban in his opinion, Adolf spurned. He taught him nothing.

During the 1940s my father began to write and publish stories and articles in little Dublin magazines. Adolf believed the family could have only one artist – him. He tried to defenestrate my father's typewriter and they stopped speaking. They must have resumed relations later. I was born in 1954 and Adolf certainly visited my parents' house. As a man, he was forbidding. He was aloof. He made me slightly anxious, even fearful. I knew without having to be told that I must not annoy him with noisy extravagant play or cheek or anything childish. He had a thick German-sounding voice with a slight Dublin edge to it: his accent was heavy, syrupy and hypnotic.

In 1956 or '57, Adolf, falsely accused of murder (the victim his now dead first wife, his Irish wife), discovered that the Irish government intended to deport him to where he had come from, a new Communist state called Czechoslovakia.

Instead, he decamped in 1958 to California with his second wife, an Austrian, which saved him and my father the bother of talking again. He died in 1963 when I was nine.

Now we cut to 1991, to Belfast, to my office. I was thirty-seven. I have a visitor with a question: will I go in to HMP Maze (Long Kesh to the truculent Republicans) to teach creative writing? I'm not surprised. I've been waiting for this for years, though how or why I've no idea. I start teaching. I appear to have some facility; later I move to HMP Maghaberry, also a Category A prison, but for Ordinary Decent Criminals rather than paramilitaries.

Now the story jumps another nineteen years. It was 2010, December (I was fifty-six), and I was in Oldcastle library for an evening devoted to the First World War internment camp.

A local historian spoke first. Many revelations followed. I'll pick three.

One: the German and Austro-Hungarian internees had had different regimes. Only the Germans were permitted butter so the Austro-Hungarians had had to buy theirs on the black market.

Two: prisoners were allowed one fifteen-minute family visit per month.

Three: after the Armistice, the prisoners and their families were deported to Germany.

Next Ruth Fleischmann spoke. Her father Aloys, founder of the Cork Symphony Orchestra, was a boy when his father, also Aloys, an organist in Cork but German-born and therefore an enemy alien, was interned in Oldcastle. Separation from his father had had a deleterious effect on her father, she said. It had marked him for life.

Hearing this, I saw my father's truth: he wasn't even born when Adolf went away, and five or six when they reunited. No wonder they had never bonded.

But why hadn't I grasped this already? After all, though I was hearing new details, I'd always known Adolf had been interned; plus, over the years I'd taught in prisons, I'd heard innumerable stories of irreparable rupture between fathers and sons arising from the father's imprisonment. Perhaps I'd never seen it because it was so obvious.

Then I thought back to my Belfast office, and my sense when invited to teach that I'd been waiting all my life for the offer. This provoked a truly revolutionary thought.

Unconsciously I'd always known the damage Adolf's internment had done, and it had primed me for prison work. No wonder when the question came, 'Will you teach in jail?' I said, 'Of course.'

This work meant I'd be with prisoners who were fathers. By teaching them to write I might help them to maintain contact with their wounded sons. My teaching would be an act of restitution and my father would love me for it, and his love was one of the things I wanted most, even if he was dead and I was fifty-six.

The awful truth, you see, whether we like it or not, is that we never grow up – never.

Built by Books 1

Carl Gustav Jung, the Swiss mystic, psychotherapist and religious philosopher, said that humour is man's only divine gift because with humour a man can make tragedy into an occasion for laughter.

I agree. Humour *is* a divine gift – but it is not the only divine gift: there's a second, the imagination, a truly remarkable faculty that allows us to relive our pasts, or to picture events or places or people that we have never known, and in that way discover what it is to live as someone else.

My family – my mother Edna, my father Ernest, my younger brother Sasha, and myself, Karl (I didn't start using Carlo until I went to boarding school many years later) – emigrated from Dublin when I was four years old.

On 4 November 1958, without prior warning, without notification or consultation, a pantechnicon van came to the house in Dublin, the family's furniture was loaded into the back and that evening, at North Wall, Dublin Port, we boarded the ferry for Wales. We reached Holyhead in the early hours of 5 November. I remember descending the swaying gangplank, moving down the quay and onto the platform where the train to Euston waited, then getting into our compartment, with its dusty seats and sliding door onto the corridor that ran down the side of the carriage.

I am sure I slept as we steamed through Wales but I was awake by the time we got to England and I remember we went to the dining car. Exciting clouds of soot and steam billowed past the windows, and there was an intoxicating smell of burning coal. I remember the cook coming to our table and forking bacon straight from a blackened frying pan onto our plates (you wouldn't get that now: Health and Safety wouldn't have it) and then – this was the high point – being given by the waiter (not the cook) miniature jars of Tiptree jam and marmalade, with the black-and-white labels and the metal screw tops exactly like those on the full-sized jars. I kept those treasures for months.

Later that day, we got out at Euston and took a taxi all the way to Morden, a suburb at the end of the Northern Line, and entered our new house, a thirties semi on Cannon Hill Lane, SW20. By late afternoon I was standing in the suburban garden, listening to bangers exploding on Cannon Hill Common, the great muddy expanse of green that stretched in front of our new house. I had no idea what I was hearing.

In front of me, beyond our back fence, which was brown with creosote, I was aware of someone at work. I went down and looked over. It was a man. I'd say he was younger than I took him to be because in the 1950s everyone looked older than they were. He had hair combed back, probably held in place with Brylcreem, and a pointy face. He was lithe and quite small and he gave an impression of energy as he bustled around gathering wood.

'Hello,' he said, as I peered over the fence. He had what I'd come to know later as a South London working-class accent. 'It's Guy Fawkes. You excited?'

No, I wasn't. Guy Fawkes didn't exist in Ireland. The name meant nothing to me. I looked back at him, blank, saying nothing.

'We're having a bonfire tonight,' he added, 'and fireworks'.

On cue a rocket appeared in the grey London sky overhead, whooshed along for a bit and then exploded. Marvellous balls of green and red were scattered through the air, where they shone and scintillated for an instant, then vanished.

The man chuckled. 'Someone can't wait' he said.

If we did talk any more, and we might have, I can't remember, I can no longer see the sticky damp fence and Mr Winifred, for that was what our neighbour was called. What I see now in my mind's eye is something that happened a bit later.

I was looking back up the garden towards our new house as my brother, on his tricycle, pedalled along the concrete path, his thin bare legs (he was in shorts) moving like pistons. I stepped back to let him pass. At the same time I felt the tubes in my chest swelling so that their gauge shrank, then heard the wheeze that came out as I tried to breathe. I sucked very hard. The wheeze became a roar. I felt dizzy.

My brother passed. I heard the clatter of the chain and the rumble of his tricycle's solid rubber wheels. I put my hands on my knees and locked my arms. My 'chestiness' – asthma – was back. It usually came from house dust or blankets or horses (still common in Dublin) but that afternoon, though I didn't understand it then, it came from sadness.

Everything I had known was lost and I was in this new, unfamiliar world that, so far, did not seem congenial or comprehensible. It was one of my earliest experiences of pain produced by separation and loss, for which the only remedy was recollection, and for that I had to have an imagination. There was no other way to retrieve what was gone except to imagine it, and in the months following I brooded endlessly on our red brick house in Dublin, with its monkey puzzle tree, its slips of coloured glass in the windows on the staircase return and in the bedrooms, its blood-red carpets and its long garden with the unruly gooseberry bush around which I used to chase, chanting mantras and spells.

The next thing I remember about our arrival in London is this. I was asleep in the back bedroom of our new home. My mother woke me early. There was something we had to do and we were late. We dressed, had breakfast, then put on our coats and hats. She opened the front door and we hurried out into the dense fog blanket (it was actually smog) that covered South London.

My mother began to rush down the hill – our house was at the top. I had to trot to keep up with her. The pavement was slippery. The fog muffled the usual morning sounds of husbands calling goodbye, banging their front doors and whistling as they walked off to work, and water drops running off the oaks that lined the street and plopping onto the ground.

Just then, a car crawled by, its headlamps like twin suns. It vanished into the thick yellow and grey smog, and then the only sounds were our shoes on the slippery paving stones.

At the bottom we turned into Cherrywood Lane. My mother continued walking fast. Several minutes later we passed through a dripping gateway. I was breathless and I had a stitch.

Next thing, I was in a classroom. My mother was gone. There was a smell of wax floor polish and Plasticine. I saw little girls in dresses and little boys in shorts. Each child was scratching away with a bit of white chalk on a slate.

A woman teacher in a purple woollen skirt and a jersey gave me a slate and a piece of chalk. She told me to sit on the floor. Then she crouched beside me. She seemed nice. She tugged at the pearls around her neck. I noticed that my mother was gone but I didn't mind. The teacher wrote 'Karl Gébler' and the date. She showed me how to hold the chalk.

I began to copy what she had written. Then I stopped and put the chalk into my mouth. It was dusty and it sucked out all the spit.

'Right,' said the teacher, 'we're going to play shop.'

A girl called Wendy was chosen as shopkeeper. She put on a brown coat and stood behind the counter in the scaled-down shop. I bought plastic tinned peas, bread, cornflakes and butter.

I paid with a plastic threepenny bit.

Without warning, a boy hit another child. Then the assailant lay on the floor and began to scream while the victim whimpered. A man with bandy legs and a crooked nose appeared. This was Mr Woodall, the caretaker. He picked up the bad boy rather than the victim and carried him away to Nurse in the sickroom.

Later, a different boy vomited. He went to the sickroom too. Mr Woodall sprinkled sawdust and sand on the sick, then scooped it up with a wide flat shovel. Afterwards he mopped the floor, using hot water cloudy with disinfectant.

'Gather round, boys and girls,' said the teacher, 'and sit on the floor.'

We gathered and sat, far from the vomit spot, and she opened a book and began to read. Her English voice was clear and smooth. The book was called *The Borrowers* and concerned a family of tiny people, Homily, Pod and Arrietty. They lived in an old house behind the wainscoting. They were called Borrowers because they borrowed things from the big people, things like drawing pins, pencils and paper. As the teacher read, I saw the Borrowers inside my head, tiny figures lugging filched rubber bands and toast crusts, thread bobbins and teaspoons.

As soon as I got home, I ran into our dining room and scooted under the sideboard. At some point when I'd explored the house I had noticed that the wainscoting was loose under there.

'Hello,' I called, through the gap at the top.

My mother came and asked what I was doing.

I explained how the Borrowers were in there and I was calling to them to come out and play. They didn't but I don't remember being disappointed. I think I reasoned that they didn't emerge because I was so big and they were so small.

It was memories of Dublin and stories told from books that lived most vividly in my imagination when I was a very young child. There was *The Borrowers*. Others included A. A. Milne's *When We Were Very Young*, Tove Jansson's *Finn Family Moomintroll* and Sean O'Sullivan's Folktales of Ireland. The story of the Children of Lir also captivated me, especially the image of the bewitched children transformed into swans beating across the sky.

Initially, these texts were carried to me by the human voice, mostly my mother's (she read to my brother and me on most nights and had a beautiful reading voice), sometimes my teacher's, and always with the same effect. As the reading progressed, the actual world vanished, replaced by the made up world of the story, with its characters talking and doing as they did in the text. In conjunction with this, there was a feeling of pleasure that surpassed anything in my everyday experience. It was like being in a trance, and even if what I was told was sad, the fate of the Children of Lir, or a bit frightening, the terrifying Goblin's hat in *Finn Family Moomintroll*, I could cope in a way I couldn't with painful real experiences. Moving from Dublin to London had given me an asthma attack, which no story ever did.

That blissful, mesmerised, almost-asleep feeling lingered long after a story ended, and in the case of certain texts, *The Children of Lir* for instance, I only had to re-imagine the swan children wheeling around the sky above the dark waters of their lake for the rapture to return.

Michael Morpurgo, the Children's Laureate from 2003 to 2005, said he wanted readings of stories by teachers to be a compulsory part of the school curriculum. If I was God or even Taoiseach or Prime Minister, every primary school teacher would read a story every day because that is how we train the imagination: by making it picture things on the cinema screen inside our head.

The next event in my own imagination's development was that I learned to read and discovered that I didn't need to have someone read aloud to me to go into a trance: I could do it myself. By the time I was eight, most Wednesdays and Saturdays I'd go to Morden children's library (beside the adult library) with my two buff-coloured slips, pay a ha'penny, borrow two books, take them home and read them.

I read Biggles and Billy Bunter stories (we had some of these at home too) but mostly I read Enid Blyton novels. I was utterly smitten by the spiffing world of the Famous Five and the Secret Seven, with the idealised mother, shadowy more-or-less absent father, and endless adventures involving treasure, sleeping in the open on bracken mattresses, and frequent feasting on tinned peaches.

It couldn't last, and where my passion foundered was on the problem of realism. As a child, the pictures I created in my imagination were constructed from the line drawings in the books, their covers (very important) and material of my own invention. They were credible and sufficient. But, growing older, I came to see that the desperadoes (usually vaguely foreign) with whom the Five and the Seven tangled were false villains, so incapable and clownish that any child could outwit them.

The really dangerous people I met on the streets and on Cannon Hill Common – Teddy boys and greasers, hooligans and yobs – weren't in Blyton's books. One day it occurred to me that she made her villains as she made them precisely so that her young heroes and heroines could outwit them. Her outcomes were rigged (just like, as I discovered about the same time, wrestling matches were). Once I realised what Blyton was up to, her prose lost its lustre: it didn't spellbind any more. Though I couldn't have put it into words (that came much later) my imagination had outgrown what it had once feasted on. Like the rest of me, it had matured. Now for the magic to happen, it was with demanding materials that were more substantial and nourishing and credible.

My Cliff Richard Moment

'Go and get bread,' said my father.

'I must pee,' I said, taking two half-crowns from him.

I went to the lavatory, counted to twenty, flushed. Then I ran into my bedroom and retrieved the matchbox from under my mattress.

I left our house and began to trot down Cannon Hill Lane. In the matchbox was a sixpence I had found in the street and hidden for an occasion like this. Scampering along, I felt the coin jiggling.

I got to the bottom of hill.

'Oi! Speedy Gonzales!'

It was a Teddy boy. They were always sitting on the wall. I slowed down: running would only provoke them.

'You – cunty . . . What's the hurry?' he shouted.

I looked ahead: eye contact was fatal. I sucked in my cheeks to stop the blush. I knew I mustn't show fear. It would only encourage them.

I passed out of their sight. I felt tired. Fearfulness was exhausting. Then I remembered my secret mission and perked up.

A few more minutes and I came to the parade with its half-dozen shops. I went straight into the confectioner's. The radio on the shelf behind the counter was playing and the blonde salesgirl, her head cocked towards it, was singing along. It was a song about the young, the young ones, as the song put it, and wherever I went that summer, it seemed, that song was playing. The singer was Cliff Richard. I thought this an odd name for a man. For a start Richard was a first name, not a surname. As for Cliff, well, a cliff was a thing like a river or a hill, not a proper man's name.

I looked at the counter: at one end, Flying Saucers, Barratt's Sherbet Fountains, Cup-Tie Chews, Fairy Milk Drops, gobstoppers, Black Jacks, candy shrimps, aniseed balls, Razzle Dazzle chewing-gum balls (grey gum surrounded with a crust of candy), liquorice pipes with red speckles on the end for embers, and liquorice laces coiled around a small red sweet, these last known as David's Slings.

The rest of the counter was chocolate: Mars Bars, Cadbury's

Dairy Milks, Crunchies, Flakes and Fry's Chocolate Creams. Sixpence would buy a lot of sweets but they would take a long time to eat. My father would then wonder why I wasn't back with the bread. His suspicions aroused, he would smell my breath and inspect my tongue when I did get home, and that way he would discover what I had done. This was how he'd caught me out before. And then I would be in trouble for having broken the no-sweets-ever rule.

I'd get the old lecture: white sugar was the secret weapon of consumer capitalism. I'd have to scrub my teeth. I might even have to go on a 'special' to the dentist (I saw him every three months as it was).

The penalties, if I were caught, were appalling. I made my decision. It would have to be eaten now, in one go. I wouldn't be delayed so he wouldn't be suspicious and I'd get away with it.

'Fry's Turkish Delight,' I said. I took the coin out of the box and handed it to her and as I did I got a whiff of match head and sandpaper. The coin had taken these smells from the matchbox I'd stored it in.

The girl, still singing, took the money and gave me a bar.

I went out, and decided on one further precaution. I scuttled round the billboard at the end of the parade and onto Martin Way, a wide road lined with factories. Nobody would see me there.

I took the wrapper off the Fry's Turkish Delight. Cars and lorries flowed by. I nibbled off the chocolate, and then ate the jelly. It was thick and sticky, delicious. It reminded me of the paste that we used at school to stick leaves and twigs to our friezes, except that stuff smelt of almond and this smelt of sugar.

A Pickford's removals lorry passed. I tried to imagine what it would be like to sit in the cab and head away. Then I realised I had no idea where I might head towards. I was eight; I didn't know anything but the regime at home, and Morden and the Teddy boys.

I stopped watching the traffic and looked at the clouds instead. They were big and white. That was when I realised I was singing the same song I had heard the salesgirl with the blonde hair singing.

My Turkish Delight finished, I went back to the parade. I put the wrapper in the wire bin where wasps nosed among sweet papers and went into the bakery.

Walking home, ignored by the Teds this time, loaves wrapped in coarse tissue paper under my arms, I carefully wiped each tooth with my tongue, front and back. I rinsed my mouth out with saliva. Then I spat and spat until the saliva was clear.

By the time I reached our gate, the chocolate aftertaste was gone.

I tripped down our path and rang the bell. As I waited on the doorstep, the involuntary singing started again: Cliff Richard's song about the young ones had got hold of me and wouldn't let me go.

My father opened the door, heard the singing, scowled. 'Oh, God,' he said, 'another victim of consumer capitalism.' I ran to the kitchen, dumped the bread and ran on into the garden.

Made by Music 1

Rock Around the Clock, Bill Haley and the Comets

There was a tallboy in my father's study with a drop lid that flapped down to reveal a Ferguson radiogram system; the controls and the gramophone arm were Bakelite; the table on which the record turned, dull aluminium with a plum-coloured vermiculated rubber cover. My father's records were thick and black and he never played one without first giving it a loving clean.

For this he used a velvet cylinder filled with distilled water; when it was damp, any dust that was on the record attached itself to this cylinder, which left the disc looking as if it was shop-new and had been drawn from its sleeve for the first time ever. His musical diet was a strict mix of classical and folk, Gustav Mahler and Woody Guthrie, Sibelius and Pete Seeger. We did not go to church, and perhaps as a replacement for this missing spiritual dimension, we often came downstairs on Sunday morning to a heady blast of Beethoven's Ninth or some Delius.

Musically I was asleep; I didn't notice music. Then, one day, I was standing by the stove in the kitchen. I was watching a wisp of blue-black smoke squeezing from the chimney pipe and curling through the air. At the same time I was rubbing my nose because the anthracite we burned was making me itch as usual. That was when I heard it: the radio was on in the study and it was blasting out the fifties classic from Bill Haley and the Comets, 'Rock Around the Clock'.

My father was out. He wouldn't have tolerated this. We had a girl who looked after us called Sally – perhaps she had turned it on. She sometimes listened to Radio Éireann when she did the housework. Sally was Irish. Or perhaps it was my mother who'd put it on. But I didn't go through to find out. I couldn't. I was literally rooted to the spot, amazed by the power of what I was hearing. Even at the age I was I knew this was a moment I was never going to forget.

And I didn't. Years later, it still being with me, I bought *Rock Around The Clock*, the LP. I have it still. It has a brilliant cover of alarm clocks and other horological objects arranged on a garish yellow background. Musically, *Rock Around The Clock* is crude, if vigorous, yet it still does sterling service as an ersatz Proustian madeleine, a memory-recall device. Like all the records I remember from boyhood and adolescence, the key to longevity isn't just the memories it evokes: the albums have to be good in their own right or, at the very least, they must give pleasure.

The Powers

Each summer while we lived in Morden we were sent to east Clare, my younger brother and I, to my mother's people, who lived in an art-deco villa called Drewsboro House. Our London house smelt of anthracite dust and the sulphur our father sprayed on the grapes that grew under the back veranda. The Irish house smelt of Seville marmalade that my grandmother made, bicarbonate of soda from the bread she baked every day, and the Gold Flake cigarettes my grandfather smoked. That summer, the magic summer, we were seven and five.

In London, toy guns were forbidden. As were toy bazookas, which fired ping-pong balls, Airfix models of the Bismarck and HMS *Hood*, Roman centurion sword, scabbard and shield outfits, and Colt .45 cap guns. No commercially manufactured military toys of any sort were permitted. Even playing with a stick that happened, by chance, to have the handle/barrel configuration of a gun was forbidden.

The injunction against war toys came from my father. He didn't like them, he said, because they were shoddy, and they encouraged youthful identification with the military murder machine. Now I am a father myself, I think he just hated the noise and high jinks that went with those toys, but back then he banned them because of an analysis, inspired by Marx, that connected consumerism and imperialism. The child who played with war toys in Morden today was happy to go to Aden and slaughter Arabs tomorrow. So, in London, we lived in a largely war-toy-free zone.

In Ireland, on the contrary, it was Liberty Hall. We were free. We made spears and swords out of ash sticks. We made Webley revolvers and Winchester repeating rifles out of broom handles. We made pea-shooters from copper pipe. We made catapults with Ys of beech and strips of inner tube. But no matter how hard we tried, no matter how inventive we were, everything looked handmade. Which it was. And nothing had the finish or the gloss of a proper war toy from a shop. It was a terrible predicament. We were free to play war but lacked that vital ingredient: the shop-bought war toy.

In the circumstances the only remedy was magic. There was a fairy ring behind the farmhouse but because of its proximity we felt its powers were compromised. Happily, there was a second ring a little further off. It was a perfect circle of beech and oak trees with wild irises growing between them. Furthermore, no matter how bad the storm, the cattle never went in there.

Off we set. Tramping along, we were in the normal everyday world of grass and birdsong, ragwort and cattle dung. But once we slipped inside the ring, we were in a different world. It was incredibly dark – it took ages for our eyes to adjust to the sepulchral gloom. It was also very quiet, while at the same time familiar sounds, like the rasping bray of our donkey, appeared to be a lot further away than we knew was the case. We had noticed the same effect in churches. The ring also had a unique smell, a chalky, musty odour, heady like the incense we sniffed at Sunday Mass.

But its most important feature, undoubtedly, was the lichen-covered stones in the middle. This was the altar. Had to be. Here, one day, we placed our offerings: a penny, a headless toy soldier, a broken set of rosary beads, a lady's finger biscuit and an old light bulb from the milking parlour. Then we knelt on the brown carpet of beech nuts and, until our bare knees could stand it no longer, we begged the powers to grant us one wish: a double-barrelled shotgun with a spring mechanism that fired cork plugs for each of us. (Presumably, inspired by the spirit of Ireland, we wanted to play at Flying Columns of IRA men against the Black and Tans.)

That night, lying in the bed I shared with my brother and staring up at the painting of the crucifixion scene hanging overhead, I saw the blood of Our Lord as blobs of sealing wax. This was no precocious painterly insight. Parcels and sealing wax were on my mind. If our wish was granted, it would come in a parcel.

The next day we went back to the ring. Our offerings were gone. Miracle of miracles. We knelt and prayed. We went back again the day after. On the night following our third visit, my brother woke me in the middle of the night. He had something to show me. I stared out into the velvety darkness. I blinked in disbelief. It couldn't be. It was. Three gold figures hovered outside: a blind fox (quite how I knew it was blind eludes me now), a bat and a fairy in a pointed hat. It was a propitious sign. I knew at once we needn't go back to the ring.

Some days later the post van pulled up and the postman fetched two long parcels out of the back. There were sealing wax blobs along the brown-paper seams. One was addressed to Master Karl, the other to Master Sasha Gébler. We carried the parcels into the kitchen and opened them. Inside were the double-barrelled shotguns we coveted. There was also a note from my mother. My grandmother read it out. My mother said she had bought the guns on impulse. She hoped we liked them. We were advised not to bring them home. Yes, I said, and shrugged. I knew what this letter meant. Grandmother had written to her. But the guns would have come even if she hadn't. The powers would have seen to it. I knew that.

I unpicked the string that attached the corks to the gun barrel ends and hurried outside to shoot a few Tans.

The Good and the Bad Brother

In November 1962, after she had published *The Country Girls* (attracting great acclaim as well as obloquy: the book was censored in Ireland) and *Girl with Green Eyes*, along with stories in the New Yorker, film scripts, and newspaper features, my father made my mother leave the mock-Tudor semi in Morden that was the marital home. I was eight, my brother, Sasha, six, and my father forty-eight.

Over the following months my father became highly irritable, very quarrelsome, and his sleep pattern went to pot. Now he wrote through the night, retired to bed around seven in the morning, got up about four in the afternoon and resumed work on his plays and novels at seven or eight in the evening.

One evening, he called us to the kitchen. He'd made one of his standard suppers, brown toast, mashed sardines and a sliced tomato. The plates were on the breakfast counter and there were three of them. He was eating with us, which usually he never did. He must be in a good mood, I decided.

My brother and I sat on either side of him. We ate. The bread was heavy and brown and came from the health-food shop in Wimbledon; it had the bitter taste of molasses. The sardines were an oily mix of flaking flesh and threads of soft bone.

When we had finished, my father slit open the buff sleeve his copy of *Time* magazine had arrived in and gave it to my brother to draw on. He subscribed to *Time* so he could savour the defeat of American imperialism across the world, and my brother always got the sleeve to draw on.

I decided to risk starting a conversation. 'Tell me about Adolf,' I said. I remembered our grandfather from his visits to the house in Dublin. He was a testy old man who smelt of cigar. He intrigued me.

'Ah, the old man,' my father said. That was what he always called his father. The old man.

He slipped from his stool and went into his study. He returned after a few moments with his *Oxford Atlas* (the 1951 edition) and a photograph. (I have both beside me now as I write).

He sat again and opened the atlas to a double spread showing the two Germanys (East and West) created in 1945, some of Poland and the western end of Czechoslovakia, the area known as Bohemia.

'There,' said my father, and he pointed at the town of Teplice-Sanov. It was just inside Czechoslovakia, a few miles south of the German border. He had ringed it in pencil. This, he explained, was where the Géblers were from. 'And these were the Géblers,' he continued. He set the photograph on the map, which he said had been taken in 1908 or 1909, when the region was still part of the Austro-Hungarian Empire. It was a black-and-white photograph, and it had been taken in a studio. Ten Géblers were arranged in two semicircles.

My father did a rundown: Wilhelm, my great-grandfather, a small-scale capitalist who owned a musical instruments factory;

Wilhelm's wife, Maria, a good bourgeois. She looked older and sadder than her husband. She wore a white blouse and a pendant around her neck. Behind Maria stood Adolf, good-looking and clean-shaven. Like his three brothers beside him, Adolf wore evening dress, but unlike them he also wore a brocade waistcoat.

My father now told Adolf's early story. He was a German speaker. He was a Czech nationalist. Following school he had gone to the Prague Conservatoire and specialised in the clarinet, though there was no wind instrument he couldn't pick up and play, just like that. He also mastered the piano, of course, as well as composition and orchestration. He had flair. He had talent. He was a virtuoso, a prodigy.

He came to Dublin before the First World War to play first clarinet in a production of *The Merry Widow* at the Gaiety Theatre. He fell into the clutches of the awful Margaret Rita, my father's mother. They married, and almost immediately there were children, first Adelaide, or Ada, who was mad, and then my father, who was not mad. After him there were four more children.

In the early 1920s, Adolf was a silent-cinema accompanist and bandmaster in Waterford. He was a good man, my father said, and wanted to help his family in Europe. His married brother, Hermann, was then living in Germany. There was hyperinflation there. The Nazis were on the rise. Adolf saved Hermann by getting him to Waterford.

Thereafter their lives went in different directions, one up, the other down.

Hermann had all the luck. He'd wisely left his wife in Frankfurt. (They would not be reunited until the 1950s). He had no children. He had no cares. He was free to concentrate on his music. He taught it at the Ursuline Convent in Waterford. He helped found the Waterford Music Society. He played with the Cork Symphony Orchestra. He was somebody in music and he was fêted.

Adolf, on the other hand, had no luck. After Waterford and then Dublin he went to Wolverhampton, in England. He opened a business selling sheet music for silent films. Then the talkies came, and his business collapsed. He ended up running a huckster's shop. The Depression came. He went bankrupt. In the 1930s, Adolf returned to Ireland. He played clarinet with the Radio Éireann Studio Players, later the Radio Éireann Orchestra. He also ran the Brass and Reed Band of the Irish Transport and General Workers' Union. He was a slave, who gave everything he had to give to Ireland: his talent, his energy, his musical knowledge and his enlightened political opinions. Tragically and typically, Ireland and the Irish, far from reciprocating, were punitive and cruel and vengeful.

For a start Adolf's Irish wife, Margaret Rita, never really cared for his music or his talent or his person, and eventually stopped conjugal relations. This obliged him to take a mistress, Marianna, and after Margaret Rita died and before he could marry Marianna, his Irish daughter, Louise, to punish him for his adultery, accused him of poisoning Margaret Rita.

By this time it was 1956, and Adolf had acquired a green passport with a harp on the front, but this now counted for nothing with the Irish Republic (as it had become). Believing they were harbouring a wife-killer, the Irish state actively began to consider deporting Adolf back to Communist Czechoslovakia.

Adolf was sixty-six years old. The Czech Communists would more than likely have arrested him and, at his age, given that he had smoked and drunk heavily all his life, he would have been unlikely to thrive.

As things turned out, however, Adolf wasn't deported. He hadn't poisoned Margaret Rita, and the case against him foundered. But Adolf's relationship with Ireland was finished. He had a sister in the US: she vouched for him and he emigrated to San Francisco with Marianna, his sometime mistress and now his second wife, and there he died.

Technically, he was killed by cancer of the stomach, but what really killed him, my father said, along with the booze and the cigars, was his failure to become a great and successful musician (that was Margaret Rita's doing: she'd hobbled him, as mean-spirited Philistine wives were wont to do) and the trauma of being accused of murder.

Yes, my father continued, his whole life, Adolf struggled to express himself musically and to succeed as a musician. He failed dismally on both counts, or so he came to believe in those last depressing American years when he eked out a living teaching the clarinet to lazy American children. Of course he had given up the ghost.

Meanwhile Hermann (and now my father was really in his storytelling stride), the less talented bad brother, triumphed. He became a civic figure in Waterford, an important personage, friendly with the nuns, going to Cork to play concerts. He was admired. He was respected. Townspeople doffed their hats to him in the street. But wasn't that always the way of the world? Didn't the good always fail and the bad always prosper?[1]

There was nothing here that I wouldn't hear again. This story of the two brothers and their different fates was part of my father's family mythology and, like Tantalus, eternally dipping his hand in the brook but never able to get water to his mouth to slake his thirst, he was compelled to tell and retell it.

My father died in 1994 when I was forty. A few years later I started writing a memoir about our relationship – *Father & I*. I wanted to include the story of Hermann and Adolf's different trajectories. It would be neat to include it, I thought, for symmetrical reasons. When my father had told the story of Adolf and Hermann to me as a child, he was really talking to

---

[1]And indeed, when Hermann died in 1982, there were eulogies in the local newspapers and a proper funeral. He also left goods and money. He certainly had prospered. Adolf, in comparison, left almost nothing when he died, was cremated unceremoniously and his ashes shipped back to my father who (somewhat uncharacteristically) wept on receiving them.

the Adolf who lived in his head. He was saying, 'I understand you, old man, like nobody else. I know your truth. Love me, please, love me . . .'

And, as an adult, writing my memoir, I was doing the same.

I was trying to show my father – the one who lived in my head– that I understood him.

Unfortunately you can't always get everything into your book, so the business of Hermann's ascent versus Adolf's decline was lost. Or so I thought. I should, however, have remembered that a book is like a message in a bottle. It goes out into the world. The bottle washes up on some foreign shore.

The cork is pulled, the message is read, and something comes back to you that you never expected.

In 2005, I was at my house in Enniskillen when the phone rang. The caller was a man named Jerome McCormick, and he was ringing from Cobh, the deep-water port in County Cork where ocean liners and passenger ships once docked on the way backwards and forwards across the Atlantic.

Jerome explained that he came from a musical family who were friends with another Cobh musical family, that of Mr and

Mrs Billy Mitchell. Both families were mixed up with the Waterford Music Society and had come across someone called Hermann, who was a Gébler, the brother of Adolf, about whom he had read so much in *Father & I*.

After Jerome's mother died in 1994, he'd found in her papers a letter written by Hermann to her. He read it to me now over the phone, including the credits above the body of the letter. The content of this letter was anodyne but as an artefact it was notable:

H. Gébler
43 Lower Newtown
Musical Director

Waterford
13.X.'44

Expert Instructor in Violin, Viola
and Orchestral Playing
Late Teacher in Frankfurt Conservatorium
Member of Frankfurt String Quartet
Member of Frankfurt Museum Orchestra
for 13 years
under the conductorship of Richard Strauss,
Mengelberg, Furtwängler, Ballin, Ochs
Carl Theatre Orchestra, Vienna

Dear Mrs Mitchell,

Many thanks for your kind letter, which I received on my arrival from Cork. I am very sorry that I had not the pleasure of seeing you at the Concert, and regret that I could not manage to call to see your brother. I do hope to meet you at the next Concert, which is on the 17th December. I am indeed sorry that your husband is not so well. I am glad to hear that the children are in good health and back at school. I was in the Ursuline Convent on Tuesday last & the nun informed me that Miss O'Shea is taking her first lesson on Monday. I thank you ever so much for your kindness and the trouble [you went to] in order to get me that pupil.

Kindest regards & all best wishes to yourself and your husband & all the family.

Kindest regards to family McCormack [*sic*].

I remain
Yours very sincerely
Hermann Gébler

Hermann's English, grammatical and fluent, was exceptional and so were his credits. If he had worked for Furtwängler and Richard Strauss (and why wouldn't he?) he was a much greater musician than Adolf.

But the letter was nothing to what came next. According to his mother, Jerome said, Hermann arrived in Cobh from Hamburg on a North German Lloyd vessel in late 1939 or early 1940. He was seeking sanctuary, but his papers weren't in order. The Irish determined to return him to Germany but Hermann 'would not or could not go back to Hitler' and threatened to jump overboard. Mr Billy Mitchell, who was the Cobh agent for the North German Lloyd line, had smuggled Hermann ashore.

Jerome also mentioned that his older brother, Malachi McCormick, a writer and publisher in New York, was gathering Hermann-related information and wanted to write a book about him. Emails between Malachi and myself followed, and yet another version of the Hermann saga took shape. There was far more to it than my father had known.

Hermann had arrived in Ireland on 17 October 1923, at the encouragement of Adolf. He had entered the Irish Free State as a tourist and found work as the bandmaster of the Coliseum Cinema Orchestra, Waterford. He was an alien, so the Coliseum's owner had to get permission from the Ministry for Industry and Commerce.

Over the following two years, Hermann received several extensions to his work permit. But in the autumn of 1925, it came to the attention of the Minister for Industry and Commerce, Mr McGilligan, that there were unemployed Irish musicians who were just as able to run the Coliseum Orchestra as the alien Hermann Gébler. Hermann was told his current work permit would not be extended, and he was required to leave the state.

Hermann consulted a local Waterford solicitor. This man

knew that the best way to make this problem go away was to get awkward questions asked in the Dáil.

On 12 November 1925, William Davin, Labour TD for Leix and Offaly, asked the Minister for Justice, Kevin O'Higgins, if he was aware that, though 'permission to continue residence in Saorstát Éireann has been refused to Hermann Gébler, of Waterford . . . Gébler's employers are anxious to retain his services and that the Executive Council and private employers are employing engineers, musicians and hairdressers of foreign nationalities'.

Kevin O'Higgins replied that as 'competent Irish violinists are unemployed' Hermann's right to remain would expire, and he would have to go.

Next to speak was another TD, a Mr Johnson, and he asked Mr McGilligan if he could categorically assure the Dáil that there were no instances where aliens were doing work that good Irish men could be doing.

Poor Mr McGilligan couldn't give this assurance and, worse, was forced to concede that in Limerick, where there was a dispute in the docks, German engineers were unloading German ships because Irish dockers wouldn't do the work. Seeing his opportunity, Mr Davin now weighed in: he asked Mr McGilligan if he was aware that a German national had recently been 'imported' into Ireland, 'as there was no Irishman available, to be chief of the Irish Army Bands.' Following this exchange, there was no more talk of sending Hermann home.

In 2008, I arranged to visit the library where the Waterford City archive is kept. I thought there might be stuff on Hermann. I drove to Waterford, checked in at my hotel and went to the library. The archivist was expecting me. Hermann Gébler, yes, she said, there was material on him. She disappeared and returned with a slim bundle.

Top of the pile was the programme for the Waterford Festival

Choral Society's production of the concert version of Bizet's *Carmen*, given at the Town Hall, Waterford, on Tuesday, 2 February 1937, at 8 p.m. The programme listed the viola player as Mr Hermann Gébler.

I was never convinced by the story of Hermann's dramatic arrival at the start of the war and Mr Mitchell smuggling him ashore, and now, seeing this programme, I became almost completely sure that it had never happened. He'd been in Ireland the whole time.

I continued leafing through the papers. There was material about the Waterford Music Club (it became a society later) and the concerts they gave at which Hermann performed, as well as various Hermann-related cuttings from local newspapers. Then I came on this from the *Irish Times* of Saturday, 16 February 1946:

NEW IRISH CITIZENS

Iris Oifigiúil announces that the following have been given certificates of naturalisation by the Minister for Justice: Aron Hersch Steinberg, 28 South Circular Road, Dublin; Hermann Gébler, 43 Lower Newtown, Waterford; Caesar Beckmann, Winton Lodge, Monkstown, Dublin; Lore Beckmann, Winton Lodge, Monkstown, Dublin . . .

There were seventeen names in all. In 1946, there were hundreds of thousands, if not millions, of displaced persons in Europe, but Ireland could take only that handful – incredible, considering the millions of Irish male and female emigrants who had enjoyed sanctuary around the world.

It was only the next morning, after my shame and outrage had receded, that I began to ponder what this cutting might imply about Hermann. Quite a lot, I decided.

After the end of the Second World War, the news that came out of Europe was dreadful. What had happened was far worse than anyone had imagined. Hermann, then a stateless person, would definitely, in case of further war, have wanted to regularise his status. Moreover, since Ireland had been neutral, which had ensured her population largely escaped the catastrophe, I imagine he'd have definitely wanted to become Irish.

However, Hermann had a problem. He could hardly write on his naturalisation application that he'd arrived in 1923, dodged deportation in 1925, and lived semi-legally in Ireland since then. He needed to arrive like a proper refugee at the war's start. Step forward Mr Billy Mitchell, with his story that he had spirited Hermann off the boat and into the Free State. Of course, shipping agents weren't supposed to smuggle illegal immigrants ashore, but now that the truth about the Nazis was out, who could blame him?

There was always the possibility that the story might be exposed as a fabrication. But if something is repeated sufficiently, it often becomes true. This applies to tales of virtue as much as to tales of vice, and this one, told over and over, became 'the truth' and the untidy detail that Hermann had actually arrived in 1923 was forgotten.

This, anyway, was what I thought (still think) had happened once I'd pondered the cutting from the *Irish Times*. I also decided my father had never been told it because when the story was fabricated in Cobh he was in London, where he'd moved the minute the war ended. He went to the British Museum Reading Room (where Karl Marx had written *Das Kapital*, he liked that) every working day and wrote *The Plymouth Adventure: the Voyage of the Mayflower* the novel that made him his fortune.

It was a shame he was away in the forties when the story of

Hermann's arrival from Germany was put together: I think he could have blended it nicely into the body of the Adolf and Hermann material he already had and used it to heighten the power of his tale of two men with very different trajectories.

In the account my father gave, Adolf laboured for music in Ireland. Moreover, he got himself properly mixed up with the natives of his new homeland. He married an Irish woman. He produced six Irish children. And – other than during the Wolverhampton years – he paid his Irish taxes. And how did the Irish state reward his generosity? By threatening him with deportation to Communist Czechoslovakia, a sentence of death.

Hermann's relationship with the Irish state, on the other hand, was a tale of unalloyed success albeit one based on deceit. First his wily lawyer had nixed the deportation order, and then his Irish friends had agreed a fake story so that he could get citizenship.

Oh, yes, my father would have worked all this, especially Hermann's faked arrival, into his narrative if he'd had it, and what a lovely ornament to his tale it would have been – the good brother nearly destroyed and the bad brother nourished by the perfidious Irish state.

And Adolf, the Adolf inside my father's head, hearing the story of Hermann's miraculous arrival at the start of the war, as sarcastically re-spun by my father, might even have been persuaded that his son Ernest did understand him and was worthy of his love after all.

Made by Music 2

Aftermath, The Rolling Stones

After her expulsion from the Morden house, my mother lived in Wimbledon; later she bought a house in Putney, in Deodar Road, named after the Australian tree famed for its fragrance.

First she bought number nine, a small terraced house that backed onto a factory and later she bought number eighty-seven, one of the road's bigger, three-storey houses, built for clerks in the 1860s and colonised by artists in the 1960s on account of the view: all the gardens on the north side of the street (as my mother's second house was) ran down to the Thames. The filthy, oily, roiling waters were literally at the bottom of the garden.

I liked Putney: unlike in Morden, I had freedom, pleasure and licence. I could do as I liked and, with pocket money, I could buy what I wanted.

One day, walking back from Putney high street, clutching an Airfix kit from which I could build a model of the *Tirpitz* or the ill-fated HMS *Hood* – it was early 1966 and I was eleven – I bumped into Malcolm, an older boy of whom I was somewhat in awe. His hair was long and shaggy, like Reg Presley of the Troggs (they had a huge hit at the time with 'Wild Thing') and he wore winkle-pickers. Malcolm was carrying a bag – Woolworth's? Golden Discs? I can't remember.

We went into his house. He lived on the other side of Deodar Road, in one of the houses with a garden that did not run down to the Thames. His mother was a typist. He produced an LP from the bag. This had cost many shillings, I gathered. I was impressed. The front of the record was purple and had a photograph of five men; they had long hair and were staring up into the lens of a camera in the same cheeky way that some of the boys would look at the women teachers at school. The Stones looked dodgy to me; appalling but also enthralling.

Silently and reverently, Malcolm eased out the white inner sleeve that was stamped with important advice: 'Take good care of your microgroove records . . . Use Emitex cleaning cloth to preserve your microgroove records. . .' then freed the record and wiggled it lovingly onto the spindle of his mother's Dansette portable gramophone.

Then he lifted the arm across, with the magnet that held the record tight, and clicked the mechanism. The record dropped and the guitar cha-cha-cha warbled from the speaker. The hairs on my neck really did stand up as Jagger launched into 'Mother's Little Helper'.

A defining moment, separating childhood from whatever it was that followed, though it was years before I understood this.

It was also years before I really appreciated the neck of Mick and the lads, starting their first original album (until *Aftermath* they'd only done covers) with a song that ridiculed Valium and other domestic drugs when they themselves were not exactly strangers to narcotics.

Built by Books 2

After Blyton, I found my way to Tolkien, *The Hobbit* and then *The Lord of the Rings*. I was captivated by the author's extraordinary make-believe yet believable world, with its hobbits and its elves, and the Dark Lord, Sauron, scouring Middle Earth for a magic ring. And yet, though Tolkien's books were better than Blyton's, less cardboard, more complex, certainly more intellectually and syntactically demanding, a pleasure to read and get lost in, I had a vague sense that I needed something else, a different kind of book though I was quite incapable of explaining to anyone what that kind of book might be.

One of our neighbours in Deodar Road (was the writer Nell Dunn, author of *Up the Junction*, a warm, funny account of working-class life, and a huge bestseller. Nell's father had an estate in Mallorca and, in the summer of 1966 we all went there, my mother, my brother, Nell, her children and others.

The house was an old Mallorcan farmhouse; the walls were whitewashed a mix of white and laundry blue. The paint was chalky, and if you touched the walls a chalky residue came away on your fingers. From the terrace one looked across parched terracotta fields to the sea and an island with a lighthouse and gun emplacements dating from the Second World War. We explored these and found girls' underwear and wine bottles. The Mallorcan young did their courting in those concrete bunkers.

I was nearly twelve now, diffident and shy, and I spent a lot of time in the library. It was on the first floor in a huge room overlooking the terrace. The shelves were heavy with the work of English writers from between the wars – Rosamond Lehmann, Evelyn Waugh, Peter Fleming, Robert Byron, and W. Somerset Maugham. There were also yards of Dostoevsky and Chekhov translated by Constance Garnett.

One afternoon, Nell found me there and put a book into my hands, *The Outsider* (its French title *L'Étranger*) by Albert Camus, with an introduction by the great English critic Cyril Connolly. The book opens with a remarkable first line, 'Mother died today. Or maybe yesterday.' I read this and was hooked. I carried the book down to the terrace, lay on a recliner and began to read. At this point the sun lit the mountains in the distance. When I finished, having read the novel and Connolly's introduction in one sitting (the novel wasn't very long), the sun had sunk below the horizon and the distant mountains were purple and shadowed.

It was a fantastic book. The language was thrillingly laconic, direct and snappy, just like in a hard-boiled American thriller but directed towards something utterly unique in the history of the hard-boiled: the decanting into the imagination of the reader, me, a picture of Algiers, with its trams, tenements and obdurate white settlers and, beyond Algiers, the Algerian landscape, sun-blasted and inhuman, rather like the Mallorcan landscape I had seen every time I had raised my eyes from my copy of *The Outsider*.

So, as a tool that generated pictures, atmospheres and sensations in my imagination, it was extremely effective, brilliant and also, because the North African world was exotic and unusual, it was intriguing and novel.

However, as I reflected afterwards, and I had Connolly's introduction to help me here, this was more than just a brilliantly told story. It was about the great lie at the heart of bourgeois society. The state sold itself as fair and just, whereas in fact, according to Camus, it was anything but. In the novel, the hero Meursault's ostensible crime, for which he's sentenced to death, is the murder of an Arab on a boiling Algiers beach. However, the actual reason he's convicted is because he fails to mourn his mother after her death – so threatening an act of social deviance that his French *colon* society has no alternative but to murder him judicially, using his killing of the Arab as the pretext.

But there was something else about the book that was even more important: it confirmed what I was just beginning to grasp about the world and the power of the state, and that was its ingenious technique.

At the age I was then, I'd already encountered George Bernard Shaw (my father idolised the playwright), whose stage works carried a strong ideological message. However, my encounter with Shaw, albeit cursory and superficial, had convinced me that telling a story while imparting a message was often inimical to pleasure. But I wasn't a complete dimwit. I knew ideas were important and had to be incorporated, and I realised from Camus that a great writer could tell a story *and* say something without putting the reader off, providing the work had two drawers, one with the narrative, the other with the message, and the reader was free to decide which to open. Grasping this (thanks to Connolly) was the equivalent of someone taking the back off a watch and showing me the mechanism. It was a real revelation.

Made by Music 3

Revolver, The Beatles

In 1967 when I was thirteen I was sent to Ibstock Place, a school run on the child-centred principles established by Friedrich Froebel, the liberal educationalist. It was mixed, and the girls wore lovely green seersucker frocks and lovely grey straw bonnets. I was becoming interested in sex.

Fanny Sturridge was a willowy Jewish girl with brown eyes and white teeth. She was in the year above but that didn't put me off: dog-like I followed her about every break and every afternoon when she was always to be found on the netball pitch.

She was school captain. She only spoke to me once and that was to tell me she was in love with Micky Dolenz, the vocalist in the Monkees. All the girls in the school were in love with someone from that damned group.

One day I noticed Fanny and some other girls gathered in a knot around the lockers. They were peering at a record decorated with four Beardsley-esque line drawings and discussing who they thought were the equivalents of these pen-and-ink drawings in the Monkees. Somebody called Ringo Starr, I gathered, was Peter Tork; Paul McCartney was Davy Jones; John Lennon was Micky Dolenz; and George Harrison was Mike Nesmith.

The bell rang and the girls vanished. I sneaked a look in the locker. The record was something called Revolver by the Beatles.

I formed a plan. I would buy my own copy and bring it to school; Fanny would see me carrying it around and this would prompt a conversation; thus would begin our courtship.

I bought the record but I don't remember if I took it to school; I certainly know I never talked to Fanny. But what did that matter? *Revolver*, from the first bar of 'Taxman' to the last bar of 'Tomorrow Never Knows', via 'Yellow Submarine' (mad, I thought, but brilliant) and 'Good Day Sunshine' (orgasmic, I thought, a word I could certainly find in the dictionary then but couldn't understand), was incomparably superior to anything by the Monkees. How could Fanny and the other girls even compare the Beatles with those fresh-faced preppies who had brought us 'Last Train to Clarksville' and 'Daydream Believer'?

Unsuccessful in love, I had become a budding rock snob. If you can't get the girl, it's the next best thing, or so I thought.

Fresh Cream, Cream

Later that year, I started at Holland Park comprehensive school. One lunchtime I sneaked down the alleyway at the side where skinheads lurked and dopeheads organised their one-pound deals – and made my way to a chipper in one of the streets off Holland Park Avenue.

Here I ran into Archimedes, a Greek-Cypriot and incredibly

stylish. He was wearing a red Victorian soldier's tunic (unlike the rest of us he managed to get away with wearing whatever he wanted at school) and carrying his books in an army-surplus cartridge bag on which he had scrawled in biro the names of his favourite bands. I noticed a new one – Cream.

'What d'ya make of them?' he asked.

Somehow, at thirteen years of age, I hadn't heard of them. Yes, I know, amazing. But I was smart. I kept my mouth shut: Irish peasant reticence was already an established pattern.

Without my knowing, I had passed a test I didn't know was a test. Archimedes invited me to his next party. Saturday night saw me in a street of crumbling stucco houses at the top end of Portobello Road. I had showered in anticipation of meeting a member of the opposite sex and my hair was still wet.

Approaching the Stefanidis residence I could smell marijuana; I could see red light leaking from the windows (all the light bulbs inside had obviously been changed); and I could hear 'I'm So Glad.'

And that's as far as I can remember. The film runs out at that point. Did I go in? Did I meet a girl? Did I turn round and go home? It's a blank. All I have is the street, and this extraordinary hypnotic music.

Naturally – but how could it have been otherwise? – I now became a Cream fan. And although *Disraeli Gears* was an incomparably better LP – after all, it included 'Strange Brew' and 'Sunshine of Your Love' – *Fresh Cream*, since it was the means by which I discovered them, always held a special place in my affections.

Santana Abraxas, Santana;
The Progressive Blues Experiment, Johnny Winter

In 1968, aged fourteen, I started at Bedales School in Petersfield,

Hampshire, a co-ed boarding school.

One afternoon in 1970, when I was almost but not quite sixteen, a Canadian boy in my dormitory called Hector said, 'I'm going to London. Do you want to score with me?'

The system in the school was that boys and girls banked their money with housemasters and mistresses. I went to mine and withdrew a pound, or perhaps two, every penny I had anyway.

'That's rather a lot, Carlo,' he lisped, but he still let me have the money. The school was not just mixed, it was progressive, and children were allowed to make decisions without being stopped or impeded by members of staff.

Hector the Canadian took my cash and went up to London. He came back that evening. In the toilets he showed me what he had: a small block of brown cannabis resin and a tiny oily pearl of opium.

We agreed to wait until the school end-of-term dance. I was to look after our stash. I put it in an empty Cherry Blossom shoe-polish tin, which I hid behind the wainscoting.

The end of term came. The dance started at seven. At nine o'clock Hector and I slipped out, made our way to the open air swimming pool and climbed over the fence, the music from the dance booming behind us; it would be the soundtrack for the scene that followed.

In a changing cubicle we chased the dragon with the opium, then smoked an untidy joint made with Golden Virginia and a king-size Rizla paper. I think the tobacco probably had a far greater effect on us than either of the narcotics. Not that we'd have either known or cared.

The sky above was bright with stars, our heads were swimming, and in the school dining room where the dance was continuing, we could hear they were playing (from *Santana Abraxas* – an album with a painting on the cover of a naked woman and a strategically placed dove; it had made quite an impression on the boys) 'Black Magic Woman/Gypsy Queen'. It was the perfect music for two stoned adolescent virgins.

But then we heard footsteps. Somebody was approaching on the other side of the fence. Oh, fuck! Now they'd got to the gate. The chain was rattling. It was Philip Harding, had to be, the German master. He was on duty – he was always on duty when there was a school dance: he had a unique talent for ferreting out boys and girls when they were doing naughty things.

Hector and I squatted on the seat, anxious lest Mr Harding should see our feet below the swing door of the cubicle, our hearts thumping.

We were fucking dead. In a matter of moments, Mr Harding would be outside the cubicle. He would call us out. We would step forward into the beam of his torch, blinking, and we would hear him say, 'Boys, you've been smoking. Now don't insult me with a lie, tell me the truth.'

Time passed, excruciatingly slowly. We were waiting, tensed up, for Mr Harding's polished brogues to clip along the concrete poolside towards us. But instead we heard – no, it was so inconceivable it was unthinkable – no, it really was, it was girlish laughter . . .

Carefully, quietly, we put our heads over the parapet of the cubicle door and saw that indeed our ears had not deceived us: it was Maeve McHenry, Maisie Baring and Emily Ferguson, and they were naked, skinny dipping, the whole scene lit by moonlight.

We sat back on the bench, relieved, delighted. When the girls had dressed and left, we smoked a second joint. Now the music booming from the dance was 'Rollin' And Tumblin'', the first cut on Johnny Winter's *The Progressive Blues Experience*, hard, driving blues-rock.

Head swimming, I looked up at the huge moon hanging in the sky and imagined it was a hole cut in the cloth backdrop of an enormous stage and that if I crawled through I would find myself in another universe . . .

Sex (or something on the way to it) and drugs and rock 'n' roll had all come together in one glorious moment. I don't think I'd ever been so happy.

· Built by Books 3

After *The Outsider* I read with new alertness, relishing the meaning as much as the story. I was also beginning to scribble – the reading provoked it – and by the time I was sixteen, about the time I had my first narcotic experience, stories, play scripts, film scripts and diaries were pouring out of me. Everything I wrote demanded to be written and was produced in great haste, usually unfinished and rarely revised. These eruptions were, I suspect, mostly rubbish. They were also filled with improperly understood ideas.

Regardless of that, I understood one thing: the place it was all coming out of was the place all the books had gone into. All that reading had strengthened my imagination by making it see all the things described in the books I had gorged on. Now, instead of words coming into my head and being turned into images, I had to conjure images and turn them into words. These would be read and uploaded into a reader's imagination and turned back into images. As an adolescent I couldn't have put this into words, but as I've got older and read more, I've understood better and now I understand so well I can describe the process. I couldn't then, of course. Anyhow, back to me at sixteen, scribbling frantically.

There were two other facts about the way I wrote then: first, I knew I had only to read a bit to get myself scribbling – someone else's work stimulated my imagination, and that continues to be the case to the present; and two, everything I wrote was weighed down with what I thought I ought to say. Of course, as Keats observed, in the letter he wrote to Joshua Reynolds on 3 February 1818: 'We hate poetry that has a palpable design upon us – and if we do not agree, seems to put its hand in its breeches pocket. Poetry should be great and unobtrusive, a thing which enters into one's soul, and does not startle it or amaze it with itself, but with its subject.' Unfortunately, but also typically, though I might have admired the way Camus separated narrative and argument, I couldn't do it. Not yet.

I was young, which was one reason why I couldn't. Another was that I was being educated. At school the focus was on reason, analysis, ideas and showing off what one knew, none of which was helpful to the practice of telling plain tales.

A Lie that Saved Me

Relationships between the sexes were common at Bedales and it was customary at the end of each school day for boys to escort their girlfriends to Steephurst, a building on the other side of the grounds from the school's campus and the boys' dormitories (known as Boys' Flat, as distinct from Girls' Flat in Steephurst).

My girlfriend, at the end of my time in the upper sixth, was called Lolly, and every evening after assembly I would wait on the assembly hall steps and then walk Lolly across. It was the summer and warm, the evenings were long, and if there was no sign of the beady-eyed housemistress when we got to Girls'

Flat, we'd abscond to the sandpit (really a quarry) in the fields behind.

The events of the first weeks of our courtship exceeded my wildest hopes. When I kissed Lolly, I found she kissed me back eagerly. When I slipped my hand under her blouse, she did not shy away but made an appreciative noise and nuzzled my ear. And when, finally, I plucked up the courage to explore downwards, she did not demur.

One June evening we sat in the twilight, watching the bats flit by and sharing a Woodbine, and Lolly described an occasion the previous summer in her local pub (she lived in Sussex) when she had been with a group of local lads she'd known since childhood. She'd had a lot to drink. When she woke up in a field some hours later, alone, all her clothes scattered on the ground around her, damp along her legs and back, but hot in the middle of her being, she realised what the boys had done.

At first, though I felt appalled and shocked by Lolly's account of her erstwhile friends' behaviour, I did not understand why she had told me this story – or, rather, I wanted to believe it was a sign but I didn't dare let myself believe Lolly meant what I hoped, which was that she was giving me permission. Then she alluded to the curious fact that, because there was a shortage of beds in Boys' Flat that term, I had been lodged in the village, at the house of an asthmatic woman who had a passion for cats. I had a room of my own, didn't I?

'Yes,' I said.

'Why don't we, then?' she said, and all was now very clear. I had no need to be inhibited by her virginity because it was gone.

'Can you get what we need?' she said.

'I will.'

On my next free afternoon I took a train to the nearest big town and eventually found a chemist that did not employ young women assistants. I was then able to make my purchase without embarrassment.

That night, at two a.m., I slipped from the asthmatic landlady's house, walked to the school, found Lolly waiting in the rhododendron bushes as agreed and led her back across the fields. On the way we met no one except a poacher who paid us no attention: he had other things to do, with his traps.

Negotiating the creaking stairs in the house where I lodged was tricky; also, the asthmatic landlady's bedroom door was open that night, and she lay asleep inside, propped up in the bed, wheezing mightily, surrounded by the cats to which she was allergic but which she refused to renounce. It was a heart-stopping moment getting past.

In my room I sat on the bed to unlace my Doctor Martens boots. When I looked up, Lolly was naked. Because of a combination of light and shadow, one of her breasts appeared larger than the other, and to my immense surprise I heard myself saying as much. I knew then we were headed for disaster.

We got into bed and kissed. After a while, I slipped my hand under the pillow and felt around for the slim envelope with a Durex Gossamer condom inside that I had placed there in readiness. I couldn't find it. I realised the slippery foil square had gone – fallen down the back of the bed. I got down on the cold linoleum and, scrabbling around in the dust, set off a mousetrap before I found what I was looking for. By the time I got back to bed, and had got the thing on the right way with the lubricant on the outside, as per the instructions, my heart was no longer in the business.

We dressed and I walked Lolly back through the pre-dawn-lightening landscape where nothing moved except a dying hare, thrashing around in the poacher's noose. At Girls' Flat, Lolly kissed me passionately and made me promise I would put the creature out of its agony. I did this on my way back with a large stick that smelt of mushrooms. The creature squealed terribly as it died, its cry almost human.

I arrived at school the next morning, groggy and tired but also strangely anxious. I felt as if a cloud hovered over my head, discernible to all but me; surely everyone in the school must know by now that I had failed to manage the business. As I slunk into the common room, where I knew I would find Lolly, my anxiety increased when I saw that she was talking to a group of girls. I considered turning around and walking out but Lolly waved me forward. As I shuffled over, I noticed that her friends were looking at me with respect. This puzzled me until the girlish innuendoes started. That was when I grasped that Lolly, whose friends were curious to know what had happened, had told a delicious little lie.

More than One Genius – How Lucky Was That?

Both my parents were writers so, of course, there were writers around during my childhood and adolescence. A few visited the house in Morden when my parents were married (including Arnold Wesker and his wife, Dusty, and on one occasion they presented my mother with Helen Thomas's two memoirs about her life with the poet Edward Thomas, *As It Was* and *World Without End*: they gave this gift because they sensed that my mother, with her capacity to feel, would see Helen Thomas a kindred spirit).

Later, when my mother lived in Putney, a lot of writers attended her parties. (She liked parties and hers were renowned) I was introduced to many writers, including the reclusive J.D.

Salinger. In fact, I spent a whole afternoon with the Hermit of Connecticut. He had his daughter with him and we went to Battersea funfair. She was seventeen or eighteen and she was wearing lime-green stockings. She made an infinitely greater impression on me than her venerable father did. I knew he was famous, I knew he'd written *The Catcher in the Rye* (I might even have read it), but he was just an old guy. I was much more interested in the daughter. I don't think she paid me any attention whatsoever.

The writer who had the greatest impact on me in adolescence was Mordecai Richler. He came to my mother's parties but I also got to see him in his own habitat, at his home, in his domestic setting, and that was why he had such an effect.

Mordecai and his wife, Florence, had five children. The eldest, Daniel, was my friend and, with my brother, I would often go to the Richler house on Kingston Hill to see him on Sundays. While I was in the house I would invariably see Mordecai and what struck me (I could hardly fail to notice this) was that he was continuously and constantly at work. Even when he didn't look as if he was working, even when he was lying on the sofa reading the Sunday papers, his brain would be churning and he would be looking for an angle, trying to think up something that he could get paid to write. He taught me that being a professional writer required one hundred per cent round-the-clock attention.

He was also important for another reason, though I didn't understand this at the time. My parents' marriage had not been a success. I discovered in the Richler household that sometimes relationships flourished. Every Sunday evening as Florence was feeding my brother and me, as she always did before we got the bus home, Mordecai would come into the kitchen. He and Florence would have a drink together and talk. This kind of domestic interlude was a revelation. Literary endeavour and marital harmony were not necessarily mutually exclusive.

The other influential literary figure from my youth was Kenneth Tynan. He was an habitué of my mother's parties. I met him frequently. Anyhow, towards the end of his life, when I was between school and university and in one of my periodic fits of depression about how I was going to find my way in the world and become what I thought I should become, which was probably a film director but one who wrote his own stuff, like Ingmar Bergman, my mother arranged for me to see him. He'd been around and he gave good advice, I was told.

I showed up at the Tynan house and was admitted. I was led into the sitting room. I sat down. A few moments later Tynan wheezed in. He collapsed into a chair and took a hit of his asthma inhaler. And then he began to speak. I wish I'd taken notes. He was brilliant.

So, I wanted to be an artist, he said. I wanted to write. I wanted to make films. I wanted to write films *and* make them. Or maybe write plays. Or maybe write stories and novels. Well, then, all I had to do was to do it. If I wanted to write – and he thought writing was more important than making films, although he admitted film was probably more appealing to a young man than literature – all that was necessary was that I put down one right word after another, and once I'd enough words in the right order I could publish what I'd written, or if it was a film script I could sell my script or shoot it myself, and if it was a play I could take it to a theatre impresario. What was I waiting for? I owed it to myself. And if I didn't make a start and apply myself, he predicted a melancholy future. I'd end up working for other people as an employee. That would be appalling. It would be spiritual death.

He was also very firm on the subject of originality. Whatever I did in the world of letters, and he was emphatic about this, I must not, under any circumstances, work as a hack or a critic. Whatever medium I went into, I must not spend my life extolling and celebrating, judging and puffing the lives and works of others. In his opinion, that was the way to get cancer. The only thing that mattered was originality. The only thing that counted was that I made works of art (literary, cinematic or theatrical) that came from the deepest parts of my psyche.

Nor did it matter, he continued, if my work turned out not to be first-rate. The point was, it would be mine, I would have made it, and I would own it. Making my work would keep me balanced and sane, wise and healthy.

He also extolled the virtues of labour. Work was ennobling; it was good for the soul. That was the future and I must seize it with both hands – a life of literary toil.

The talk lasted about an hour. Then I said goodbye and left. I don't think I ever saw him again. But his words never left me. They remained in my unconscious and gradually came to exert a greater and greater influence.

What Tynan did, which was why I never forgot what he said and would be permanently altered by it, was to size me up in a moment, decide I was going to do something creative, then tell me to go and do it and to stick with it. When you're young and callow, as I was, an authority figure, who reads you right and tells you what to do, will have a profoundly transforming effect.

I'm not saying I wouldn't have become what I became (which is primarily a writer) if we hadn't had our talk. I would have found my way, I feel sure, because I was driven by an intense psychological need (though I had no idea about this then) to propitiate my father and to please my mother by creating literary artefacts with some sort of value and aesthetic substance. But Tynan cut the journey time by years – though first, before I could get to literature, I had to make a little detour into film-making and directing.

The Kafka Lothario

I went to the University of York to read English in the autumn of 1973. I was nineteen. Before long I wore a beard (ill-advised), a donkey jacket (pretentious) and I was in love. The object of my affections was my tutorial partner: Victoria was blue-eyed, blonde, and spoke with a burr in her voice. Victoria was Cornish. Victoria wore long, floaty dresses (like Stevie Nicks from Fleetwood Mac) and sometimes an anklet with bells.

Our tutorials with Mr Durwood were on Tuesday afternoons, and we'd always have lunch together beforehand. One day, as we queued at the servery of the college cafeteria, we fell in behind a student in a beret with Martin Amis's first novel *The Rachel Papers* on his tray.

'Worth reading?' Victoria asked him. He was a postgrad, linguistics, and he said he wouldn't comment on the content but he had a lot to say about Amis's transitive verbs, all of which apparently he'd counted.

I got my food and sloped off disconsolately. Victoria followed two minutes later.

'He looked interesting,' I said, not meaning it.

'From linguistics – interesting? Are you mad? They're worse than the biochemists.'

We laughed, and she added ruefully, 'I've only myself to blame, of course. I see someone with an interesting book, I can't help asking about it. I've met all my boyfriends that way.'

I'd heard about attracting girls with interesting books but I'd never heard it confirmed. Well, now I had.

The following Tuesday I had Robert Pirsig's *Zen and the Art of Motorcycle Maintenance* with me at lunch. It was a good beginning. Victoria liked what I said about it. I followed with Jack Kerouac's *On the Road* (she loved my account), Knut Hamsun's *Hunger* (a bit on the bleak side, she thought, judging by what I told her) and then Samuel Beckett's *Molloy*. Bad idea, worse than Hamsun: Beckett most definitely did not impress – or, at least, my report did not. Too gloomy, too depressing, she explained. I was crushed.

'I don't want a book that just tells me how awful life is,' she said. 'I want a book that makes sense of the world.'

I went straight to the university bookshop. Kerouac had been the high point since which I had made little progress. But now I had new intelligence: where was the book that wasn't about the awfulness of life but that explained the world? A book from abroad would surely do the trick. And there I spotted it. The following Tuesday when we sat down to lunch, I set it in front of us – cover up, naturally.

'Oh, *The Trial*,' she said. This edition had a picture of Kafka on the front. 'You look a bit like him, you know.' I'd a beard and he didn't but I wasn't going to argue.

In our post-tutorial conversation, which extended from tea through dinner and on in to the small hours, and included two bottles of Hirondelle and some Red Lebanese hash, I made my pitch. If we wanted to understand the twentieth century and all its miseries – the Holocaust, Fascism, Stalinism, totalitarianism, state violence, colonialism, imperialism, consumer capitalism, Maoism and anything else you cared to add to the list – then *The Trial* was your book and Kafka was your man. Moreover, *The Trial* had been written before most of what had gone wrong in that century had happened. So Kafka was clairvoyant as well as accurate.

Thirty-plus years later I reread *The Trial*. It was a chastening experience. It is never nice to remember the nonsense one talked but in this case the idiocy seemed of a particularly high order. It seemed wilful. It wasn't just that I was wrong-headed: I'd said what I'd said in defiance of the evidence provided by a text I had actually read.

First, which I completely ignored, *The Trial* is a comedy, and second, an even bigger solipsism this, it is emphatically not about what I'd said it was. I should have known this because the author very thoughtfully announced the subject on the cover. It's called *The Trial* for the excellent reason that that is what it is about: it is about a legal process, a trial, and the travails of the accused K. as the state tries him. Kafka's legal system may not be realistic but it is a marvellous construction with its own worked-out logic, perfect according to its own terms in every detail. If *The Trial* were a watch it would have a Swiss mechanism and it would keep perfect time.

Perhaps if I'd said this to Victoria, I might have got what I wanted. Instead I was sent on my way with a peck on my cheek, friendly but not amorous. Oh, if only. But that's the trouble with life. We live it forwards; we understand it backwards.

Made by Music 4

The Songs of Leonard Cohen, Leonard Cohen

After our Tuesday afternoon tutorials with Mr Durwood, Victoria and I would usually spend the evening in her college room, ostensibly for the purpose of a post-mortem on the writer we'd just 'done' but in truth to gossip, drink and take drugs.

Despite her aversion to sad books, most of the musicians Victoria liked made music at the melancholy end of the spectrum: she liked Joni Mitchell, John Prine and Johnny Cash, concerned was Leonard Cohen, or 'Ole Lugubrious of Montréal' as we jestingly called him.

On one of those Tuesday evenings, the curtains of Victoria's college room were closed – we didn't want the college porter looking in and seeing what we were up to; Victoria was sitting on the bed, turning her anklet and tinkling the bells; I was sitting on the floor, the album sleeve *The Songs of Leonard Cohen* between my knees with its sepia photograph of melancholy Leonard staring up at me while I cut speed on Victoria's small mirror; and all the while, the pained voice croaking from the speaker sang of Suzanne, tea and oranges, and her place by the river . . .

During our Tuesday evenings I'd become as big a Cohen devotee as Victoria so I was delighted by what I was hearing. Of course, self-interest was also at play. I was secretly hoping, thanks to the mood created by Cohen's music, that Victoria would tap the bed and ask me to sit up beside her, and that after I had sat up beside her we would kiss and one thing would lead to another . . .

But she didn't. I finished chopping and we snorted and Cohen sang on. We were never intimate, not that evening, not any evening. All we did was talk and take drugs and drink until, at four o'clock in the morning, I would say my goodbyes, stagger back to my room and fall asleep to the half-remembered words of 'The Sisters of Mercy' or 'Hey, That's No Way to Say Goodbye'.

It's a cliché – an unfulfilled student relationship with Leonard Cohen droning in the background – but that doesn't mean it was any the less real when it happened. And I really liked the music too. Still do.

Tubular Bells, Mike Oldfield

I got nowhere with Victoria but then I met Fiona at a fancy dress party. (I was in tails; she was in a Biba nightdress, furry slippers and curlers – this was the seventies).

We started living together in a flat above a hairdresser's.

Everything tasted of lacquer; it even got into the toothpaste. The landlord belonged to a fringe religion and several of his relatives were buried in the garden.

It was my first adult relationship and I did what I thought then was the adult thing: hugely embarrassing though this is to admit, I bought a copy of *Tubular Bells*.

Yes, it was superficial musically but it was also sweet and engaging and it *seemed* new; we came to love it, Fiona and I. We ate to it; we worked to it; we smoked dope to it; we made love to it.

Sex and drugs and rock 'n' roll had finally fused together.

Pretzel Logic, Steely Dan

Money was tight at college and I used to frequent the local Book and Record Exchange buying and selling textbooks.

One day when I was in, a record sleeve caught my eye; it had on it a picture of a monkey-faced street vendor in the middle of some heartless American city. I shouldn't have but I bought the record on the strength of the picture. I wasn't disappointed. I thought *Pretzel Logic* was magnificent, and it rose even higher in my estimation when someone pointed out that the Duke Ellington standard, 'East St Louis Toodle-O' (which ends side one), quotes directly Mozart's Requiem.

Here was rock (or a part of it) doing the same sort of thing as the literature I was reading: quoting others; celebrating a tradition.

The downside to this realisation was that I now bored more easily: glam and stadium rock, Slade and Cockney Rebel, they just didn't interest me. Too much attitude, not enough content. In that sense *Pretzel Logic* was a demarcation line marking the end of something: after I'd bought it I stopped listening to the charts, I stopped buying records, I withdrew from contemporary music. I just wasn't interested any more.

Built by Books 4

When I went to the University of York, despite having scribbled a lot at school, I decided I wanted to be a film director. I joined the university drama society and directed some plays, including Beckett's Play and Happy Days, and, on account of the drama work I'd done at university, I got a place at the National Film School or NFS (now the National Film and Television School).

I graduated from York in 1976 and, aged twenty-two, started at the NFS in the autumn. Like most of my peers I wanted to become a writer-director and, which was part of the training given to all aspiring writer-directors, I had to videotape dramatic scenes under the supervision of a professional. I was assigned to Bill Douglas, the Scottish director (and writer) whose reputation rested then on two dark but exhilarating autobiographical films, *My Childhood* (1972) and *My Ain Folk* (1973).

Bill provided the actors and the short script – a two-hander about marital breakdown. Though I had anticipated the script's bleakness it had an unexpected, and novel, typographical feature. There were no full stops in the stage directions and only occasional ones in the dialogue. Bill explained that as films didn't have full stops he didn't see why scripts should either. By avoiding them where possible, he continued, the script replicated the one-thing-after-anotherness of film.

Bill's thinking was so startling and original that I opted to work with him on my graduation project, an adaptation of a story by Anton Chekhov. 'In the Ravine' was about infanticide and corruption, and my plan was to relocate it to nineteenth century Ireland. I would shoot it in Connemara using local non professional actors, except for the main role, the woman who murders the child. Marian Richardson played the part.

At Easter 1977, I presented my first draft to Bill Douglas.

Sitting opposite me in the NFS canteen he went through it with a pencil, cutting, paring, querying. Then he returned the typescript and asked me to write a new draft. Over the following months I wrote many more drafts (perhaps twenty), all, in varying degrees, long-winded, laborious and febrile reproductions of Chekhov's story.

My failure to please Bill was at first puzzling, next exhausting, and finally infuriating. Then one day it came to me: my whole education had been devoted to making my thinking faculty big and strong, and now it kept coming up with criticisms and demands that threw my imagination off its delicate business, which was inventing.

If I was going to write this script, I was going to have to write without criticising what was flowing out of the pen. The inner critic could not be allowed into the room when composition was occurring. He had to wait until the work was finished. Then, and only then, could he come in, read the text and advise.

The other thing I grasped somehow was that the key to telling a story, to a story succeeding, was flow, forward motion. A story was like a line of falling dominoes (where the first knocks down the second knocks down the third), and if my story was to have the same perfect forward motion, there must be neither gaps nor obstructions nor, indeed, full stops. Only what followed from what had gone before could be included, and everything else had to go if it got in the way of the flow. And, of course, those extraneous things that obstructed were always the work of the inner critic.

So – all I had to do was ban the critic and take my hands off the handlebars. It sounds easy, couched in those terms, but it was not because, of course, my education had been directed towards training and enabling the inner critic. It was hard to make him wait outside.

But somehow I managed. I wrote (let's say) my twenty-first

draft without the critic present and I noticed as I was writing it and as I was reading it over afterwards, that I had a trace of that tranced feeling I got when I lost myself in other people's stories. Eureka! I realised I had a story of sorts. It was like learning to ride a bicycle: I'd had to fall off a lot but now I'd managed my first wobbling journey from A to B.

I shot my film in Ireland (it was called *The Beneficiary*) and graduated from the film school in July 1979 aged twenty-five. Over the following eighteen months I made *Over Here*, a documentary about the Irish in England for the Arts Council of Great Britain, and *Rating Notman* for the National Film Finance Corporation. This was a cinema short based on a powerful true story Rebecca West had told in *The Meaning of Treason*, about a Second World War Royal Navy rating forced to become a Gestapo spy after he was taken prisoner. Like 'In the Ravine', *Rating Notman* sprang directly out of reading. Someone else's words, in my imagination, had a tendency to grow into something new.

I was lucky to make those films, but while I was making them I was struck by an unexpected feeling. I didn't want to just direct or even just write and direct. This was partly practical. I had come to realise that to be dependent on the film and television industry was hazardous. I'd also decided it was unhealthy for my psyche if, in order to express myself aesthetically, I had to depend on others approving what I wanted to do in order to get that work made as a film or a television programme. I needed to be able to make work that could have a life without having to undergo the complicated vetting process that every film and television programme, no matter how modest, had to endure. I wanted to be free of all the palaver and I wanted to be my own master and therefore what I needed to do, I'd decided, was not to direct; what I wanted to do (and what I'd always wanted to do but it had taken me until now to realise this) was to write for publication. To be sure, I would then have to find someone to publish whatever I wrote but that was a lot easier than getting a film made of a script I had written or a proposal taken up for a documentary I'd concocted. Once someone had been found who would publish it, the work would be autonomous: it would live out in the world in a magazine or a newspaper or a book, and anyone who wanted could just pick it up and read it. It didn't need to be distributed and then projected or transmitted before people could have access to it, as films and television programmes did. Writing, I had come to understand, offered an easier means to get material across to people than film or television and, of course, literature being my parents' area, I was unconsciously attracted to writing because I believed it would please them.

So, at the same time as I was making *Over Here* and *Rating Notman* I started trying to write short stories for publication. I tried various styles and techniques but none of these stories worked. They'd no lift, no heft. I couldn't interest anyone in them. And then one day I had an inspiration. I'd go inside myself, to my memory bank, and I would mine a buried seam of childhood hurt.

In the summer of 1961 I was seven years old and 'home' on holiday with my maternal grandparents in County Clare: a day at the seaside had been arranged for my grandmother, a great aunt, my younger brother and myself, and a car hired to take us to the coast. The car, Mr McNamara's Morris Oxford, could only take four: if there were more than four their weight would damage the axle, he believed.

On the morning, as we were about to leave, an elderly female appeared and wanted to come. As Mr McNamara would only allow four in his beloved Morris, one of us would have to stay behind. I was the older child and it was believed I *would understand*, so I, rather than my younger brother, was left. Well,

I did not understand. This seemed like a terrible violation of natural justice. I minded very much and I went on minding all through the day that followed, which I spent with my irascible, dangerous and slightly frightening maternal grandfather. In my imagination I cooked up the image sequence that told the story, me waking, going downstairs, the elderly relative appearing, the hire car coming, being told I would have to stay home for the day because my place in the car had been taken by our surprise visitor, and so on. To give it specificity I furnished it with details remembered from my childhood holidays in Ireland. These were not inventions. When you tell a story about the past there are always parts you have to fabricate but they have to be made out of what you would have seen, or could have seen, or even did see, but never what you would like to have seen.

Then I wrote the story in the simple past, in language that was clear and direct (to this day it remains my conviction that plain and simple is best). *The Literary Review* accepted 'The Speech of Birds' and paid me thirty pounds. I had crossed the chasm separating never having been in print from being in print, an event of colossal significance. From now on I could expect to get paid for the work my imagination did. I was on my way.

The Graduate Society (London Branch)

It was 1982. I was twenty-eight. I had published some short stories but no novel yet. I had no girlfriend either.

One afternoon the phone rang in the flat I shared with a Dutch cameraman.

'Are you Carlo Gébler?'

The speaker was a young Dubliner, her voice breathy and lovely.

'Yes.'

'I've read some of your stories' she said. Her name was Olivia, she added.

No sooner had I got her name than an image of Olivia was cast up before my mind's eye. She was tall and graceful, sensitive and charmingly diffident, a Celtic Charlotte Rampling.

Olivia explained she was calling on behalf of the London branch of the graduate society of an Irish university. She was the new secretary.

'We meet every month,' she said. She mentioned an Irish Centre in north London. 'We always have a speaker,' she continued. 'Usually from sport or business. But I want to broaden things out, so I wondered, would you read a story?'

Of course I would. Anything for you, Olivia, I thought. But, lest I appeared eager, I asked about the evening.

'There'll be a bit of society business first and then you read – for half an hour, say. Afterwards everyone will pile into the bar. And we'll pay you.'

She offered fifty pounds – a week's rent. It was a done deal. I noted the time, place and date in my diary. We said goodbye.

Time passed, and finally what I had recklessly come to consider as the evening of my date with Olivia arrived. I dressed carefully. Assuming all the males at the meeting would be Price-Waterhouse-Cooper trainees in suits, I opted for the conventionally unconventional look of leather jacket and red tie. This would impress her.

Then I went to the street and eased myself into my car – a very fogeyish 1962 Morris Oxford saloon. To avoid being seen behind the wheel (I couldn't be sure such a car would impress Olivia), I parked some way from the centre and walked the last quarter-mile.

The venue was a sixties monstrosity with posters of shamrocks in the windows. The bar was decorated with shillelaghs and rank with the smell of old Guinness. I hardly noticed or cared. I had eyes only for O. But striding towards me across the awful carpet (stiffened by the dried remains of who knew what fluids), I was surprised to see (quite contrary to what I had expected) a tiny girl (under five foot, I thought), with shiny knees and bobbed hair. It couldn't be, could it?

'You must be Carlo,' said the throaty voice. Oh, yes, it was: this was Olivia.

My mouth opened but no words came out. This was because an incredible act of fantasy reassignment was under way in the brain. Instead of the willowy woman of my dreams, Olivia had turned out to be a lively, chirpy Audrey Hepburn lookalike. Could I like her? I asked. You bet! came the reply.

'Yes, I am,' I said, beaming. That was when I noticed a man lurking behind her, tall and gangling and bespectacled. He was, I immediately guessed, the boyfriend, a figure I had not included when, over the preceding weeks, I had imagined this evening.

'This is Declan,' said Olivia, embracing the etiolated love object. 'He's also the society president.' I shook my rival's hand.

The next part of the evening was a blur. I had a drink and made small talk. The room filled as fifty members showed up, mainly lusty men and cheerful girls from the west of Ireland. Among them was the society's treasurer, a behemoth called Keith. As we were introduced I couldn't help noticing that Keith refused to acknowledge either Olivia or Declan and that no sooner had he finished shaking my hand than he darted off.

'My ex,' whispered Olivia.

Ex-boyfriends hadn't been part of my picture of the evening any more than boyfriends had. 'Oh, right.' I said grimly.

We adjourned to the Limerick Lounge. I sat at the back. The

members sat in rows with their backs to me. The committee – Olivia, Declan, Keith and two or three others – sat behind a table at the front facing us. Olivia had said there'd be a few minutes of business and then she'd call me down. I leafed through the typed manuscript of the story I had brought to read.

The meeting opened. Declan said something. Keith sniped viciously at him. Members hissed. Declan called for calm, adding, 'It's nobody's business but ours.' What must have happened, I now realised, was that Her Loveliness Olivia had only recently switched from Keith to Declan. The two love rivals had murder in their hearts, feelings shared by several members on the floor.

The rhetoric got nastier. I decided to leave. I would just walk out and no one would notice. I got up and headed towards the door. As I moved, unobtrusively I believed, Olivia saw me. She looked puzzled. She shrugged as if to say, 'What is this?' I mouthed, 'I'm going.' I got to the door. She slipped off her chair and began to come towards me. Even though she was on her way to me it was too late to turn round. I opened the door and went out. Before I could pull it closed behind me, Olivia opened it. She came out and pushed it to.

'What are you doing?' she said.

'I thought . . . as everyone's so very . . . preoccupied,' I said, 'there won't be time for the story so I should just slip away.'

She shook her head. 'No, you can't go now,' she said. 'You must come back in. Everyone's dying to hear you.'

'But what about . . .' I pointed at the door, on the far side of which loud grumpy voices were clearly audible.

'Don't worry about that,' she said. 'That'll all be done and dusted any minute now.'

She wasn't going to let me go. I would have to go through with this. She reopened the door. I slipped back in. She followed. She closed the door noiselessly behind her. I went back to my seat and she to hers.

Of course, what she'd assured me would happen didn't happen. The bad-tempered meeting did not stop. It went on for what seemed like eternity but was probably an hour. But then, at last, it did end. My turn had come.

I stood up, holding my typescript. Olivia explained to everyone that I would read an unpublished story. She motioned to me. I ought to go to the front, I thought. Obviously that was the place to read from. But my legs wouldn't move. They wouldn't carry me there. Panic and dread surged in my gut. No one wanted to hear me. They all had other things rather than literature on their minds. It was obvious. And the room had an evil atmosphere. It felt like a bar before a fight erupts.

'What do I do?' I asked myself.

'Don't waste any more time,' came the reply. 'Just get this ordeal over and done with.'

And no sooner did I get to the end of this thought than, without knowing I was going to do this, I blurted out the first sentence of my story to the backs of the heads before me. Olivia looked slightly startled but only for a second. Then she sat, crossed her legs and gave the impression that, although I'd chosen an unorthodox place from which to read, she would give my story her undivided attention.

Well, now I'd started, I thought, I'd best continue. I remembered the advice of my speech teacher. When reading aloud, pick someone in the audience and read to them. If they're captivated, so will everyone else be.

There could only be one candidate for this practice. I locked my sights on Olivia and began to read to her. She did not disappoint. She looked back at me, her eyes full of attention and interest. I began to feel slightly optimistic. Perhaps I could win this audience round, I thought. Perhaps I could make them listen and like me and my story.

This was a mistake. Olivia had to pay attention. How could she not? After all, she'd brought me there. But the crowd was quite another matter. They didn't feel they had to make an effort. Nor did they. I registered a change in their mood. Something was going on. At first I couldn't tell what it was or where it was happening. Then I saw. Keith had moved his seat back from the committee table to a place where his rival couldn't see him and he was now, dumbshow fashion, satirically re-enacting intercourse between the diminutive Olivia and the stringy Declan. This involved some ugly fingerwork.

Alerted by the tittering, Declan twigged. He turned and saw. Then he picked up the glass in front of him, and threw its contents in Keith's face. The sodden treasurer smirked and muttered, 'You eejit.'

I broke off from the story and said, 'Do you want me to finish?'

'Not really,' said one voice in the audience.

'No, we fucking don't,' said another.

A third was making mock-farting noises.

For a second I contemplated saying something nasty, and then running out, hopefully with Olivia in tow. But she was holding Declan's hand while giving Keith, who was wiping his face with a handkerchief, the finger.

I hurried through the door, across the bar and out into the street.

I never did get paid.

Albert Camus

It was 1984. I was thirty years old. I'd a partner, Tyga, a daughter, and I'd published several stories. A magazine offered to send me to Algeria. I was to find Camus's house, his schools, and the places he'd written about in his books. I was to see what remained of his white colonial world in now Islamic Algeria; I was also free, said the editor, to describe the contemporary scene.

Albert Camus was born in 1913. His ancestors were among the thousands of settlers who had flooded into Algeria after the French annexation of the territory in 1830. These people, as distinct from the native Algerian Arab population, were called *pieds-noirs*, or black feet, according to some because of the black leather shoes worn by French soldiers, and according to others because the stokers on the French cargo-boats that sailed regularly between France and Algeria worked barefoot.

Camus grew up in the city of Algiers where he later worked as a journalist. During the Second World War he went to France and joined the Resistance. After the liberation he published *The Plague* to great acclaim. Nineteen-fifty-four saw the start of the Algerian War of Independence. In 1957 he won the Nobel Prize for Literature. In 1960 he was killed in a car crash. Two years later a peace agreement was concluded between the Front de Libération National (the FLN) and the French government. Over the following weeks, almost all Algeria's *pieds-noirs*, one and a half million of them (accompanied by an equivalent number of Algerian Arabs who'd fought for the French or were otherwise compromised), quit their homeland for France rather than live in FLN-governed independent Algeria.

Before leaving for Algeria, I reread all of Camus's books; they were better than I remembered, especially the lyrical essays, and particularly *Summer*. One essay in this lovely collection made a huge impression: 'Return to Tipasa' started with a description of Algiers as 'the city of summers', and went on to describe, in unforgettable, rapturous prose, the honeycomb-coloured Roman and Phoenician ruins on the coast near Chenoua. In my mind and inspired by 'Return to Tipasa' I settled on an itinerary: first, Algiers city, Camus's home town – here I would do the hard work of research; then, Tipasa, the place in Algeria he loved above all others and site of the only memorial to him in modern Algeria. It would be a fitting climax to my journey.

What is it they say about the best-laid plans? We arrived in Algiers, Tyga and I, on a boiling afternoon in June. It was Ramadan, when Muslims fast between sunrise and sunset. Algerian tempers were frayed. Just how frayed we found out the next morning, on a bus going to Belcourt, the working class suburb of Algiers where Albert Camus had grown up. It was crowded, and everyone was hot and hungry. Tyga was wearing a modest long-sleeved dress but this did not deter a man in a burnous calling her a *pied-noir* bitch and telling her to fuck off back to France. A couple of other passengers shouted at our accuser – my partner was a guest: so what if she was a *pied-noir*? The driver stopped the bus and we offered to get off. No, shouted our defenders, this was a matter of honour. There was a bit of a tussle. Our team won. The man in the burnous was ejected and we drove on.

We alighted in the old Rue de Lyon where Camus had lived. Miraculously, the old French numbering system appeared to be intact. I counted the numbers and then there it was, ninety-three, the low, two-storey home of the Camus family. The owner opened the door, holding a stave of loaves bound with a twist of paper. He showed us in and around the three meagre rooms. His wife was picking grit out of semolina, exactly as Camus might have seen his mother doing.

'He won the Nobel Prize, you know,' said the owner, 'the boy who lived here.'

He was blithe. It seemed he was used to literary tourists like ourselves.

The next day we were standing outside Camus's old *lycée*. A girl in a sundress was sitting on the steps, smoking a cigarette. She looked a bit like a young Jane Birkin, with her elfin face and clear eyes. After she had studied us for a while she came over and introduced herself. She was fifteen, she said, she had a penfriend in Italy, and her name was Nora. The name seemed quite unlikely but she seemed pleasant and together we walked in the direction of the great *pied-noir* church, Notre Dame d'Afrique, on the heights of Bouzareah.

Sandwiched between us, Nora chattered away. Did we have an apartment? Yes. Could she write to us? Yes. Could she visit? Yes. Then she told us she hated Algeria, she wanted to emigrate. The only trouble was, she had no passport. Of course, they were hard to come by – here she laughed sarcastically – because if Algerians could get passports, the entire population would leave. She laughed again. However, she continued, now that we had met, she'd had an idea. She knew a man who took brilliant passport photographs. How about she got her photo taken and she put it in my passport? Then she could leave her stinking country posing as my daughter. She would come and live with us, she continued. She would cook, she would clean, she would be our slave. She would do anything, in fact, to get out of Algeria. Please, please, she begged.

We came round a bend and there was Notre Dame d'Afrique, a huge nineteenth-century church with a cupola, a monument to *pied-noir* piety. As we sauntered through the gates into the dusty precinct, and fended off the gang of boys who made a half-hearted attempt to steal my camera, I explained to Nora that her proposition would not work. Immigration officials were smart, I said. They'd spot the forgery immediately. Besides, I continued, she must stay, she must finish her education.

We entered the church. It smelt of incense and old stone. It was filled with memorials to early *pied-noir* pioneers who had died civilizing, as they saw it, the newly conquered Algeria, but perhaps the most telling inscription ran around the frieze below the cupola: NOTRE DAME D'AFRIQUE. PRIEZ POUR NOUS ET POUR LES MUSSULMANS. Pray For Us and For the Muslims.

In this stony, silent place where nobody came to pray any more, Nora rattled on. Her parents had gone to France when she was three. Her mother's name was Francine. That was a French name, wasn't it? Now she lived with a woman, an 'aunt' of some sort, although she had no idea how they were related. The aunt was cruel. Nora lifted her dress to show that her legs were bruised.

'This aunt beats me because my name is not a proper Algerian name, but a pied-noir name,' she said, 'but my aunt is a Madeleine, and that's another French name, isn't it?'

As we sidled out of the church, Nora slyly blessed herself with holy water. I asked her if she was a Muslim.

'Of course,' she said. 'I couldn't live in Algeria as a Christian.' She stared at us without blinking.

'But your parents or your grandparents were *pied-noir*?' I said.

'Grandparents,' she said. 'Grandfather married an Arab girl.'

Camus had had a vision, I remembered, of an egalitarian multi-racial society in Algeria with no bars on miscegenation. This was not how he would have wanted things to turn out.

We began to descend from the heights of Bouzareah back towards Algiers. Camus often made this very walk and wrote about it. On one occasion he had come upon an Arab boy who had been hit by a bus and was dying on the roadside.

'You see?' said Camus, pointing at the heavens. 'You see? He says nothing.'

On our third day we went to look at the *monument aux*

morts, the old memorial to Algerian victims of the First World War, only to discover that the FLN, though they had left the memorial, had obliterated the roll of honour listing those who had died.

As we stood in the blazing heat puzzling about this – why leave the memorial but obliterate the names? – a man came up to us. His name was Ahmed, he said, and he was a teacher of French literature. He asked what had brought us to Algiers. When we told him, he beamed and said he was a devotee of Camus. He would be happy to show us around.

We went to a café and talked. Ahmed seemed very pleasant. He was single, mid-thirties, had nice even white teeth. He wore a suit, and told us he had spent many years at a French university. He also sang us several *pied-noir* songs in a plaintive, plangent voice. We were seduced.

Two days later we rendezvoused in the afternoon at the Gare de l'Agha bus depot. The plan was to motor to the village of Tipasa, seventy kilometres west of Algiers. Tomorrow we would rise bright and early and visit the Phoenician and Roman ruins at Tipasa, but tonight we would sleep in the house of a Berber family who were Ahmed's very special friends.

But when we arrived at the house, the friends were somewhat puzzled. They seemed more like acquaintances. However, as custom dictated, they asked us in without demurring. Then the young girls of the family gave us chrysanthemums and kissed us on the cheeks. In the corner, a child called Marika sat doubled up on an orange box, laughing to herself. 'She's mentally retarded,' Ahmed shouted at me in English. Then he turned to the child and continued in English, 'You're stupid, aren't you, Marika? You're terribly, terribly stupid!' Marika smiled with pleasure. She only spoke Berber but she assumed that she was being complimented. I began to sense I might have misjudged the character of Ahmed.

We ate outside after sunset with bats beating overhead. We had *loubia*, a stew made with tomatoes and peppers; *tamisa*, a dish of courgettes and chickpeas; and *chackchoucka*, a dip of onion, cumin and peppers. To drink there was Algerian cola, which set the teeth on edge.

Then it was time to sleep. We were shown to a shed where a spotless bed had been made up for the three of us. Ahmed undressed, proposing a threesome, audaciously suggesting our 'love-soiled' sheets would be 'treasured' by our hosts. A Berber custom, he explained. Everything became very clear now. We declined and spent a sleepless night listening to the rats, and Ahmed snoring. Camus, where have you led me? I wondered. Sometime in the middle of the night, young men started shouting in the village half a mile away. Ahmed woke at four a.m. Mysteriously, he now needed to take a taxi to Algiers. He found my wallet in the darkness, pulled out some notes before I could stop him and, promising he would repay the money, he vanished.

An hour or two later, our Berber host put his head around the door. He was delighted Ahmed was gone. 'That makes two pieces of good news,' he said. 'Oh, and what's the other?' I asked.

Ramadan, he explained, had been scheduled to last two more days, but in the middle of the night the end had been brought forward by forty-eight hours. It was over. That was what all the cheering we had heard had been about.

'So,' he chirped, 'we will have breakfast together, now, in the daylight.' He gave us the thumbs-up sign.

'And Tipasa?' Tyga and I chorused in unison.

'Tipasa?' Our host looked crestfallen.

'Don't tell us today's a public holiday?' said Tyga.

He nodded. Yes, indeed. Today was a public holiday, a public holiday that had come two days early. Every Algerian had the day off and – just as everywhere else in the world on a public holiday – swimming pools, parks, ancient monuments, everywhere was closed.

We went to the gates of Tipasa anyway. It had a sentry box attached with guards inside. We begged. We cried. We even tried bribery.

'Come back tomorrow,' the guards said.

We explained about our flight. They were *désolé*, but rules were rules, they said, with Gallic shrugs.

I got up on a rock to look over the fence. I saw a single honeycomb-coloured pillar. That was all. We caught the bus back to Algiers, we never got our money back from Ahmed, and the next day we left.

Working at Writing 1

I had published stories based on or inspired by things that had happened to me. Now I decided to be a bit bolder. I decided to take facts and improvise a story around them.

Fact: my grandfather drank and raced horses. Why not, I thought, imagine an eleven-year-old boy who was like me but not me (I called this alter ego Paul Weismann) going with his grandfather and his grandfather's favourite horse to a provincial Irish race meeting, the horse breaking a leg and having to be put down, and the grandfather going back on the drink because of the death of his horse?

I wrote this as a short story. Then, when I had finished writing, I had a surprising but totally convincing intuition that what I actually had was the start of a novel. Moreover, I knew a lot more. I knew it was a *Bildungsroman* about the character Paul Weismann looking back as an adult on his childhood when he had lived in Ireland with his grandparents. I knew what happened over the course of the novel. I knew it had a prologue and an epilogue set in the 1980s, bracketing twelve chapters set in the 1960s, and I knew the title: it was called *The Eleventh Summer*.

I also knew from both parents that only blockheads wrote for free: I needed a commission. The young English novelist John Milne arranged for me to meet Julian Evans, an editor at Hamish Hamilton. I showed him the opening chapter of *The Eleventh Summer*. He asked to see the second and third. I wrote them: he liked them and commissioned the novel. It was as simple as that.

The Eleventh Summer was published in 1985 when I was thirty-one. It was reviewed well. It sold a bit and the American publisher Dutton bought it. British publisher, editor and author were delighted: a US sale was a sign that I was an author with a future.

The publisher put the US edition out with an illustrative cover that showed a mop-haired Irish lad peering out from behind a bush. Dear reader, it said, between these covers lies some pleasing Oirishry. Though this was not true – the novel was slightly bitter – I said nothing. Privately, however, I wondered if my publisher might not end up in court, charged with contravening the Trade Descriptions Act.

As it turned out, American book buyers didn't seem to notice the finesse. The book was a modest success. My American publisher, a genial *bon viveur*, expressed interest in the next book. Of course, the contract gave him right of first refusal but he let it be known his interest was more than mechanical. He thought he could do something with me. What he wanted, of course, was a repeat of the first.

Now, had I been cunning, that was what I would have done. But I was callow and idealistic. I believed each book must be as different from its predecessor as the writer could manage. Otherwise the writer would die.

So, eschewing repetition, I wrote a novel tracing the life story of August Slemic, from his troubled childhood in Poland between the wars, through service in North Africa during the Second World War with the Eighth Army, to melancholy middle age in London, to the day Prince Charles and Lady Diana Spencer tie the knot in 1981 and the sad Polish *émigré* is overwhelmed by domestic calamity.

The manuscript was delivered. My British publisher was positive but not a word did I hear from across the pond. Months passed. I attended a literary party. My American publisher loomed into view, grinding ice cubes between his teeth. He'd read my manuscript. He wasn't having it and, what was more, he was disappointed. He'd gone to huge lengths building my platform in the US on the strength of the first novel. With the second, had it been more of the same, I could have broken big. Surely I'd understood that. Hadn't he sent me a message to that effect? Yes, when he had let it be known his interest was more than mechanical. But I'd ignored him, hadn't I? I was just another know-it-all young novelist. I was also an idiot. By changing tack from Ireland to Middle Europe I'd thrown away a promising future. If he could sue me, he ended, he would. And with that he stamped off.

Hamish Hamilton published this second novel, called *August in July*, in 1986. The book received favourable reviews though even I understood – good notices and the kind words of friends notwithstanding – that the next effort had to be less melancholy and have more oomph.

And I certainly tried to be more cutting edge with novel number three. *Work & Play* told the story of Fergus, a middleclass Dubliner and ex-heroin addict at large in 1980s London. It was published in 1987. It had bags of topicality, plus it was a social novel, brittle, even comic, and I hoped it would be popular, a seller. (It wasn't, really). Evelyn Waugh might seem the obvious influence, but my biggest debt was to Anthony Powell's astringent, socially acute pre-Second World War novels, especially *Afternoon Men* (1931). Jay McInerney's *Bright Lights, Big City* (1985) (which was not an influence because I hadn't read it then), having recently done so well, and with mine seemingly telling the same sort of story (how a nice lad is ruined by drugs), *Work & Play* was bought by a US publisher (different from the first), who hoped it might appeal to the same readership as McInerney's. Sadly, it didn't, but at least someone in the US had liked it enough to buy it.

I felt chuffed: I'd overcome the second-novel hurdle and now I'd managed a third.

Julian Evans was keen on travel writing (which enjoyed a renaissance in Britain during the late 1980s) and had noticed that Cuba hadn't been the subject of a travel book for some years. Since I'd published pieces on Greenland, Algeria and the Falkland Islands, he believed I could do a book about it, and in January 1988, with Tyga and our seven-year-old daughter, I flew to Havana to start.

There, having swapped our dollars for pesos on the black market, we travelled around the country for four months while I tried to locate a particularly beautiful motor car made by Cadillac, the 1957 Eldorado Brougham, a pillarless sedan (with both doors open there was no column supporting the roof to impede the view of the interior), a brushed-aluminium roof and, its most unusual feature, a unique suspension system. On the Eldorado there was an air spring at each wheel, fed by a central compressor. Thanks to a system of valves and solenoids, the system continuously adjusted to the load and road conditions with the result that the ride was unbelievably smooth. Visually, with its tail fins, sculpted exhausts and sweeping lines of chrome, it was one of the most extraordinary if exaggerated cars of the fifties.

I never found an Eldorado (though I did meet a man who had had one once), and when I returned to London, I'd several full notebooks. With this material I wrote a book that mixed a chronological first-person account of the journey and my search for a 1957 Eldorado Brougham with sections of narrative history. It was published as *Driving through Cuba: An East-West Journey* and was also (which was one reason I wrote it) bought by an American publisher.

Cuba, for all its virtues (its fantastic free public-health system, for instance) was a totalitarian state and I came back determined my next adult novel must describe the miseries visited on the innocent by ideology.

This book (my fourth novel) also sprang from the humus of family history. My father's first wife was an American, Leatrice Gilbert, and they had had a son, Karl. In 1953, when Karl was a year old, Leatrice returned to the US and divorced my father. In 1954 he married my mother. I was his second child and he called me Karl, too; this replacing of a lost son with a second of the same name (as if the first son was gone forever or had never existed) was my starting point for my next novel.

In *Malachy and His Family* there are two half-brothers called Malachy, both born in the 1950s. Malachy 1 is the American-born son of John Garrett, an illegal Irish immigrant in the US, and Amy, an American girl. Malachy 2 is the British-born son of John Garrett and his second wife, Teresa, an exile from Budapest following the 1956 Hungarian uprising; Malachy 2 also has a sister, Eva. In early adulthood, Malachy 1 visits London to meet his father and half-siblings, and the novel shows what happens during that visit, in particular his incestuous relationship with his half-sister, Eva.

It's a bleak book with a depressing emphasis on the inability of people to escape from the social and political structures imposed on them by the state, but Hamish Hamilton thought it was my breakthrough novel and promoted it energetically, hoping it would appear on the Booker long list. Sadly, it failed. Neither did it find a US publisher.

Christopher Sinclair-Stevenson, who then ran Hamish Hamilton, suggested that I might succeed as a travel writer where I hadn't as a novelist, and noticing that Sicily, like Cuba, hadn't been much written about recently, he proposed I go there and write a book about it.

In the summer of 1988, having agreed to this, I went on holiday to Donegal with Tyga, our daughter, India, and our newborn son, Jack. While we were there I had to collect a friend from Irvinestown in County Fermanagh and, as we drove back towards Donegal, she talked about the places we were passing: here, where a policeman was shot; there, where a head had been found in a litter bin, and so on. (The head in the litter bin made a huge impression). As I listened, it occurred to me that all the Troubles books I'd ever read were about Ulster's conurbations. Maybe, I thought, rather than Sicily, I'd come to County Fermanagh, Northern Ireland, specifically Enniskillen, which was still hurting after the IRA's bombing of the Cenotaph on Remembrance Sunday 1987, and write about that.

When we got back to London I went to the London Library, where books were grouped by subject rather than Dewey number, to see if I was right that all Troubles books focused on cities, and it was as I'd thought: they were all about Belfast or Derry and there was next to nothing about the countryside and the small towns.

I wrote to Christopher Sinclair-Stevenson suggesting, instead of Sicily, a travel book about Enniskillen and County Fermanagh. He thought it a great idea and agreed to commission it.

In the months before we left for Enniskillen, I read Jean Rhys's novels, which I'd not read before, and was much taken with them. I agreed with her description of society as pitiless, impersonal and unfair, and I also agreed with her counsel that the only response to the awfulness of life was to endure it.

At some point, as I read, I began to wonder what, if anything, had changed since the 1920s and 1930s, the period she mostly wrote about. Dentistry was certainly better and abortion easier to procure but otherwise society seemed as capricious and vindictive as ever. As these thoughts were swirling around, my agent, Antony Harwood, urged me to publish a novel in tandem with the Northern Ireland book so that critics and readers wouldn't think I now wrote only non-fiction. As I had realised that I ought to try to manage my career (rather than doing one thing after another without heeding the consequences or anticipating the future), I agreed.

I started *Life of a Drum* (from the German proverb 'What is born a drum is beaten to death') in the spring of 1989. It tells the story of Catherine Janowski (née Baring), who lives on the outer fringes of London's Bohemia with her husband, a petty criminal, and who, after he dies, is passed from one lover to the next, literally, like a parcel. I wrote it like a fairy tale, albeit a very black adult one. The fairytale form, I thought, where the narrative is always cast-iron and inescapable, was the right one for a story with the cast-iron and inescapable downward tilt of this one.

In July 1989 I was thirty-five. The unfinished manuscript of *Life of a Drum* was in the car boot as we drove to County Fermanagh. We rented the top floor of an old house about six miles from Enniskillen and enrolled our children at the integrated (that is, non-denominational, neither Catholic nor Protestant) primary school. My plan was to finish the novel while researching the non-fiction book (I estimated that that would take six months), then go back to London and turn my research into a publishable manuscript. Very quickly, however, I discovered that rural Northern Irish society was so complicated, and the process of gaining trust so difficult, that six months wouldn't be enough. We'd have to stay longer. Never mind, I thought. More time in the field meant a better book.

I got the title for it soon after I arrived, from Val Rogers, the ex-headmaster of Portora Royal School. At a party he told me that a glass curtain divided Fermanagh's Protestant and Catholic communities, and that you never saw it until you crashed into it and broke your nose. This, I decided, would be my theme as well as my title. All I needed now was the substantiating material.

I started research. I interviewed some people; I attended some big events – for instance, the Relief of Derry celebration by the Royal Black Institution in Maguiresbridge on 12 August 1989; I gathered information on the bombing by the IRA of the Enniskillen Cenotaph on Sunday, 8 November 1987; I investigated the reconciliation efforts catalysed by the bomb. I wrote up my investigations as chapter-length narratives. I also kept a diary in which I recorded quirky details thrown up by the conflict.

From the outset I knew the book would span the twelve months from July 1989 to July 1990. On 1 August 1990, my research period finished, I laid out everything I'd written on my study floor, and began to create the book. Like a film editor working with rushes, I extracted the best bits, assembled them in sequences, then arranged these into sections, contriving startling juxtapositions (I hoped) as I went. After a couple of weeks, I had a book with four sections corresponding to the four seasons, eight chapters in each section, and each chapter comprising a single narrative and a diary piece. I remember the job as being easy, but my memory may be playing tricks. A fortnight was all I had to do the work because on 23 August I was getting married and it had to be dispatched to Hamish Hamilton before then.

Nineteen-ninety-one saw the publication of the two books I'd been working on in parallel. *Life of a Drum* came out in the spring, coinciding, as we'd decided to settle permanently in Enniskillen, with the purchase of our house (an old schoolhouse built in the Lutyens style in 1930), and *The Glass Curtain* the following autumn, just after we'd moved in. The books didn't fail – they got reviews and they weren't bad – but they didn't fly either: they didn't sell. If ever there was a time to be in London, schmoozing and trying to navigate a course this was it, I now realise, but then I didn't know that.

A Catastrophic Day

I looked at my watch. It was ten past ten on a Monday morning. I shouldn't, I thought, but what the hell? I'll go and make a cup of coffee.

When I came into the kitchen I detected the sinister smell of burning plastic. I sniffed the stove. I peered into the rubbish bin in case there was a cigarette burning in it. (It was possible: I smoked roll-ups in those long-ago days). I checked the refrigerator plug. Nothing. I was about to abandon the search when I heard fizzing and popping. I glanced up at the fuse board and saw a pale grey box with dirty yellow flames jabbing out of it.

I tripped the switches on the main board above the burning box. I ran to the bathroom. My wife was in the shower. 'Electrical fire,' I shouted, like an extra in *London's Burning*. I ran around the house quicker than Sebastian Coe ran the 1500 metres pulling out every plug. I went back to the bathroom. My wife was draped in a towel. Alas, no time for the Badedas moment. The shower was still running. Hadn't I turned off the electricity? I rushed back to the fuse board. I now realised that the burning box, which served the shower, was still very much alive and sparking. From first aid class at school I dimly remembered that wood was a poor conductor. I found our wooden spaghetti tongs and began to tug at the industrial fuse sitting in the middle of the melting case. It was like pulling at a pencil stub stuck in boiling chewing gum.

Finally, however, success.

'Shower's off,' my wife called.

By coincidence a builder appeared. He'd come to fix a door.

'I'll find a spark,' he said. He returned forty minutes later.

'This is Giovanni,' he said. Giovanni was Irish, he added, though his grandparents had been Italians who'd come to Ireland to sell ice cream to the Irish in the 1920s.

I looked at Giovanni. The man before me was wheezing and his eyes were bulbous. He really didn't look good. 'Hello,' he whispered. 'Show me your problem.'

I led him to the kitchen where, with enormous difficulty, he climbed onto a chair the better to see the damage. 'Oh dear,' he croaked. 'No trip.'

'Giovanni just had a heart attack,' the builder muttered.

'Heart attack!' I said.

'Who wired this?' asked Giovanni.

'Actually, Giovanni was in bed when I called round,' the builder continued.

'Because they don't know their arse . . .' Shortage of breath stopped Giovanni continuing his sentence to the end. I thought he might fall and moved closer to catch him. But he didn't and, after a long question-and-answer session about the various electricians we'd had in the schoolhouse when we were doing it up, Giovanni decided that the faulty box was the work of an apprentice electrician from Cavan whom he knew to be reckless.

'Free Stater, you see,' said Giovanni, as if that proved the point.

Now that we all knew whose fault it was, repairs proceeded. Shaking and gasping, the dying electrician levered off the smouldering box and clipped the live wires.

'Coffee?' I asked.

'Yes,' said Giovanni.

'Sugar?'

'Four.'

I put four spoonfuls into his, as requested, and stirred. That should keep the Angel of Death at bay for an hour, I thought. I gave him the mug and he took a gulp.

'I wonder what the old angina will make of that,' he gasped.

He departed, finally, alive. I returned to my study, hoping to continue the page I'd left at ten past ten. My muse, however, had fled – banished not by the man from Porlock but a small electrical fire.

As I couldn't write, I left the study and drove to town to do various errands. I achieved as little there as I had at my desk. At the end of the afternoon, when I got back home, I was morose and annoyed because, not having written, I had failed to propitiate my Catholic work ethic. Now a second electrician came. He was going to redo our entire board so that no fires would ever start again. He climbed onto a chair and stared at the melted box.

'Lucky,' he said. He ran his finger along the scorched bottom of the main fuse box that was immediately above the box that had caught fire. 'Look at that,' he said. His finger ends were black. 'You're lucky the big box didn't go because the whole house would have followed.'

In my mind's eye I glimpsed myself and the family in the hostel accommodation the local Housing Executive people provide for emergencies. But even with that picture in mind, I couldn't feel grateful that we hadn't lost our home. All I could think was, I haven't written.

Later, when electrician number two left, my wife thought to cheer me up. 'Look,' she said, 'you mightn't have written anything but think what you did achieve. You stopped the house burning down. Imagine if you hadn't done that. There'd have been no writing for months.'

She was right, but the trouble with being a catastrophist, who must see everything in the worst possible light, is that feelings will always override facts, even in defiance of reason. Once I feel annoyed, resentful and thwarted, no amount of sound counsel is ever enough to banish the damnable catastrophic feelings.

The Garage Man

In the village by the lake, on the border between the Republic and Northern Ireland, there was a sprinkling of frost on the tarmac as I crunched across the bridge. There were new buildings everywhere, and painted signs acknowledging the International Fund for Ireland, which had paid for them all.

'It's a morning for porridge,' an old man called out to me. He stood on the greasy forecourt of an abandoned garage, hidden by trees.

We started a conversation. His garage had gone bankrupt, he told me, in 1972, when the tourists stopped coming because of the Troubles. 'Come into my parlour,' he said, 'as the spider said to the fly. My name is Joe.'

Joe led me into a small, concrete box with a huge dusty picture window – it had once been the garage office-cum-shop – and invited me to sit on a leather seat cannibalised from a car that sat under a shelf heavy with dusty chamois leathers and 1966 World Cup keyrings. As I sat I noticed, leaning against a wall, a metal sign for Firestone Tyres and a Shell logo that had once adorned a pump.

'Mind now,' he said, as he sat, 'those Jacksons.'

I didn't follow. 'Who?'

'The Jackson boys,' he said, and pointed out the big window towards the bridge I had just crossed. 'The Jacksons!' He looked at me as if I were deliberately ignoring the obvious.

'The Jacksons,' I murmured. 'Yes, the name rings a bell. Did I read something about them in the local paper once? Weren't they brothers? Weren't they all in the Ulster Defence Regiment or something?'

Joe snorted and nodded. 'And wasn't the oldest John,' he said, 'and wasn't he the first to go?'

'I wouldn't know their first names.'

'It was John, don't you remember? He worked the little farm where the mother lived, four miles out the road here.'

'Right,' I said quietly, and tried to gauge what direction Joe was taking this in.

'He had a little council job and he was a part-timer. And they put it about he was on the take, didn't they? The Provos. They said he was taking cement from the council roads depot and flogging it off. They got him when he was mowing the lawn at home, didn't they? And because they'd put out the word that he was pilfering, the people round here said, "Well, maybe John had it coming!" Didn't they? Didn't they?'

His question had a certain menace. I nodded uncertainly.

'You remember the second boy?' he said.

'No, I don't.'

'The second boy was Tim – you must remember Tim?'

'No, I don't.'

'He worked in the quarry out the road here and he was a part-timer too. And they put it about – he was married, you see – they put it about he was having his way with a woman who wasn't his wife. They got Tim when he was driving the dumper at work, didn't they? And because they'd put out the word that he was seeing this other woman, the people round here said, "Well, maybe Tim had it coming!" Didn't they? Didn't they?'

'Yes,' I said.

He had wrung an agreement from me at last, an acknowledgement that I knew this story although I didn't really. It made him smile.

'The third brother was Mark.'

'Oh, yes. Mark,' I said. 'I remember him,' I lied.

'He had a van with a grocer's shop in the back, shelves, counter, cash till, and he was a part-timer too. He drove all round the country selling stuff. And they put it about, didn't they, that if he saw a little boy on the road, he'd stop and invite him into the van and give him a lollipop and sit him on his knee? They got Mark when he was stopped at a house here in the village. They shot him and they walked off down the street like footballers after a game. And because they had put out the word that Mark lured little boys inside his van, the people round here said, "Well, maybe Mark had it coming!" Didn't they? Didn't they?'

'Yes, yes,' I said, with all the fervour I was able to muster, and Joe stared back at me with his dark, angry eyes.

'With her three sons gone, the mother couldn't manage the farm. Not alone. No, no, she had to put it up for sale, which was part of the plan of the ones who did this mischief, of course. One of their "friends" bought it, and Mrs Jackson went away to Belfast. She lasted six months up there, died of a broken heart.'

There was a long pause while I waited to see what was next.

'We did bad,' he said finally. 'I heard Father O'Leary say that with my own ears.'

'Did they catch the ones who did it?'

'Course not.' Joe snorted again, and shook his head. 'Now there's talk of peace, and the International Fund is here, but all the peace and all the building in the world,' here Joe leaned forward and began to whisper confidentially, 'it won't make them go away, you know. They're here, and they're here to stay.'

'Excuse me, who's here to stay?'

'The Jackson boys. Didn't you see them? John and Tim and Mark? You just walked past them. Standing out there on the bridge.' He pointed through the dusty garage front window. 'Have been for years, and haven't budged once.'

I took the view that the best policy at this point was to say nothing.

'And them three Jackson lads will go on standing there with the holes in them, and every time we pass them, they'll look at us with their awful eyes, and we'll know in our living hearts we're cursed, and one day we're going to pay.'

Joe rubbed his hands and turned away, cleared his throat, then spat into his handkerchief.

'Well now,' he said, getting up and shuffling over to the counter where there was an old Primus and a box of matches. 'I think I'll boil the kettle. I'm sure you'll have a drop of tea.' He lit the burner. There was a whiff of gas.

'I'm just going to pop over the bridge past them Jackson boys to the shop,' he said, 'and get a pint of milk. You do take milk in your tea, don't you? And I might pick up some Hobnobs while I'm at it.'

Abroad

The town of Siros was in two parts. The new part, early nineteenth-century, was built when Siros was temporarily the capital of Greece. As we drove through we couldn't fail to notice how many of the streets were paved with marble. Oh, yes, they knew a thing or two about grandeur in the nineteenth century.

On the edge of the new town we found the road we were looking for and began to climb the steep hill to which the other part, the old town of Ano Siros clung. Unlike the new town, where we'd come from, with its straight roads and grand squares, all the streets here were crooked and bafflingly higgledy-piggledy. Of course, they'd made the old town this way to confuse Turkish marauders who, as a result, had always got lost in these streets. Consequently, throughout the centuries of invasions, the Turks were never able to sack the Roman Catholic cathedral at the top of the hill, the principal church of the island's majority Roman Catholic population, because they were never able to find their way there.

But we got through. We followed the signs, and then we passed out of Ano Siros and into the island's agricultural hinterland. After driving for a while the tarmac dribbled away and we found ourselves on a dirt road that ran along the edge of high hills. I gripped the wheel, white knuckles showing, as we crept around one unprotected corner after another, nothing between us and a drop of thousands of feet. I agreed with my wife in the back, the infant on her lap – it was our second son, Finn, the newest addition to our family – that to slip over the edge and fall to the bottom would not be a good way to die.

After several miles on this treacherous road we saw, coming towards us, a farmer on a donkey, with several huge bright plastic bottles of water strapped to his wooden saddle. Terrified that the car's movement might startle the donkey and cause him to bolt, I pulled up, and while I waited for him to pass, the engine idling, the bitter smell of exhaust fumes hanging in the air, I gazed around at the landscape. There were terraces everywhere, some as little as six foot square, and walls of honey-coloured stone that marched in straight lines up and down and across the countryside, enclosing every precious plot.

Presumably, with earth so precious, the Siriots of old had needed to mark their territory definitively from their neighbours', regardless of the hours of back-breaking work it had involved. Oh, there was no mistaking it: the past life of the people who eked a living here was very hard indeed. Even now the life of those working the land, judging by the state of the man and the donkey, wasn't that much better.

I went on and we met a couple of other donkeys laden with farmers and bottles of water and stopped so they could pass too. Then the landscape got poorer and more wretched, and there were no men on donkeys, and we didn't have to stop once for anyone. A handwritten sign appeared, nailed to an old post. It said, *Taberna, 500 metres*, and although it seemed inconceivable, an inn in the middle of nowhere, half a kilometre further on there it was – a square white building with four shady pine trees.

As we parked I could hear techno music coming from a Subaru Jeep; the volume on the cassette player turned to max The owner of the bar was unloading crates of ouzo from the back. He wore a back-to-front baseball cap. He stopped work, stroked our sleeping child's naked stomach for a moment, welcomed us in and called his sister. She came, a well-made woman with a body that had obviously been fashioned by manual work, strong and sturdy, but not toned and athletic She wore an ancient dress, and her eyes were light blue and piercing.

We wanted ice cream but the proprietor had none. We

wanted the phone to ring the house where we were staying so we could tell them we'd be late back because we'd travelled so far, but there was none.

'No phone!' I said. I shrugged. I looked incredulous. They must have a phone. It was impossible to live out here without a phone.

The owner's sister pointed at the telegraph poles by the road outside. 'Follow the wire to the widow's house at the end,' she said in English. 'The widow has a phone. We all use it.'

We sat on the terrace then, drinking Coca-Cola out of dusty ribbed bottles, and I stared into the distance. I saw a brown scorched landscape, a faraway village with just half a dozen dwellings, and the shimmering Aegean. Thirty miles away, two neighbouring islands floated in the afternoon haze. They looked unreachable, unattainable.

The music was off now. A donkey brayed, a bird trilled, and Finn pulled at the straw in his drink. Suddenly I felt as if I was on Aran or in West Donegal, and had a powerful sense that the brother and sister who ran the bar lived lives of aching solitude, not unlike those of some on Ireland's western seaboard.

Of course, this pair had techno music and baseball caps and other bits of flotsam carried to them from the world beyond, but essentially they were alone. Like their ancestors, they eked out a precarious existence in an inhospitable place – and, just as in certain parts of Ireland, the strongest element in their lives was a sense of sexual deprivation. There was little here by way of the comfort of others, and I felt that lack stretched back for generations. This is what I thought.

In this hot, dry place, I had not expected that the inner eye would turn towards my colder, wetter home and her sorrows – but wasn't that what always happened on journeys? You never found new things out, you simply rediscovered what you knew already – which in turn suggested to me, as I sat on that terrace, something about the vanity of the traveller.

We finished our drinks and got up to go. The owner took off his baseball cap and sunglasses to bid us goodbye. He had one blue eye, one brown.

'It must be lonely out here,' said my wife.

'I have no problem.' He smiled.

We got into the car and set off down the hill. The telephone wire was on my right. I followed it to the end, to the house of the widow.

An Incident

It was a glorious summer's day, early afternoon. We arrived in Rossnowlagh in Donegal with friends, the Brankins. We planned to pitch tents and camp. We nosed the car through the entrance to the car park above the beach. Donegal County Council had a sign up at the entrance, 'No Camping', but we paid no attention, us and the Brankins. Like so many others, we'd been camping here for years.

We found a grassy corner near the dunes, and put our tents up. Round about four o'clock, several dozen Escorts and Ford XRis arrived, filled with young people. They parked beside the toilets on the other side of the car park, hauled huge speakers from the boots of their cars and turned on their music.

Next thing, a group of eight or ten separated from the rest and drove across to our corner. They got out of their cars and lay on the ground and drank. When they had finished, rather than carry their bottles to the oil drum that Donegal County Council had provided for rubbish, they chucked them onto our pitch. We said nothing. Perhaps that was our mistake.

They had two tents and they started to erect them. There

was a lot of 'cunt' this and 'fuck' that. The most vociferous was a boy with two earrings – we nicknamed him 'Croaker'.

Once their tents were finally up they went back across the car park and rejoined the others. Then everyone drove off, heading for the beach. That was where the party was going to be.

It got dark. We could hear their music in the distance. David Brankin and I got talking. 'Mid-forties,' he said, 'as we are, we think we're young, or youngish. But then you meet real young people like those ones, and you realise you're middle-aged.' Half eleven that night, being middle-aged, I turned in.

And I slept fairly well. I slept very well. But when I got up in the morning David had quite a story to tell.

In the middle of the night, they had come back, the ones who'd camped beside us. They'd sat round our food table, helping themselves. David had reproached them. 'We're hungry,' said Croaker.

'Get your own food,' said David. 'Now, get out of here.'

'Can we take a light from your fire?' Croaker asked. He seemed reasonable and David didn't want trouble. David had pulled a burning plank out of the embers and handed it over. Maybe that was another mistake. Next thing, they'd picked up all the firewood we'd gathered earlier on the beach, strolled back to their tents with it and lit their own fire.

They'd started drinking. David couldn't go to bed – he knew that – so he sat and waited. We were forgotten for a while. Then they remembered us.

They came over with a ball. 'Game of football?' they said.

'Your two tents, they're the goalposts.'

'No,' David said. 'That's where our wives and children are sleeping.' They'd started playing tag, untying guy ropes, crashing around. David said, 'Why don't you get the fuck out of here?' which was not like him at all. That had brought them up short.

They had retreated, swiping an empty Camping Gaz canister. They threw it onto their own fire for the 'craic'.

'That'll explode,' David had called across anxiously.

'That's the whole fucking point,' Croaker had roared back.

It didn't, and that had made them angrier. They piled into their cars and circled round us.

Then they stopped, their three cars in a line, with our tents caught in their lights. 'Come on, cunt.' They wanted to fight David but not on our site, out in the darkness, down on the beach. He wouldn't budge. Eventually they screeched off, vanishing into the night on some mysterious errand of their own. David rescued the Gaz canister, then sat up to wait for them to come back. He had the kitchen knife by this stage.

They had returned towards dawn but now they'd sex on their minds. They'd piled into their tents and got to it, and then they fell asleep.

When David had finished his story, the Géblers and the Brankins (the wives were up as well) went over and prowled around the neighbours' site. They were still sleeping and we were going to slash their tyres or make a few sneaky incisions in their tents to let the rain in. But then my wife noticed their car doors were open, and the keys were in the ignition.

My wife opened the door of Croaker's Escort – a purple number with 'No Fear' on the back – lifted the keys out, walked over to the oil drum that was the bin, and dropped them in. Bingo!

It was noon before he noticed and then the cry went up. 'Anyone seen my fucking keys?'

'Didn't you put 'em in your pocket, like I said?' shouted his girlfriend. She was really helpful.

'Have you lost something?' my wife called. No sarcasm, just pleasant.

'Mind your own fucking business,' said Croaker's girlfriend.

She was beside herself with rage.

'You know, they've not said sorry,' my wife said, 'and I'm not going to lift a finger till they do.'

They didn't say anything, not a word. They just went on searching, while we went on watching.

By afternoon, the oil drum was heaped with rubbish and wasps swarmed all over it. They passed it a thousand times, but they never thought to look in it, of course.

Early evening, we left. As we drove away, I could see them in the rear-view mirror, still searching.

Working at Writing 2

As an adolescent I had met the Anglo-Irish sage Hubert Butler, and now that I was living in Ireland I read his essay collection *Escape from the Anthill*. One essay in particular caught my attention.

'The Eggman and the Fairies' was the story of Bridget Cleary, a young, married, childless countrywoman, living in County Tipperary. In March 1895, after she had been unwell for some weeks, her husband Michael, along with about a dozen relatives, decided that the fairies had stolen Bridget and left a changeling in her place. The only way to banish the impostor and bring the real Bridget back was with fire, so Michael and the relatives put Bridget into the grate, twice. She took three days to die from her burns, after which Michael buried her in a shallow grave.

But you couldn't kill someone in the Irish countryside and it not be noticed. It wasn't long before the police found the body. Everyone who'd participated in Bridget's burning was arrested, charged, tried and sent to prison.

In Butler's opinion the catalyst was jealousy. Michael believed his wife was amorously involved with a tradesman who bought eggs from the local women, including Bridget. Naturally he had felt anger and shame about the affair (though it had never happened) and vented his feelings, which couldn't be openly admitted, as fantasy: the woman in their bed was a changeling and the real Bridget was a prisoner in an underground fairy palace. Maybe there was a novel in this, I thought.

I rang Butler to canvass his opinion. 'I'm not quite certain I got it right,' he said, and explained that he no longer thought Michael's jealousy had caused the tragedy. He couldn't have encouraged me more if he'd said, 'Go and write it as a novel.'

I found the transcript of the Preliminary Inquiry (the interrogation of the defendants by the local magistrate to determine if there was a case to answer) in the *Nationalist*, the local paper, and read it carefully. If Bridget's adultery wasn't the explanation for what had happened, could I find another?

By the time I reached the end of the transcript I thought I had. It was mass hysteria. March 1895 was wet and miserable. The defendants were locked up in the Clearys' cottage for days, ideal conditions, with everyone urging everyone else on, for the poisonous fantasy to flourish. This wasn't a nineteenth century opera plot, as in Butler's thesis – husband unable to admit jealousy murders wife on preposterous pretext that she's a changeling – but a twentieth-century story about mass psychosis.

This resonated with me. In Northern Ireland, I'd noticed, most people on their own were pleasant and reasonable; however, when a lot of individually reasonable people were put in a group together they often became unpleasant, unreasonable and sometimes violent. In the Bridget Cleary story I thought I saw a way to describe some of the dynamics at work in the society in which I had settled, but on a scale that was small, domestic and, more importantly, not overtly political.

I had written my early novels quite quickly, usually taking between six and nine months. This one took a lot longer. Having already written five novels, I was now a tougher critic of what I wrote and far readier to cut what didn't work.

The Cure took two years to write and was published in 1994 (when I was forty). It was a considerable critical success. Nonetheless, shortly after publication Kate Jones, my editor at Hamish Hamilton (Christopher Sinclair-Stevenson had gone), said she had to let me go. I didn't sell, apparently.

To secure a new publisher I needed a book. I'd no new novel in my head but I'd had fourteen stories published over the previous ten years. Write a further three, I thought, and I'd have a collection.

I put together the volume *W9 & Other Lives* and while I hawked it round various publishers, I wrote a couple of books for children, *The Base* and *Frozen Out*. It was a strange time. I couldn't understand why no one wanted to publish the stories. (In the end Pat Ramsey of the Lagan Press in Belfast took *W9 & Other Lives*). Gradually it began to dawn on me: I'd had a lovely run of good fortune but now I'd entered different times. To get through I would have to be indefatigable and cunning.

At the Depot

It was the last Friday of the summer. The bus from Belfast to Enniskillen was moist and hot. At the Enniskillen depot there was no sign of the taxi I'd ordered to take me home. Typical.

I went into the bus shelter, with its drinks dispenser and painted metal bench. I'd wait five minutes; it might turn up. A very old woman sat in the corner. She was in a brown dress and a black gabardine coat. Balanced on her lap was a large cardboard box containing two packets of dog biscuits.

'Well, do you reckon the peace'll last?' she whispered, meaning the ceasefire the IRA had recently announced. Her lower front teeth were missing and she pushed her tongue through the gap, and then, before I was able to answer, she continued, 'There'll be fighting again, you watch. They're burning Orange halls and chapels and churches. Oh, they're awful rough now, the Irish.'

Then she leaned forward and stared out at the crowded forecourt; there were coaches pulling in and out. 'Is that the Cavan bus?' she asked, and pointed at the closest coach.

'I don't think so but I could ask that inspector over there,' I said.

'Huh! Inspectors! There's six counties now in Ulster – there was nine, but there's six now, and they won't come into the state, and why should they? And they've said they won't come, so leave them alone, that's what I say.'

In the car park opposite the bus station, a woman staggered and fell flat on her back, dropping her cider bottle. Her male companion rolled her onto her front and got her to her knees, but he couldn't pull her to her feet. She was too heavy, too drunk. He swore at her and lurched off in disgust. The woman screamed after him. I couldn't hear her words because of the plate glass of the shelter between us.

'The Irish, they have England bombed entirely,' continued the old woman, shifting her box of dog biscuits. 'They have her ruined from head to toe. They have her on the run. That's why we have ceasefires. Have you the time?'

I showed her my watch.

'Plenty of time. The one who made that stuff made plenty of it. I was in England in the fifties and the sixties. Very nice people. Never had a bit of bother. I was a domestic. On the timetable it says the Cavan bus is six-forty, but one time it came early, and I missed it!'

In the car park the drunk woman crawled to the pay-and-display machine and, using one of the supporting poles, hauled herself to her feet. She staggered off.

'When I was a child we lived in poverty on a small farm in Cavan, and we had no money, and my mother, may the Lord have mercy on her soul, she made do without money. De Valera ran the state then, and he cared for the poor. But now no one cares for the poor, and a taxi now – just a three-minute ride – it's too much.'

Then, pointing, she said, 'Where's that bus over there going?'

'Belleek.'

'The Church was very good to the poor. But now, on account of this one who's in prison, I won't say his name – you know the priest I mean?'

'Father Brendan Smyth?'

'Him, yes. I went to church all my life, but now I don't bother.'

A youth in a T-shirt strode by. The picture on the front was Ireland without a border and the message '26 + 6 = 1'.

'The Church don't care anymore for the poor, and in the state now, they hate the poor. The Six Counties'll not come, and why should they? And our atrocities, they'd shame you.'

A coach wheezed to a standstill in the sunshine outside.

'Your bus,' I said.

'Yes, that's my bus,' she said. 'They're very nice people, the English. But since this Father What's-his-name, Father Brendan Smyth, like I said, I don't bother with the Church any more and I don't think I'll be going again.'

Her eyes were wet. She got up and went as far as the door. Then she stopped and turned.

'Everything I had is gone. Even the timetable is worthless.

It's all gone. It's all worthless. Everything. That's how it is.'

She padded away, the ribbed soles of her plastic boots sticking to the hot concrete. I watched her get onto the bus. She waved as it drove away. I didn't know if she was waving to me or even if she'd see but I waved back anyhow.

After the bus had gone I went to the telephone box and rang the taxi company.

Personal

'Carlo, how would you explain this place?' asked the English guest as he settled into the front of the car beside me. 'So beautiful and yet there was all this violence.'

At the wheel I felt my heart sinking. This was the question every guest asked when they came to Northern Ireland. They expected an answer that was neat and simple and pat. The trouble was, there was no such answer.

What I wanted to say at this moment was, 'Look! You've got to live here to understand the place.' Whenever the question came up, that was always the answer I wanted to give. I never did, of course. Those words were always going to sound rude, however I said them. What I always said instead was, 'Look! You've got to remember, it's always personal here.'

In fact, this was a hopeless answer because it raised more questions than it answered. However, what it did have going for it was a certain gnomic authority and sometimes that did the trick. Tonight my luck was in. The Englishman at my side went silent and stayed that way for the rest of the journey.

At last, we arrived at a small farmhouse and went through the back door and into the kitchen. There was a party going on. We found Raymond, a policeman, sitting at the table with his wife, Alicia, who was Italian.

I introduced my guest, pulled up a couple of chairs, and we sat down opposite them. Raymond poured us all a drink.

'How are you?' I said.

'Oh, well, if I don't grumble, I'll be breaking the habit of a lifetime,' said Raymond.

Alicia rearranged her plait of long dark hair, sighed but said nothing.

'Heard about Rosemary?' asked Raymond.

'Oh, God!' said Alicia. 'I don't want to hear another word about her.'

A marital spat followed. In the end Alicia said, 'Go on – give yourself a heart attack! Talk away,' after which she whispered, 'bloody woman.'

'I've got this business,' began Raymond, 'trout farm. I do it as a sideline to the police job. I needed help and I got this friend, Rosemary, to come and work for me. I think it would be fair to say I trained her.'

He topped up the glasses.

'Then, one Friday, last year, Rosemary quit. I got back from work – there was this letter of resignation waiting. I rang her up, she said, "Sorry, Ray, family commitments, please send on my P45." I was disappointed, but I thought nothing more of it.'

'You sent her some flowers,' Alicia interrupted.

'Yes. I did,' Raymond swallowed a mouthful of wine. 'The very next Monday, Alicia took the children to school, then drove out to see someone on the other side of town from where we are, and she saw this sign that said, "Such and such a trout farm, under construction", and who should it turn out is the manager? Rosemary, and she's got the backing of some guy who's her new business partner.

'Then I started to ask around – you know how it is in a small place – and I learned this was planned from the day she started with us, although she'd never bothered to tell me. I learned she arranged all her grants while she was working for me, even fixed her planning permission, using a different name, of course, so I wouldn't know. Next thing I learned, she'd photocopied my address book and was writing to all my customers and giving them the good news about her bloody business.

'Anyway, now we roll forward in time. Her business is up and running. We are in competition. I don't talk to Rosemary any more. Then, out of the blue, I hear she's made a complaint. She says I'm in cahoots with the guy in the DoE who checks the water we discharge from the fish tanks into the river. She says I'm paying him to overlook the fact that it's dirty. It's absolute nonsense, but the guy's suspended immediately – and that's where we are now. He's not being paid, I can't do any business, and we're waiting for some tribunal to deliberate.'

'Oh dear,' said the Englishman.

'Yes,' said Alicia. 'But she's cut off her nose, this Rosemary.'

Raymond snorted.

'It's bad for my Raymond,' said Alicia, 'but it'll be worse for her. Alan, the DoE guy, very nice, totally non-political. Alan's brother, on the other hand, no! Member of the Provisionals, big in the movement, not at all nice.

'Now this brother, he doesn't worry me or Raymond,' she continued, 'and Ray is a policeman. But Rosemary, her husband, he's a part-timer. If it all starts again properly, they'll go for him straight away. Why not? There's a black mark against his name. In fact, I'd say they will for certain.'

As we drove home in the darkness, several hours and many glasses of wine later, I heard the Englishman saying, 'I see now what you meant when you said it was personal.'

A Proustian Moment

My wife shouted, 'She's going to be sick! Stop!'

I stopped the car but it was too late. My elder daughter's sick jetted out like water from a burst pipe. It seemed to have a lot of kiwi in it.

We were ten in the car: my wife and our four children, Gina and her three children. The young ones in the jockey seats at the back were all shouting, 'Ugh! Stinky!' and the baby, Georgia, I noticed (she was our fourth child, our second daughter, and she was asleep), had our elder daughter's sick between her toes.

We piled out onto the verge. All the young children skipped about like young colts, except for the five-year-old, Finn: with his plastic bow and arrow slung over his shoulder, he climbed into a field full of sheep.

'Take off your jeans and you can have my tights,' said my wife to our teenage daughter, who was covered in her own sick. 'And you're not to laugh at my hairy legs,' my wife added, pulling off her boots.

The fourteen-year-old needed a certain amount of encouragement.

The day was cold and damp – not a good one for changing in the open. Also, we were on the public highway. I looked around: I saw a few crows, and some bleating sheep running terrified from the boy with the bow, but otherwise no one, nothing.

'There's nobody around,' I assured her blithely, at which point, on cue, a long line of cars with Tyrone number plates came around the corner and drove past us. Fresh from church or chapel, the occupants of the cars could not help but stare in surprise at the milling children, and the clothes draped over the five-bar gate. They even pointed.

Cleaning operations took an hour and then we resumed our journey. To our amazement, we found our destination, the Gortin History Park, less than a mile down the road. Unfortunately the gate was locked and the notice outside informed us that Sunday opening only started on 1 April. This was 31 March. Obviously God had different plans for us today.

We drove on to the Ulster-American Folk Park – same story. This left us with only one option: we would have to go to Omagh, find a restaurant and treat the children.

But, inevitably, because it was a Sunday, Omagh was closed. A solitary pedestrian commiserated and advised us to try the Coach Inn.

The name conjured up the nineteenth century, but in reality the Coach Inn was very much late-twentieth. It was a huge white building, standing on a ring road, quite close to a flyover.

However, it did have a painted board outside that read, 'À la carte meals 12.00 noon to 9.00 p.m.' Even the children cheered when they saw that.

We parked and tried to get into the Coach Inn but all the doors appeared to be locked. The only one that wasn't opened onto the lobby outside the toilets, where the air was thick with bleach and the gassy sound of flushing urinals. It was an ill omen, and when we got through to the lounge, we found it empty and hushed.

'You are open?' said my wife, bullishly.

The young barman shook his head.

'Oh, please,' she begged. 'Three adults, seven kids, it's the middle of the afternoon, we're starving. There must be somewhere to eat.'

The barman looked at his watch and said, 'Ah, right enough, Sunday, twenty to four, never a very handy time.'

The Kentucky Fried Chicken restaurant was open, he thought.

'Oh, God!' moaned my wife, but five minutes later, there we were, sashaying through the doors into the square glass box that was KFC, Omagh. There was not a window open in the place, and the air was thick with the fug of cooking oil.

Chaos ensued as each child ordered, then changed his or her order fifteen times in the light of what the other children were having. It really was extraordinary how many permutations there were to be had from a menu that was basically chips, chicken and soft drinks.

But we did it. We got the food and spread ourselves over half a dozen tables. I ate my first French fry and, just as the taste of a small rich cake, a madeleine, soaked in tea, provokes Marcel in *Remembrance of Things Past*, so this KFC chip did the same for me. On the inner screen where memories are shown, a scene from my past flickered into life.

The place was London, the time 1982. It was a winter's night and I was in a flat in Elgin Crescent in Notting Hill, and I was pounding away at my portable typewriter, an Olivetti Lettera 22. Then I ran out of coffee. Disaster.

I had no money but I had a vast green seduction sofa where I hoped I might find some. I carefully searched the crevices. Eureka! In the cracks I found enough change to buy what I needed.

I left the flat, hurried round to the KFC in Portobello Road and went in. It was also a glass box where the air was filled with the fug of oil. London or Omagh, the KFC inner atmosphere was always the same, it seemed.

As my funds would stretch I bought coffee and chips. I went back out into the street. There was a vague smell of rotting vegetables (the odour came from produce the market stallholders dumped at the end of every working day) and I could feel the heat of the chips and the coffee through their respective containers. It had begun to rain and the pavement felt slippery underfoot. I went forward slowly so it was a few minutes before I got into the flat and back at my desk. I eased the top off the coffee and opened the chips, sprinkled on KFC salt and ketchup, then ate one. It was hot and I had to breathe out quickly to stop it burning my tongue.

And there, despite my urging the projectionist to run it on, the film stopped, and in the inner cinema where I'd watched the fragment the lights came on and I was back in Omagh, surrounded by seven screaming and delighted children.

Eddie

It was the summer of '95, and I'd a desk and a job in Belfast in a first-floor office with two lovely windows. It was the end of the day and I was standing with Mary, the office cleaner. She was in a blue overall, bare legs. It was hot. We looked out of the windows as the sun streamed in. It had been glorious for days.

'It's our reward,' she said – and not for the first time, alluding to the ceasefire, the first, of the year before.

'Oh, right,' I said.

Our gaze dropped to the small public square across the road from the office. There was a patch of grass, a few flowerbed and some benches. Around the bench closest to us, half a dozen street drinkers were gathered, a vodka bottle whizzing clockwise from hand to hand. Then, as it was about to pass into the hands of a large, red-faced woman with dyed red hair, the bottle reversed and started going back the way it had come.

'Trouble!' said Mary, and elbowed me.

The red-faced woman tried to snatch the bottle back. A man covered with blue tattoos shoved her away. Now everyone was jeering except a fat, dumpy fellow with curly hair. He shook his head, shouted, 'Not fair! Give it back to her,' and stepped forward.

'That's Eddie,' said Mary.

'You know him?'

'Oh, yes. Well, Belfast is small, isn't it? You know everyone, really. He lived in our street when I was a girl. Very good parents, very strict, chapel every Sunday, not that you'd know now.'

Eddie tried to wrestle the bottle from the tattooed man. Their tussle seemed amiable – until the tattooed man put his fists up. Eddie, breathless, sweating, took two savage punches to the head; he buckled and sank to the ground.

Mary exhaled. 'There was no call for that.'

Some other vigilant office worker must have been watching like us and made the call, for the next second, it seemed, the cops were there, grinning as they spilled from their Land Rover and strode towards the mêlée.

'Eddie was such a lovely boy,' said Mary. 'He used to have a go-kart he'd made himself, and he'd pull me round the streets on it. He was called "Go Faster" because that's what I would say – "Go faster, Eddie, go faster."'

As the police did their police thing, Mary gave me a thumbnail sketch of Eddie's life. He was an only child. His father had died when he was twelve. He'd got a job in a tannery at fourteen and begun to drink. His mother had died of despair when he was twenty. He'd lost the house and moved onto the street. A cousin had found him sleeping rough up the Falls. She'd brought him home. Disaster. Eddie set his bedroom on fire and went back to the streets. That was thirty years ago, and since then nothing had changed.

'Would Eddie recognise you now?' I asked, as the cops led away the tattooed man who'd assaulted Eddie. He was shrieking and waving his arms at an imaginary swarm of flies.

'Oh, aye, I see him on the streets, and if he's not half-cut he'll say, "It ain't great with Go Faster! Give us fifty pence."'

The steel door shut on the tattooed man, and the Land Rover drove off. Then one of the remaining drinkers noticed that the woman with the red face was holding the bottle and, worse, that it was empty.

'That was smart,' laughed Mary. 'She's drunk the lot while no one was looking.'

The other drinkers were not so amused. One man pulled her red hair, while two young drinkers took it in turns to kick her bottom. Only Eddie, still on his knees, like a supplicant, spoke up for her. But nothing he could say would calm them. The party was over. Everyone stormed off in a rage. Now there was just her and Eddie.

'He's got a job, you know,' said Mary. 'Cleans the buses at night.'

Down below, the red-faced woman was trying to pull Eddie to his feet. But Eddie could not rise. He was stuck.

The red-faced woman went and spoke to the black railings around a tree.

'What's she doing?' I asked.

'She thinks the railings are a policeman, I bet,' said Mary. 'She's asking for help.'

Eddie began to laugh. He evidently thought the woman's mistake was hilarious. She didn't. The woman went back to her defender, gave him two half-hearted kicks and staggered off.

'We'd better go down and get him back on his feet,' said Mary, 'or he'll die there.'

At that moment two crusties with matted, dreadlocked hair and much pierced ears swooped by, took an armpit each and lifted Eddie to his feet. He thanked them and began to waddle his slow, sad way towards Botanic Avenue.

Now he'd been pointed out to me, I often saw Eddie

afterwards, in doorways and entries, and once, with Mary, I met him in the street, a vast scab on his chin like a squashed toffee.

'Hello,' she said, and he looked at her blankly. 'He's going downhill,' she whispered. 'He doesn't know me.'

Then, one evening, she came in to clean the office and found me at my desk. I asked her, 'How's things?'

She shrugged. 'I'll make the tea,' she said. I followed her to the kitchen and found her looking out of the window. The red-faced woman and the tattooed man were on the bench, a cider bottle passing slowly from one to the other.

'You know how cold it's been? she said. 'Well, Eddie got into a wheelie bin when it was snowing. He went to sleep and he never woke up.'

The Boys

They boarded the bus in Belfast, three of them, late teens, early twenties, very snazzy with their big puffy jackets, curtain ring earrings and back-to-front baseball caps emblazoned with messages from the dance floor, 'Young Love', 'Party On', 'House Rules'. They each had something under their jackets, held like a wounded bird, but as the bus turned out of Glengall Street, the clatter of bottle tops on the floor at the back indicated what they had carried aboard.

The bus hurtled westwards under an evening sky of mauve, then black. The boys in the back began to hum 'The Sash'. Half of the passengers shifted nervously. Then the trio broke into words, not the original ones of 'The Sash', but new, satirical lyrics. So they weren't bandsmen, after all.

At Dungannon, where the bus stopped for five minutes, the

boys nipped to the bog, then swaggered back, buttoning their flies and smirking at every woman they passed. After a short conference, several passengers decided to get off and catch a taxi. The bus went on, emptier. From the back came the chink of rolling bottles and the Republican song 'Foggy Dew' but performed house style; one sang the lyrics, while the other two shouted the drum and bass lines. Was it a piss-take, or just irony? Whatever the answer, everyone now felt spooked by the boys in the back.

At Ballygawley, after another pit stop, the driver announced that drinking was forbidden. Too late now, said the boys, it was all gone. There was more beery laughter, and the last of the passengers ran. Now everyone was gone except myself, the driver and Fun Boy Three.

A few minutes later the bus pulled up at a bus stop in the next village, Augher. A pale-faced youth came aboard, saw the three older ones in the back and bolted into the seat across from where I sat.

Within seconds the three heroes were around him, smiling, charm personified, dripping with fake bonhomie.

'Hello,' purred the leader, a fellow in a canary-yellow jacket.

There was a brief exchange about some event at which Canary (as I decided to call him) had seen the new passenger. 'I mind you there,' said Canary. His voice was sweet as treacle. 'What do they call you now? I can't remember.'

'Graham.'

'Oh, yes, it's Graham, isn't it? That's a very nice name, isn't it, boys? Isn't Graham a very nice name?'

Effusive noises came from the cronies. They all wished their name was Graham, apparently.

'What does your mammy call you, Graham? I bet she calls you Grahamy-Wayamy.'

'She just calls me Graham.'

'You'll have to speak louder. I can't hear you, Graham.'

'She just calls me Graham.'

'Just Graham. Just plain old boring Graham? Doesn't your mammy have a nice pet name for you, Graham? You look like a boy who'd have a nice mammy, doesn't he, lads? Doesn't he look like a boy who'd have a nice mammy who'd have a nice name for her nice boy?'

Graham swallowed and said nothing. I felt as if I had stumbled into a Pinter play. Canary looked out of the window at black fields, black hedgerows and a black sky, then back at Graham.

'A little bird tells me you're going to Enniskillen, aren't you, Graham?' he said.

Graham was pale and silent.

'We're going to Enniskillen as well, did you know that, Graham? I'm going there and my friends are going there. So we're all getting off together at the same stop. Now, is that a very good idea? You get off, we get off, together. Do you really want to do that, Graham? What do you think your mammy would say? "Don't do it, Grahamy-Wayamy," is what I think she'd say. "I don't think you should get off where they're getting off, Graham pet. No, I don't think so. I definitely don't think so."'

Graham stood and ran down the aisle. 'Stop the bus,' he shouted. 'I have to get off.'

The driver stopped the bus. We were in the middle of the Fermanagh countryside, not a light in sight.

'Have you got a problem?' asked the driver, as the door hissed open.

Graham dashed down the steps and into the darkness.

The door closed and the bus pulled away. Canary and friends banged on the glass and called, 'Goodbye, Graham, you made the right decision.' But Graham stood on the verge, his back to the bus, his face turned to the hedge so he neither heard nor saw their farewell.

At last we got to the Enniskillen depot and parked. It was the end of the journey. The driver was writing something in a book as the boys filed past him. They were brazenly swigging bottles of Miller that they'd obviously kept for now.

'We'd like to thank you,' said Canary, 'for conveying us so beautifully.' He put his hand out but the driver wouldn't shake it. 'Oh, well, if you won't be friends that's your lookout,' he said. Then he said to his friends, 'Come on.'

He led them down the steps and across the depot's forecourt, and I could hear them whistling in the darkness long after they had disappeared from sight.

Letter to an English Friend after Canary Wharf

Saturday, 10 February 1996

Dear W–,

This morning I went into Enniskillen, sashayed into the Lochside Garage Shop and said, '*Daily Telegraph*, please.' (Now, I'm an old colonel, what else would you expect me to read?)

'No *Telegraph*,' said the girl.

'But it won't be Saturday without Oz Clarke's wine column . . .'

Then my eye fell on the other papers arranged along the counter. The forces of National Liberation had bombed Canary Wharf. Hence no *Daily Telegraph* because Canary Wharf is where it prints. I hadn't listened to the radio the previous night or that morning and that's what happens when you omit to do so. Things happen and you don't know about them.

And yet – well, pompous and self-inflated as this sounds, I can't say that I was exactly surprised. No, not exactly.

Julian Barnes starts his great adultery novel *Before She Met Me* with a long quotation from a medical textbook of which the gist is this: the brain is in three parts; there's a bright bit at the top – that's the computer terminal, full of smart girls and Microsoft buffs; then there's a very large middle section where the brain does its paperwork and this is filled with civil servants and pen-pushers; and then, finally, there's the basement, the oldest part of the brain, and here dwells our guardian, old Mr Reptile, whose speciality is sniffing out danger and seeing into the future on the strength of the slightest and most seemingly whimsical evidence.

For instance, I remember once, when I lived in London, walking down Portobello Road in the early hours and seeing a bank of red tail lights under the M40 Strange, I thought, so many motorbikes lined in a row Then beady-eyed Mr Reptile stirred in his basement lair and shook his head, and I knew, in the darkness, out of sight, the bikers were waiting. I turned around and walked away; some other pedestrians weren't so lucky.

Nearly seven years ago, I left London and came to live in Northern Ireland, and I have to say, since I arrived, he has been very, very helpful. A story, I think, will do to illustrate. One evening, a few years ago (the Troubles were in full spate), I was in

Belfast, cycling towards the house where I lodged, when I saw a group of men on the corner. Now, in that area, there were always groups of men; it was that kind of area, a proletarian area where men stood around on street corners.

But Mr Reptile saw things differently. 'Vigilantes,' he murmured. He was right!

I was all for turning around but he shook his head. 'Big mistake,' he said. That would attract attention. That would make me look suspicious. The way through, he advised, was to affect blithe insouciance and act like I belonged.

So I sailed towards the vigilantes, pointed in the direction of my house, shouted I was going home to my dinner and carried right on. Nobody so much as lifted a baseball bat. Of course not, because I was a local on his way home to his tea. Thank you, Mr Reptile.

As you know, I work at HMP Maze sometimes, doing 'creative writing'. Driving there recently I found the motorway closed. I was diverted into Portadown. I found myself on the outskirts of a Republican estate – tricolours on every lamp post, green, white and orange kerbstones, and lots of Liberation graffiti.

As I was driving along, looking for diversion signs, the words 'Clegg out. All out.' flashed past, scrawled on a wall. (Private Lee Clegg was one of a party of paratroopers who opened fire on a stolen Vauxhall Astra in the Glen Road, West Belfast, on 30 September 1990; at his trial he was convicted of the attempted murder of the car's driver, Martin Peake, and the murder of Peake's passenger Karen

Reilly; the Life Sentence Review Board, however, on account of 'exceptional mitigating factors', subsequently released him from Wakefield Prison in July 1995). Seeing 'Clegg out. All out,' Mr Reptile sighed in the basement and that was it. I knew the peace wasn't going to last.

Now, you could say, 'Come on, Carlo, you're just making this up because it's a good story and it reflects to your greater glory.' Yes, and there's no way I could disprove that. But my question – one I think worth asking – is how come he made this prediction?

I can only say it was because of what those four words of graffiti said so emphatically about the Republican idea of equivalence. Within the hermetically sealed world of the movement, if Clegg gets out, then everyone should get out, because that's the way the world *ought* to be. Theirs is a world full of oughts, of which the biggest is: they generously declare a ceasefire, everyone ought to come to the table. But if not everybody comes, as everybody *ought* to know, the only alternative is to go back to basics, back to explosives. Hence Canary Wharf.

When I put it into words, this seems long and cumbersome, yet the beauty of Mr Reptile is that he grasped it all in an instant.

He's asleep now, so I can't ask him for his thoughts on the weeks and months ahead. Anyway, perhaps that's not necessary. I can work some things out for myself. When I drove back from the Lochside Garage Shop this morning, I saw what I haven't for months: a line of army helicopters sweeping towards the border. Later, I heard on the news that the army is back on the streets of West Belfast.

This future, of course, bears an uncanny resemblance to our not-too-distant past. But will we have the courage to just say, 'No, we're not doing this again, forget it, no more killing'? I'm afraid I don't know, but if Himself down in the basement were in a position to speak, I suspect he'd say, 'I don't think so, no, not for a while anyway.'

Yours gloomily,
Carlo

Fear and Loathing in North Belfast

I was in an entry, the passage running along the back of two rows of terraced houses. It was narrow, about four foot wide, dead straight, high walls of Belfast red brick on either side and uniform doors at uniform intervals, which opened into the backyards of the uniform houses.

The BBC had sent me to North Belfast to investigate punishment beatings I was looking for the scene of a crime and it was not hard to find it. I just counted down the doors and then I was there, outside the back of number eighteen, where the victim had lived. She was a woman who had been accused of 'anti-social behaviour'. One evening, a few months ago, she was taken out of her house and brought here to the entry. She was beaten, her hair was shorn off, and then she was covered with green paint: there were splashes and puddles of dried paint everywhere, testament to her punishment.

I slipped from the entry back into the street. The sun was shining so brightly I had to blink. On the corner there was a lamp post, the remnants of a shredded Sinn Féin election poster lying in the gutter below. It was Thursday, 30 May 1996, polling day for the Forum, and I could hear an amplified voice in a nearby street. I presumed it must come from an election car with a PA system that was driving around exhorting the faithful to vote.

I turned up the street, counting again, until I came to the front of number eighteen. The doors and windows were covered with sheets of metal painted a hideous brown and scrawled with messages: 'Sharon sucks Seamus,' and 'Up the RA'. Number eighteen had become uninhabitable since the punishment, yet the houses on either side were occupied, net curtains in the windows, children shouting within.

As I stood there, contemplating this Belfast phenomenon, the way violence can sully a home, a piece of ground or the corner of a street and turn it into a place where no one will go, I heard a woman calling, 'This place is shite. The devil walks here.'

I turned and saw that the speaker was somewhere between forty and sixty. She had bright blue angry eyes and her arms were folded across her chest. She stood outside the house opposite number eighteen. Except for the boarded-up doors and windows, number eighteen and her house were mirror images of one another.

'Good morning,' I replied, and walked across. A teenager shuffled up and stood behind her. He had wide, girlish hips and narrow shoulders, and his face was covered with thick, blond down. He nodded, smiled, detached a brace from his upper teeth and pulled it out of his mouth. It was a mix of plastic and steel.

'Your woman in eighteen was done,' she said. She had correctly guessed what I had come to see. 'It was the RA.'

I smiled to show that, yes, I knew, and that, no, we weren't going to fall out about it.

'And wasn't it after the Housing Executive putting in new chimneys and a damp-proof course!' she said.

'They did a good job.' I could see that all the houses in the street had new chimneys.

'Ach,' she said, and repeated her mantra. The place was shite and the devil walked here.

A group of glue-sniffers staggered out of the entry where the punishment had happened, white bags held to their mouths.

She said, 'Look at them hoods!' She nodded in their direction. 'They like to hang around here outside my house. And if the husband goes out to speak to them, they tell him to fuck off. You can do nothing with them. Out all hours of the day and night, and have been since they were bairns. The parents don't care.'

A girl, sixteen if she was a day, pushed past with a new baby in a pram. The glue-sniffers whistled.

'Last week, over in Andytown,' the woman continued, staring after the young mother, 'these ones you can see over there, they got a boy in the toilets, raped him and then, God help the poor fellow, they tried to get the brush up.'

'Really.' It sounded like an urban myth but I said nothing.

'The peelers came looking for them the next night. Chased up and down the entry, over there and at the back of my place. Pouring rain it was, and the peelers, they got absolutely soaked. They didn't get those hoods, of course.'

A car nosed slowly up the street. Four hard men sat inside. The car stopped and the men glowered at the glue-sniffers, who, quick as fish fleeing from the shadows of approaching fishermen, vanished up the entry from which they had just emerged.

'That's the Shinners,' said the woman. 'They're what pass for the police round here.'

I nodded.

'Now, make no mistake, those hoods should be punished, but not like the girl in number eighteen. Hand them to the peelers, I would. But that doesn't happen. Not round here. You see, this place is shite. The devil walks here.'

'Where would you like to live?' I asked.

The men in the car had turned in their seats and were now staring at us.

'On a mountain,' she said. 'I don't care about my house My husband hasn't got a job. And those bastards, forgive my language, running round in their big fancy cars, and having their foreign holidays, and they never did a day's work in their lives, not a day's work, and them always throwing their weight about like they're the lord and master, why would I want to live here?

'Other than Mass on Sundays, I just keep to myself. Don't socialise except for the woman next door. She has her windows broken now and again by them. Like, she's a Protestant. I mind that. I haven't brought my son up bitter. See. We're not bitter. She's the best neighbour in the world. But we keep to ourselves. I wouldn't let my son out to run around. Between the hoods and the Shinners, you wouldn't know what trouble he'd get into. And I mind the UVF too. They come down here and break windows and riot as well, you know.'

The men in the car were still staring.

'Look at those now,' she continued. 'They're out looking for the vote. But I won't be voting. Not after what happened in number eighteen. Up the top, that's green, white and orange up there, but not down here. They won't get the vote down here. No way.'

The crunch point had come for the four men. Either they were going to have to talk to us or move on. Mercifully, they decided on the latter. The driver engaged the car in gear and drove away, very, very slowly, just so we'd know the woman hadn't out-stared them; he had simply, and very graciously, decided to move on.

'Hooray!' she said, sounding almost happy. She turned to the youth behind and saw he'd taken his brace out. 'Put your brace in, son.'

He jammed the brace against his palate, then forced the metal tracks over his buckled front teeth.

'Who do you think pulled down the Sinn Féin election poster?' I asked.

At that moment the glue-sniffers reappeared. They gathered round the lamp post at the foot of which lay the poster. The woman looked back at me fiercely. 'I'd rather see my child dead than running round with that lot or the other lot.'

It was a very Belfast moment. I'd asked a question and what I'd got back was not the answer but an existential statement. Between the lawless youths who roamed her streets, and the forces of National Liberation who claimed to police them, there was nothing to choose, and she really would rather her son was dead than running around with either.

'Well, goodbye,' she said. 'It's been nice to talk to you.' She gave me a weak handshake. 'And remember, this place is shite. The devil walks here.' She hustled her son through her front door, closing it carefully behind herself, and the last thing I heard was the sound of locks turning and bolts sliding home.

Lorra-Lorra-Lorra

This taxi driver had the face of a Roundhead—jutting cheekbones, high forehead and wild, wispy hair.

'Surprise, surprise,' he shouted, as I got into the front seat beside him. 'Cilla-Cilla-Cilla,' he continued, at top volume. He gunned the gas, and shot into the traffic.

If he were twenty, I'd have said he was on amphetamines. But this man was fifty if he was a day.

To get the conversation going, I said, 'Do you like Cilla Black?'

He said, 'It's my birthday today.'

Not the segue I'd expected.

'Lorra-lorra-lorra,' he bellowed, and then he explained, 'I'm a great fan of *Blind Date*. You see, I was in it myself.'

I had visions of my Roundhead driver behind the sliding screen, his date waiting on the other side. 'You were on the show?'

'No,' he said. 'I was in the dating line. Twenty years of marriage, then I had a messy divorce. To get back in the swim, I joined an agency.'

'What – a singles club?'

'No! Introductions agency! You filled in a card with your details, and the women did the same. Then the cards were circulated and you met.'

'Any joy?'

As he drove, he pulled a banana out of a paper bag. Off came the skin and the cab was filled with the smell of the fruit.

'All men lie about their height,' he said, talking and eating simultaneously, 'and all women lie about their age. I learned that.' He chomped meditatively. 'If someone put "drinker" it meant raving alcoholic. "Petite" meant midget. "Own business" was a stall in St George's Market.' He roared with laughter.

'So where would you and the women meet?'

He dropped the empty banana skin into the bag. 'Car parks usually.'

This, I thought, I cannot be hearing. 'Really?'

'The women liked it that way,' he explained. 'Easier. And so it was, "See you in Castlecourt multi-storey at eleven on Tuesday. Level three. Mine's an Audi. I'll be wearing a carnation."'

I hadn't forgotten his birthday. 'Will you be doing something nice for your birthday?' I asked.

'Oh, yeah.'

'So you've . . . found love?'

'But not through the agency,' he said quickly. 'I met her through a friend.'

'And she's waiting at home for you?'

'Lorra-lorra-lorra,' he shouted. 'Surprise, surprise.'

My Roundhead was clearly off his rocker.

'No, she's not waiting at home,' he said. 'It's just a casual thing. She's her own place. And she has to work. I'm very strong on that. She's got to earn her keep. I'm not making the mistake I made before.'

'What was that?'

'Hitching to a housewife.'

'You've lost me,' I said.

'I went bust, you see, and wifey couldn't take it.'

Next second, a metaphorical weight appeared to settle on his back: his voice cracked, his shoulders drooped.

'Had a franchise business,' he explained. 'Security company. Lorra-lorra locks.'

A bottle of chocolate milkshake came out of the paper bag. He unscrewed it using his teeth, spat the top into the footwell, and took a swig.

'One day there was a stream of money, next day the stream was dry. I was the overall boss here in Northern Ireland. What happened? Hand-in-the-till job. Anyway, overnight I was ruined. Employed twenty men, had to let 'em go.'

He slotted the brown milkshake bottle into a holder attached to the dashboard.

'We needed money. I said to the wife, "Get out there, girl, and skivvy. There's a lorra-lorra electricity bill we gotta pay this month." But the wife, she'd never worked. She couldn't handle it, couldn't get her head round it.

'So, one evening, I came home to nothing. She'd taken every stick of furniture, even the light bulbs, and cleared off, left me the four bare walls and the twin boys. She'd just decided to cut her losses and get out with what she could.'

The despair in the front seat was almost palpable. He began to whistle the theme from *Blind Date*.

'When I had my business,' he said abruptly, 'I played golf at Sunningdale with Georgie Best. That's how successful I was!'

I didn't know what to say, so I said, 'Have you seen your wife since?'

'Aye. When Barry married, one of the twins, she was at the reception, all pally. Oh, yeah, we talk *all* the time now.'

It was the way he said 'all' that encouraged me. 'She wants back?'

He looked at me, his eyes bright with joy. 'I could lift the phone tonight and she'd be home tomorrow like a shot.' He clicked his fingers. 'She says leaving me was the worst mistake she ever made.'

I felt sorry for this wife. 'Couldn't you take her back?' I shifted into Relate-speak. 'Twenty years of marriage, after all, plus you have children . . .'

He shook his head. 'I might build it all up and then she might get a notion in her head and take off again.'

'Not if she says leaving you was the worst mistake of her life, surely not?'

'She's done it before, she'd do it again.'

We had arrived at my destination. He pulled the handbrake and smiled. 'Just look at the Provos. Look what they said and then look what they done. Lorra ceasefire, then they call it off.

Oh, yeah, course she'd leave me.'

He punched the meter and that, as far as he was concerned, was that.

Fergus

There were no buses or taxis, so I went into the garage and the owner said he'd fix me up. That's the nice thing about Ireland – you can always ask, even for something as ludicrous as a lift home.

A minute later Fergus, a mechanic, opened the door of a battered Ford Cortina and asked me to step in.

'Sure you don't mind running me home?'

It was no bother, said Fergus.

He nosed the car onto the road where it began to lurch and buck.

'Could we be out of fuel?' I asked nervously, pointing at the gauge, which indicated the tank was empty.

Fergus gunned the engine. The car shuddered. He pointed a finger with a ragged nail at the radio in the dashboard. 'Did you hear some frigging imbecile let off two bombs in Lisburn?'

I asked the predictable questions. Was it the army barracks that were hit? Was anyone killed?

'Don't know. Just heard it on the news. Twenty hurt. Frigging idiots.'

In reply I told him about a dinner in Dublin I had just been to, and a woman who had said to me that when we have a united Ireland, all the Protestants can go back to England and Scotland. They came from there, she had said, so surely they'd be happy to go back home. She wasn't joking, and she ran a newspaper.

I had intended to suggest that stupidity was everywhere, not just in Lisburn. A big mistake because, as I should have known, the road to Hell is paved with good intentions. An oppressive silence now filled the inside of the bucking Cortina. Fergus stared ahead. I saw his cheek moving as he sucked air in and out.

'It all begins in the home,' he said. 'All this shite's pumped into them about the united Ireland. Then they grow up to do this. But not in my home, it wasn't.'

He mentioned a village on the Monaghan border. I said I should have recognised his accent.

'And all this oul stuff with parades and flags,' he continued grumpily, 'I've no time for it. It's just provocative.'

Just as I began to wonder exactly which type of parade he was on about, he said, 'It's stupid, all this marching and carrying on because of some wee battle in the arse end of nowhere, four hundred years ago. Sometimes I think the Protestants love King Billy more than they love God.'

I remembered the old adage, 'In Ireland we say, "To Hell with the future, let's get on with the past!"' but since my last intervention I knew silence was the better course.

'It's been getting bad for me with the security forces,' he said, 'these last lock of months since the RA stopped their ceasefire, and now it's going to get worse again.'

'Do they pick on you because you're a Catholic?' Surely I was on safe ground here.

'Sometimes,' he said, with surprising geniality, and then he added enigmatically, 'they do and they don't.'

'They do and they don't?'

'They do a job but . . .'

I could see him trying to decide. Could he trust me? Was I going to be offended? In the end I saw him take a deep breath. He had decided to risk it.

'Last week I was going out with the girlfriend to a nightclub in Ballyconnell, and there's a checkpoint at the border there, you know. It was a quarter to three in the morning when we went into it, and do you know what time they let us out?'

I shook my head.

'Quarter to six. They stripped the car right down – seats

away, panels out, tyres off.'

Our own car juddered, but Fergus pushed on.

'I can understand with the army, the pressure they're under, and the anger they feel when one of their mates is killed, but they definitely bring hatred on themselves.'

I waved at my gate and he turned onto the driveway.

'So you'll get more of this sort of treatment?' I said. Which was presumably part of the Republican strategy, I thought, although I kept this idea to myself.

'Without a doubt,' he said bluntly.

He turned off the engine and settled back in his seat, a man about to make a statement.

'You can say the English shouldn't have come and taken our land off us and then made us pay rent to have our own land back. You can get angry about it and plant bombs but there's no point. That was hundreds of years ago. You can't go back to the way something was. You've got to forget it. I just want a wife, and a house, and a quiet life, and kids. I want to go forward. I don't want to go back.'

He turned the key and the engine coughed back into life.

'And they're still arseholes, them ones, who did that thing in Lisburn,' he finished.

There was another long silence. I thanked him for the lift. He thanked me for listening so patiently to his ranting and raving. We said goodbye.

Working at Writing 3

My next published adult novel, *How to Murder a Man*, owed its existence entirely to HMP Maze where I'd worked intermittently as a part-time creative writing tutor since 1991 (before I moved to HMP Maghaberry in 1997, of which more in a bit). The prisoners I taught wrote about everything, including what had got them into jail, the fiendish complexities of killing, getting away afterwards, and the courage they had brought to the murder business.

One evening, discussing with an old school friend a play I'd just read (it was by a Loyalist and contained information on such things as how to get a gun through an army checkpoint), I remarked that this play was a manual on how to murder a man.

'*How To Murder A Man*,' said my old friend. 'There's the title of your next book.' He was right, I thought. But what exactly would that novel's story be? Then, as often happens, I got my answer from literature: I read a Victorian memoir, *Realities of Irish Life*, by William Steuart Trench.

Trench was a professional landlord's agent and his book describes his working life. In 1851, he went to work on the Marquess of Bath's estate near Carrickmacross, County Monaghan. His brief was to make the estate pay by clearing out rent defaulters and putting in reliable tenants who would pay rent regularly.

And this is what he did; he made an offer to the rent defaulters that they couldn't afford to refuse: he'd waive all rent arrears; he'd let the tenant sell all he had and keep the proceeds; and, finally, he'd give the indebted tenant and his family a one way ticket to America. All that the tenant had to do in return was surrender his lease to the estate rather than 'sell' it to a new tenant, as was his right.

Trench's scheme got going (how could it not?) but it wasn't long before some tenants realised it was a bad thing, which, if it took root and established the principle that tenancies instead of being 'sold' to a new tenant reverted to the landlord instead, would lead to the end of the Ulster Custom and the loss of their most valuable asset. Those who were Ribbonmen (an underground, agrarian, largely Catholic organisation, dedicated to defending their members' rights and privileges against the depredations of the law, the police, the Orange Order and strong farmers) decided that Trench must be stopped; they recruited two assassins, put them on a weekly retainer and warned Trench to leave or be shot dead.

Trench, never a quitter, reviewed recent Ribbon killings to determine his chances of survival. He noticed that whenever anyone was shot, bystanders immediately rushed to the dead or dying man, which allowed the assassins to get away. Here, Trench realised, was a way to stay alive.

Trench armed his bailiff and his adult sons and put the word out. His bailiff or his sons would be with him at all times. If he was shot, Trench explained, they would never, under any circumstances, come to his aid; on the contrary, they would chase whoever had shot him and kill or catch and hang them.

This strategy unnerved the assassins. They had a blunderbuss, which they could fire only once, and now, magnifying their problems, it wasn't only a matter of getting close enough to kill Trench: they also had to be certain of getting away.

Over a year Trench's assassins made numerous attempts (which failed) to kill the agent until eventually they were caught. In return for a new identity one opted to testify against his comrade. The second man was convicted, sentenced to death and hanged.

Trench's account, vivid and compelling, was also intensely familiar: here were all the preoccupations with the difficulties of paramilitary practice that I had encountered in the work of prisoners in HMP Maze. Whatever the century, whatever the weapons, it seemed the Irish political assassins' problems remained the same: one, you had to get close enough to do it, and two, you had to be sure to get away. I took a proposal for a novel based on Trench's experience to Little, Brown and Co and was rewarded with a commission to write *How to Murder a Man*.

In March 1997 (I was forty-three), by which point I'd nearly finished the novel, Billy Wright, founder of the Loyalist Volunteer Force, was jailed for eight years for threatening to kill a woman. Shortly after his arrival in HMP Maghaberry, Christopher 'Crip' McWilliams, a Republican serving life for murdering Belfast bar manager Colm Mahon on 15 December 1991, took a prison officer hostage in the Education Department, using a smuggled gun. He claimed later that he had intended to kill Wright when he arrived for a class. McWilliams was disarmed before he carried out his plan and, following the incident, both he and Wright relocated to HMP Maze where each now believed he'd be safer than in Maghaberry. (As paramilitaries, both had automatic rights of transfer).

I started at Maghaberry in April. I worked from the Education Department. In my security briefing I was told what to do if I was ever taken hostage by someone with a gun. Over the following weeks, as I floated around the wings, I heard a lot about McWilliams and his antics, his gun and how he had smuggled it in. I suspected the willingness to tell me things was a reflection of changing times, a collective sense that tectonic plates were moving, a sense confirmed on 19 July 1997 when the IRA announced their second ceasefire. But not everyone was affected: some were stuck where they had always been, McWilliams among them. On 27 December 1997, he and others, again using smuggled firearms, killed Billy Wright inside HMP Maze.

Spurred by this, and all the stories I'd heard, and because by now I'd finished *How To Murder A Man*, I started *A Good Day For a Dog*, a novel about guns and a jail vendetta. But I would work on it only intermittently in the years ahead as I had other calls on my time.

Diana-Week in Ulster

A fresh-eyed child careered into his parents' bedroom and said, 'Diana's dead.' I said nothing and attempted to sleep on. But my wife struggled into her dressing gown, disappeared, and a few seconds later was back, shaking me frantically with the news, fresh from Paris, of the crash. This was Sunday, 31 August 1997.

The next day, Monday, 1 September, I had to get to North Belfast for nine o'clock; the traffic in the city was horrendous, so I took the back route via West Belfast. In Beechmount, the paint-smeared fort-like police station flew the Union flag at half mast, but otherwise it was tricolours in every direction as far as the eye could see.

Nothing here, I thought, to emulate what had already started in Britain. No books of condolence or piles of flowers. The elimination of the Crown from Ireland has always been assiduously sought by Republicans. From the Treaty negotiations and the argy-bargy in the 1920s about the Oath of Allegiance to the foundation of the Republic in 1949, it didn't seem to matter to De Valera *et al* that Ireland was tied to sterling, that Ireland's principal trading partner was Britain, or that the civil service, especially its upper echelons, was composed of appointees of the *ancien régime*. No: what mattered more than anything was the removal of all Crown connections. And this spirit lives on. When they went to the talks on 15 September, now that there was a new ceasefire in place, Sinn Féin would be arguing for a thirty-two-county republic, Ireland, a monarchy-free zone.

That same Monday evening, on the way back home to Enniskillen, passing through a little village of the other persuasion – only Red Hand of Ulster flags here – I noticed a flagpole had gone up, muddy earth, a daub of wet concrete around the base and the Union flag at half mast. It hadn't been there when I'd passed in the morning. Now it was. That was astonishing.

Tuesday I went to the local sports centre, nicely printed special notices on the counter. As a mark of respect, in view of the funeral, the place would be closed on the Saturday coming, it said. A cluster of lantern-jawed men in the corner were passing one of these communications from hand to hand, guffawing and grumbling. They couldn't believe it; this was ridiculous; she wasn't their princess; why should they be deprived of their Saturday morning footie because of her? And wasn't Diana the honorary colonel of some British regiment, and hadn't she'd been photographed driving around in a tank on some junket, fetchingly dressed in army fatigues? She had indeed. She was a warmonger. Heads nodded. Oh, yes, closing the sports centre was a bad business.

The woman behind the cash register rolled her eyes at me. I kept my counsel. It was a government building – the sports centre – used by both sides, so in a sense, I reasoned, sloping off to the changing room, they had to close it. But those grumbling men wouldn't have to put up with the kind of total Saturday closure on the day of the funeral as they would if they were in England, Wales and Scotland, I thought. That wasn't going to happen here. In Fermanagh, the western extremity of the kingdom, we were too far away to be affected by mass hysteria centred on Kensington Palace.

Then, on Thursday, notices with a picture of the princess began to appear outside garages and inside shops all round the county. As a mark of respect, they would be closed for the funeral. It was one shop, then two, then four – and then it was everywhere, even the twenty-four-hour garage open every day of the year. The pull of something happening hundreds of miles away was growing stronger and stronger.

On Friday, a lightning trip to Belfast. Everywhere there was closing as well, more predictably perhaps, and outside City Hall and council buildings there were mounds of flowers with sniffling sightseers surveying the bouquets, reading the messages.

Friday night to Enniskillen, chauffeuring the elder daughter to the pub. The place was empty, a ghost town. No short-haired boys revving their Ford XRis around the Cenotaph, no crowds in Chippy Street milling around the fast-food joints, shouting jocularly or barfing in the gutter. The mood of the town was quiet, subdued, meditative; it reminded me of nothing so much as the town before Remembrance Day. At the start of the week I would not have thought it possible but I was wrong: the mood of grief really had swept across the sea from the land of the ancient enemy and gripped us by the heart.

Saturday was, well, like that Saturday everywhere – there was complete shut-down as people gathered around their television sets to watch the service. Afterwards, in the afternoon, the sun shone weakly, and the streets filled with people, their mood assuaged yet also contemplative. There was going to be no whooping it up like after an Irish funeral.

Sunday I left Ireland for Ottawa, Canada, but not before someone reported to me that there had been complaints. Diana's pall-bearers had been Welsh Guards, flown to London to do the carrying and now *en route* back to Ulster, to Crossmaglen. Ah, it was sweet while it lasted, our little interregnum, but now hostilities were resumed and in Ireland, Northern Ireland, it was business as usual.

Ottawa Diary

Some years ago, I was in an hotel outside Cienfuegos, Cuba. A large group of middle-aged Francophone Québeckers sat by the pool and hissed at the old waiter in the disgusting, time-honoured Cuban style, then fell about laughing at their brilliant mimicry and their Québec daring.

Over at the bar a Cuban whispered to me, 'Capitalism, compañero,' and shrugged his shoulder. It seemed that the Western economic system not only exploited its poor but it also produced ill-mannered yahoos like these visitors.

Now spool forward many years to Ottawa airport and my next encounter with Québeckers. I was at the luggage carousel when a young woman with the face and black hair of the silent screen actress Louise Brooks came up to me.

'My bag is too heavy,' she explained. She spoke English with a French accent. It was charming. I lifted her case onto a trolley for her. Not heavy at all. When she asked, I told her I had come to Canada to attend a literary festival. Telephone numbers and other details were exchanged.

That evening, in my hotel, which was on the south side of the Ottawa River, in Anglophone Ontario, I turned on the television, as one does. Forty stations and rising. On North American television there is no distinction between programme and advertisement, so content and commerce are part of the same seamless flow. On the Shopping Channel I watched a woman who was mostly made of silicon interview Mr Juice Man, maker of the JuiceMan Juicer.

'You put the apples and bananas in here,' he explained to her, 'push the plunger and out comes the juice. Now you do it.'

'Oh, can I?' she purred. Now she pushed down the plunger, and as a thick white substance spurted from the spout, she smiled lasciviously at the camera. It was terrific bad porno.

In between the demonstrations there were testimonials from happy customers, soft-focus close-ups of well-spoken Canadians who pronounced on JuiceMan and their consumer satisfaction. For these people, and presumably for the rest of us watching in English-speaking North America, consumption was the principal civic virtue. To enjoy complete product satisfaction was the mark of the good citizen. It also had the additional bonus of getting you on television.

The next morning, to the mall – where else? At every turn I was greeted by shiny-uniformed retail staff, all eager to midwife my purchasing decision. There was something almost loverlike about their attentions. 'They have to be tarts,' said a droll Canadian, when I related the experience later. 'There are twenty people waiting in line for their McJob.' So, unemployment is driving up standards in the service sector.

During the evening that I was reading, the Louise Brooks lookalike came along, bringing a friend. In the bar afterwards, the friend, Charlotte, shook my hand quickly and began to talk. Her mother was Anglo, her father a Québecker; she was raised in English-speaking Ontario. Her temperament, she said, was Latin passion overlaid with Anglo-Saxon reserve: she was passionate but also punctual, reliable and honest, and a dedicated enemy of corruption. She told me the Canadian national character had much to be admired – energy and a belief in fair play, for example, qualities she had in abundance, she claimed. But on the downside, when it came to back-stabbing, Canadians were in a league of their own.

'Look at Greg Rusedski,' she said. 'He gave up his Canadian citizenship and became British to advance his tennis – and why not? Then the guy nearly wins Wimbledon and the press here trashes him. Could we say well done? Oh, no. Not now he'd become British. That's typical Canada.'

From this she returned to her character. She was placid, she said, and she had a ready knack for getting on with people. And as she rattled on, it seemed that this was not so much a conversation as a sales pitch. Her personality was just one more product for consumption. If she failed to get me to like her, and I turned away showing no interest, that was a lost opportunity, but if I liked her, she could ring up another sale.

On my last day I left the hotel and crossed to the northern side of the Ottawa River, to Gatineau, in Francophone Québec and went to a small roadside inn. In Anglo-Canada on the Ontario side, where I'd been all week, all the waitresses had worn shorts and sweatshirts with corporate logos, but here in Québec it was different. Here the waitresses wore their own clothes and each one was in a dress. There were no artificial tans or expensive teeth on display. I won't say they were more real but certainly these were women as I recognise them; and certainly they had not embraced the virtues of the Anglo-Saxon retail world.

As I sat at the table I remembered Cuba. On the strength of that scene of French-Canadian unruliness I'd thought Québeckers were foul but now I was having to revise my opinion. Now the retention in Québec of a French-speaking anti-corporate identity, here represented by something as simple as waitresses wearing their own clothes and speaking like human beings, not like graduates of the McDonald's College, seemed nothing short of a miracle.

No Handles, No Cross

That Saturday morning, late January 1998, my wife lay on the sofa, nine months pregnant. The telephone rang.

'Hello, Nurse Corrigan here.' The caller was speaking from the nursing home in Dublin where my father resided. He suffered from Alzheimer's.

'He has a chest infection,' said Nurse Corrigan. 'He's really not well.'

I had received many calls from the home over the years but

none quite so emphatic. I put down the phone and my wife said, 'You must see him tomorrow. I can do without you then but I need you on Monday.'

The next day, Sunday, the morning was bright and crisp. I left the boys, Jack and Finn, but took the girls with me, India, sixteen, and Georgia, three. Georgia was excited and kept hooting, 'We're going to see my grandpa, everybody.' My brother, who happened to be staying, came as well.

Filing into the nursing home in Dublin, I smelt its familiar smell, a mixture of cabbage water and wax polish. A nurse saw us and hurried over. 'Your father's dying,' she said bluntly. Wisps of her hair had come away from the bun in which the rest was contained. She tried to gather the loose ends and stuff them back but the bun fell apart. 'I'm useless with hair,' she said.

We found my father in his room, asleep on his side, wheezing heavily. The skin on the top of his bald head had puckered and ribbed as if the skull underneath was shrinking. India, my eldest, looked around the room anxiously. 'What are those?' she asked, and pointed to a huge pile of incontinence nappies. 'No, don't tell me,' she added, horrified. She had realised. 'And look at the size of that!' She nodded at an industrial tub of Sudocrem. 'Ugh!' she said, and fled. I sat on a chair. My brother took the second, empty, bed. Georgia clattered around in her shiny patent shoes shouting, 'Shush! Grandpa sleeping.'

My brother produced a camera and she said, 'Take my picture.'

She climbed up onto the bed, took Grandpa's crooked hand and assumed her photograph posture – straight back and best smile.

The room was bathed in flashlight. The figure under the bedclothes slumbered on, oblivious. The child slithered down. India returned. Her disgust had subsided. I cut a lock of hair from the sleeping figure and put it in an envelope. We all said, 'Goodbye.' I looked at the figure in the bed and was reminded of a torch bulb, yellow and wavering, in those last moments before the battery dies. He was drifting away. No doubt about it.

We left, and I said goodbye to my brother in the car park; he was going to Dublin and then on to London. I drove back home to Northern Ireland without stopping.

The next morning I took the older children to school, and Georgia to the childminder. Then I went to the hospital where I found my wife in her hospital room. Her room smelt of acetone. The day before, while we'd been in Dublin seeing my father, she had painted her nails, 'ready for theatre', as she put it, and now she was being made to clean off the polish. She wore a gown, white and stiff, with ties at the back. For the umpteenth time she gave her details to a nurse, then a catheter was inserted and a pre-med given.

At two o'clock we set off for surgery. My wife played her Walkman as we trundled along the corridors, and I could hear the voice of Victoria de Los Angeles through the headphones, tinny yet still sweet. We arrived at a pair of scuffed doors with 'Theatre' written above. This was the end for me. I kissed her. Then she vanished inside for her Caesarean section. I went out to the car park.

I smoked a cigarette and stared at the reeds in the River Erne below the hospital. They were the colour of broom handles, a woody yellow. I went back and waited at the scuffed doors. A midwife rolled out an incubator. Our new baby lay inside, his face very red under a waxy coat of vernix.

We trundled to the recovery room. The midwife weighed and measured him. 'I'll turn on the television,' she said, in a voice that brooked no opposition. Nowadays, the TV is always on, like there always used to be a fire lit; television is the new hearth.

She fiddled with the zapper and the television came on. It was an ancient episode of *Blankety Blank* hosted by a very young Terry Wogan. As the programme played I watched my new son open his sticky lids and look at the world for the first time.

My wife was wheeled in. She woke up. Our other children appeared. Everyone got a chance to hold the baby and have their photograph taken.

We left at seven, and as we got home the phone was ringing. India rushed to pick it up. A boyfriend, perhaps. She put the receiver to her ear, listened and then said, 'It's the home in Dublin, Dad, and I don't think it's very good.'

By ten o'clock that night, I was on the phone to a Dublin undertaker, ordering the coffin. Pine veneer, no handles, no cross.

Devil in the Detail

As luck would have it, I was in HMP Maghaberry on Good Friday (10 April 1998) when the peace talks came to an end, the day the parties, or most of the parties at any rate, signed on the dotted line and we took another faltering step towards peace in God's own country after nearly thirty years of mayhem and more than three and a half thousand deaths.

I hit the prison at two o'clock and went to the Education Department. I usually have no difficulty getting in because there is always an officer in the pod behind the grille. But that afternoon there was no one anywhere.

'Hello,' I called. 'Anyone home?' I looked through the metal bars. The corridor beyond was eerie and desolate. Was everyone at church? It was only an hour away from the Lord's crucifixion time, three o'clock. Then I saw a telltale flicker on a patch of ceiling. Television flicker.

After a lot of shouting and rattling of bars, I got the attention of the principal officer who, like everyone else in the department, was watching the telly in the staffroom. The exception were the prisoners in the Braille unit, who were getting ready to type up a Braille text of the Agreement. Since the ink was still not dry on the original, it had not yet arrived, but soon it would and they would set to work. They didn't have a radio or a TV but they didn't need one, did they? They would have it from the horse's mouth when the text finally arrived.

But television told us what was happening, and if I have one overriding memory of that day, it was that television was absolutely everywhere. When I got into the jail proper and wandered the wings looking for this prisoner who'd written a poem or that prisoner who'd written a short story, the plummy, concerned, confident voices of political pundits and television news reporters followed me. Every television in the jail was on (and with one in each cell that makes for a lot of televisions). And everyone in the jail, it seemed, had been up half or most of the night, waiting to see if what was supposed to happen was actually going to happen, and now that it had happened, they were still watching. They still couldn't quite believe it had happened (as I couldn't) and they wanted to know more. They wanted to know what was really in the document and that was why they kept watching.

Now, one thing that was known on that Good Friday afternoon was that some 'political' or 'paramilitary' prisoners were likely to receive 66 per cent remission on their sentences – in other words, they'd serve just a third of their tariff. It had long been expected that something like this would be incorporated as part of any settlement: the early release of prisoners was one of the rare areas where the fringe Loyalist parties and Sinn Féin were in complete agreement.

What is it they say about not being able to please all of the people all of the time? When I found Minty in his cell, instead of the normally optimistic and ebullient Ordinary Decent Criminal (ODC) serving a life sentence for murder, and with whom I always looked forward to spending ten minutes, I found a rather grim-looking fellow staring, yes, at his in-cell television.

'Well, we'll have that off,' he said, as I came in, and off went the set. Ah, blessed silence, although televisions droned all around us. And then Minty started, his tirade obliterating all other noise. Why were 'they' (by which he meant the paramilitaries) getting remission? Why not him? Why not all the ODCs? As he saw it, either everyone in jail in Northern Ireland had committed a crime and therefore should stay in prison until they'd served their sentence, or no one had committed a crime, in which case everybody should get 66 per cent remission.

From there he went on to make his other point. For more than twenty-five years, he said, paramilitary prisoners had been treated by the courts as criminals, and described by most politicians and commentators as criminals. But now, apparently, they weren't criminals any more. A wand had been waved. They'd been decriminalised. They had to have been. Otherwise why were they getting out? But everyone else, himself included, was still a criminal, and they were staying in. It wasn't fair.

Up to this moment I had felt, well, if not exactly optimistic, not exactly pessimistic either about the peace process. Something amazing had been brokered and maybe, just maybe, I thought, it might work. Now I told myself, well, Minty, he wants out of prison – who wouldn't? Of course he's going to focus on why others were getting remission and he wasn't. He wouldn't be normal if he didn't. But after I'd said goodbye and walked off down the landing, it occurred to me that Minty was behaving exactly as everyone else would behave, myself included, only he'd got there more quickly than the rest of us.

It's an awkward truth about human nature but we have to face it: although most of us in Northern Ireland were generally committed to peace because we were sickened and disgusted and ashamed by what had happened here, we were also selfish and self-centred, and had a well-developed capacity to view legislation not in terms of what it did for everyone but solely in terms of what it did for us. We were also very talented at seeing legislation not as something that advanced, corrected or ameliorated, but as a mechanism that created, on the one hand, some winners, and on the other, some losers. The saying 'The devil's in the detail' was one I'd always loved, but given our national predilection for asking, 'What's in this for me?' and 'Am I losing out here?' I suspected it would be uttered so often in the weeks and months ahead that I might well turn quite against it.

Bumped

The publicity person from my publishers rang. *Newsnight* wanted me for their post-Good Friday Agreement referendum special from Belfast.

Saturday afternoon, 2 May 1998, I rolled up to Broadcasting House. The front looked very closed. Moments later, sashaying through the back gate, I had a metaphor attack. On the day after a referendum in which, uniquely, Protestants and Catholics had acted together, the only way into the state broadcaster was through a Portakabin. It was like going into a dodgy warehouse to buy some porno. Not my best conceit. I rejected it instantly.

The Green Room was an RTÉ/*Newsnight* co-production. Guests and technical staff from the two jurisdictions were co-mingling and troughing. A blonde PA, plate on lap, was on the phone to Ken Maginnis, MP for Fermanagh and South Tyrone. I overheard a short, tetchy exchange. She put the phone down.

'He's insisting on eating a rather nice piece of liver,' said the irritated PA, forking an enormous piece of something into her mouth, 'and he's not coming.' Her munching colleagues nodded agreement. Unconscionable. How dare the man eat rather than come straight on the box?

I went off to the lavatory. Jam-packed with *Newsnight* guests. I opened the door of a cubicle. A man was already in there, doing what men do with a lavatory bowl. His crop of curly hair seemed familiar. I knew this man. But who was it? Of course. It was the other Maginnis but spelt McGuinness. It was Martin McGuinness. Excuse me, I wanted to shout, this is my traditional pissing route. Then I became aware that a shaven-headed minder wearing a suit was hovering just behind me in case I did something to Mr McGuinness and I saw that the joke was as cheap as the last literary offering. I really was going to have to pull my socks up if I was going to scintillate for Jeremy Paxman.

A few minutes later I was back in the green room. By now Martin and Co. had arrived, and everyone else who had been in the room had, for some unaccountable reason, scarpered. This left just me and another man I didn't recognise. We each sat in a corner, like old timers in the American Wild West, invisible on the edge of the saloon.

Meanwhile, the McGuinness gang hogged the bar, so to speak, which in this case was a table laden with BBC fare.

From my perch I watched Martin. It was interesting. When I trough I pick what's nearest. Not Martin. He peered intensely at the food, his forehead furrowed, and he appeared to be thinking, Will I eat that? No, that one looks better. No, no, that one looks better still. And the sandwich selected for culling was then placed with fastidious precision on his plate. I could feel another metaphor just about to heave across the horizon, like a battleship. His manner at table was like Sinn Féin's pick 'n' choose attitude to the Good Friday Agreement: we'll have this but none of that . . . I dropped the idea quickly as another quip well below par.

Now Martin had his plateful. His face wore a look of excited anticipation. The first morsel, gripped fastidiously between finger and thumb, was arcing towards his open mouth. At that moment the *Newsnight* PA popped her head around the door and said in her lovely English voice, 'Mr McGuinness?' He glanced up, startled. In the flesh, he didn't look like the faintly demonic Harpo Marx we knew and loved from television, more like a poor impersonator of the real McGuinness. A virtual Martin. It's a sad fact but in life no one looks as good as they do on the box. In life one looks fake but on the box one looks real. 'Makeup,' trilled the assistant.

Mr McGuinness said something about being on the verge of eating. But, like all Brits, the assistant was intransigent. Jeremy Paxman'd started, the show was rolling.

Martin stood. His expression was dolorous. Once again Irish history was following its old tragic trajectory. At the very instant poor Paddy was about to tuck into his tea, up popped Britannia to drag him off to the Calvary of beige foundation.

Martin slouched away, minders in tow. I heard the other old timer chuckling. Poor Martin, he'd been so looking forward to his tea. I would have laughed myself but I didn't because at that moment the PA slid back and sat down across from me. Her face was rueful. I'd seen that face before. On *The Larry Sanders Show*. This was the standard television face adopted by young female assistants when they had to break the bad news.

'You've bumped me,' I said, before she did. Yes. She was terribly sorry. Too many items.

'Really, it doesn't matter,' I said emphatically.

She was puzzled. Was this sarcasm? Ulster irony?

I wondered how to explain that I'd brought this doom on myself. Three crap literary conceits and you're out. That's God's way. The slightest sign of bad literature and He will have you bumped. Simple as that. But would she understand this? No chance. I picked up my coat and reprised, 'Really, it doesn't matter.'

And it could have been worse, I thought, slinking out through the Portakabin. Thank goodness Martin and Co weren't present to witness my humiliation. Oh, yes, if He'd wanted, he could have made the bumping so much worse.

The New Kitchen

I found the house, just as Mrs Lampin had said I would. It was at the end of a straight road with the river behind. The river was the border between north and south, between Northern Ireland and the Republic. The old bridge across the river was gone; only the stumps on either bank were left. There was a new, half-built concrete bridge a few yards upstream. I was there to talk about a distant Victorian relative of hers, a minor writer. Mrs Lampin wanted to republish his books.

I got out of the car and went to the garden gate. Mrs Lampin's house was built of stone. I categorised it without thinking: eighteenth-century, planter. I must read less Pevsner, I thought.

I went to the door and knocked. Mrs Lampin must have been lurking nearby because she opened the door immediately. Grey hair, clear blue eyes, no jewellery, except a plain gold band on her wedding finger; mid-fifties, I guessed.

She led me to the kitchen, gave me tea, and told me her best friend was the local priest, although they worshipped in different churches. And then somehow, as happens, the conversation segued to the new kitchen she wanted.

'What's wrong with this one? I said. 'Oh, I don't mean here,' she said.

Ah. I realised I'd misunderstood.

'I meant in the old house,' she said.

She took a key from a hook. We went outside. Across the road I glimpsed another building. It was a yeoman's house, I thought, early eighteenth-century.

We crossed to the gate of this yeoman dwelling. The garden behind was overgrown: I smelt honeysuckle. 'I haven't touched the place for twenty-five years,' Mrs Lampin apologised, pushing the gate back. 'After the tragedy, I just closed the door and never went back.'

I followed her up the cracked tile path.

'But I know the roof's sound,' she chattered on. 'Father Daniel checked for me. He couldn't see any light through the slates.'

Her husband was dead, I guessed, casting my eye across the roof; hence the priest, a safe man around a Protestant widow. 'The slates look fine,' I agreed, and wondered what the tragedy was. 'Whose house was this?' I asked. That might give me the answer.

'It was the family home,' she said. She turned the key in the lock. 'When I married my husband, we took across the road. My husband's big brother, James, he lived here, with his wife. There was twenty-two years between the brothers.'

So, the much older brother, James, was dead, as was James's wife, I thought. It seemed to me that in Ireland, or Northern Ireland, there was no story that didn't come without a genealogical back story, and usually a long and complicated one.

Mrs Lampin pushed back the door and I followed her into

a dusty hall. There was a 1972 Northern Ireland telephone directory on a table. 'This is the kitchen,' she called. I followed her into a big room with tongue-in-groove walls.

The damp floorboards sagged beneath me. Bird droppings studded the stove. 'Lovely,' I said. 'So what are you going to do? You're not going to take out these lovely presses, are you?' I pointed at the big pine cupboards. 'My granny had ones just like those in the kitchen in her house in east Clare.'

Mrs Lampin stared wildly and blinked. 'It's for my son.' Then she said, 'You know, the gunmen just walked over the old bridge, before it was blown up.'

She pointed and I saw both bridges through the window, the old broken one and the unfinished new one.

'They sauntered up to the front door and knocked. Bessie answered, that was James's wife.'

I saw that she had spotted my look of incredulity. Then I saw an expression of great effort on her face as she turned her thoughts away from what had happened and back to the kitchen.

'My son's worked in Toronto these last ten years. He married there, and now he's coming home with his wife and their boys. Coming to live here. Now we're normal again.' Her face changed again. 'They shot Bessie straight in the face and ran down to this kitchen. James was eating his tea. His gun was in the holster on the back of the door. He tried to run for it but he was fifty-three. Too slow. They got him right where you are.

'I saw photos of the house in Toronto. Lovely, all-white kitchen, with a washing machine and wide worktops. I want my son and his wife to be happy here. I want them to have what they had in Toronto.

'They went back down the hall. Bessie wasn't dead. Do you think a white kitchen might suit, or is that too cold? They shot her again. And do you think I should leave the tongue-in-groove?

Father Daniel said people'd pay a fortune for pine like that nowadays. We heard the shooting. We were over in the other house. And I want lots of power points – you can never have enough. We watched them, the two gunmen, as they walked back across the old bridge to the south. The daughter-in-law'll have a juicer and a blender and a Magimix, of course. In the Free State papers, it said James and Bessie were shot because he was in the UDR. And what about a breakfast counter, right where you're standing? I just got a kitchen with a Belfast sink and a plain table when I married and that was it. I never designed one. So tell me, please, you're younger than I am, you must know about these things, what do you think I should do in here?'

Hibernaphobia

At four a.m. we piled into the car, myself, my wife and the new baby, Euan, and drove away. The thorn hedges were dusted with snow-like blossom, and the fields were filled with pillows of mist. The world seemed newly minted that morning.

In Belfast, at the Seacat cross-channel ferry terminal, we got into line. A Stena stewardess was checking boarding cards. Men in shiny green football jerseys swaggered past. I paid no attention.

The line rolled forward. We were one from the front behind a Ford XRi. The driver produced his boarding card and the stewardess bent and looked through the back passenger window. At this moment the driver put his head out of his window behind her and deposited his breakfast on the tarmac without her hearing or seeing; ham and potatoes and lager. The stewardess tapped the roof; the XRi accelerated away.

I drove forward, shouting a warning. Too late. The stewardess stepped back into the puke.

'Oh, God!' she said, trying to wipe her soles on the tarmac, as I pulled up.

Ten minutes later, stepping into the ferry passenger lounge, I saw why I should have paid attention earlier to the swaggerers in green. Our companions, to a man, were Celtic supporters. My wife found corner seats and we formed a sulky, middle class huddle while the fans roistered around us . . .

At half past four in the afternoon, I found myself in a genteel Edinburgh hotel. I had done the wedding (which was why we had come) and this was the reception. Beside me sat a woman with cornflower-blue eyes and a cut-glass English accent. We were eating roast beef.

'Where're you from?' she asked.

'Enniskillen, Northern Ireland.'

'I know where it is,' she said tartly.

'You're not from Ireland, are you?'

'Goodness, no,' she said, 'but Gerry, my late husband, was.'

Five minutes later, I had the story. Gerry's family were Catholics. His father, a career soldier in the British Army, had returned at fifty to Ballymena, and a sinecure as an RUC armourer. Gerry, the son, wanted to study engineering at Queens but was obliged, as a Catholic, to settle for Celtic Studies.

'It made Gerry bitter,' said his wife, 'and as soon as he graduated, he left. We met in the Middle East. He took me back to Ballymena after we got engaged. I couldn't believe it.

My father was South African, my mother was Dutch, I grew up in Java. I'd seen some things in my life I can tell you but I'd never seen anything like I saw in Ballymena. It was so . . .' She waved her hand in the air. 'The bigotry. It beggared belief.'

'A few years ago,' she continued, 'Gerry was dead and a

relative of his died in Ballymena. I'd never taken our daughters there, and I thought, I'll bring them to see where Daddy came from and go to the funeral.

'We went over. The three days there were the longest of my life. On the last morning, walking in a lovely park, the four of us stared at our watches continuously. We couldn't wait to get out of that vile place.'

I wondered what to reply to this woman whose basic message was, *You live in a shithole*. In the end I decided to say nothing. I had another piece of beef instead.

It was night when we arrived back at Troon to catch the ferry home. Knots of green shirts were dotted around. We joined the line of waiting cars. A figure loomed out of the darkness. I wound down the window. It was the stewardess from that morning, the same one who'd stepped into the vomit.

She'd had a long day. She looked awful.

The previous sailing from Troon, she explained, the eight o'clock, had been delayed leaving because it had had to wait for Celtic supporters. As a result that ferry would be late coming back from Belfast for us.

'Why did the last sailing wait?' I asked. 'The fans could have caught this one.'

'Ah, no,' she said drily, 'this sailing's for bandsmen and Rangers supporters who've also been in Scotland today.'

Hadn't she seen the Celtic supporters waiting in the shadows? Well, maybe not. I decided not to mention them.

The boat, when we got aboard, was packed with Rangers and Celtic fans and bandsmen, and the atmosphere was febrile. We found a seat. The ferry cast off. Men began to pace around. Many wanted to fight, even with their own. There was a scuffle behind. The security staff pounced. A youth was led away. It was the pattern of the next two hours: would-be combatants cruised the aisles looking for a ruck, but every time something was about to start, staff stopped play.

While my wife slept with Euan in her arms, I fumed. I remembered the woman at the wedding reception and found myself agreeing that, in sum total, we comprise nothing but ugliness.

Arriving in Belfast, just before dawn, acute Hibernaphobia still dogged me. We drove out of the city and back into the rural world of snow-dusted hedgerows and mist-filled fields. And it was only here that I was able, at last, to believe that we're not quite as bad as we sometimes seem. I suppose it's what's called the Wordsworth effect.

Drumcree

Friday, 3 July 1998

My friend from London, Gina, arrived at Aldergrove, the airport outside Belfast. She was with her son Vassili, friend of my son Jack. She was here to have a weekend in the country with us – not Wiltshire, alas for her, but Fermanagh.

We piled into the car, drove past the checkpoint and came to the roundabout at the top of the Moira road. The airport behind us, with its British Airports police in their peaked caps decorated with black-and-white check braid, its ring road and its Novotel, felt British. And in front of us, in the form of a bog-standard roundabout, was the point where one crosses out of Britain and into Northern Ireland. It was the flags, you see. There were always a couple here, a Union flag and an Ulster flag (the cross of St George with the red hand in the middle) fluttering from the lamp posts that ring the roundabout. And they were usually old and frayed. But not today. Today there were flags on every lamp post, and they were new, they were big, they were clean. It was an unmistakable sign and Gina didn't miss her cue.

'Drumcree,' she said.

'Uh-huh.

'Of all the weekends in the year,' said Gina, 'I have to pick this one to come to Northern Ireland.'

Sunday, 5 July 1998

It was the end of Gina's weekend. To find out what was happening in our little world I turned on the television. Images instantly appeared of a ludicrously green County Armagh landscape, a grey Irish sky and a black stone steeple – the spire of Drumcree church. It was crunch day. The Portadown Orangemen had been refused leave by the Parades Commission to walk down the Garvaghy Road after their church service. The Lodges had given notice of their intention to walk down their traditional route. And the army had created a 'sterile area' around the Garvaghy Road. Yet another light-the-blue-touchpaper-and-retire situation.

And the route to the airport, I reflected, along which I would be taking Gina and her son a little later, lay quite close to Drumcree. Two years before, during earlier Drumcree disturbances, there had been trees on the motorway, and pickets around the airport. Hapless travellers were turned back by men in balaclavas. Hundreds if not thousands of passengers failed to make their flights. Aldergrove was in effect closed down for several days.

My own experience of similar Drumcree-related difficulties (also two years earlier) was less dramatic but every bit as ominous. It had involved a journey with Ulsterbus from Belfast to Enniskillen. I had caught the last coach out of Belfast and there were only four passengers: myself, and three unfortunate travellers who'd come up from Dublin and had to get back to

Fermanagh. A mother and her only daughter who had just got back from a bonding holiday in Spain, and a nervous Catholic from Derry, who had lived in Arizona for fifteen years and had just flown in for his uncle's funeral in Enniskillen. The Drumcree stand-off was news to him, he explained. It wasn't in the Arizona newspapers.

We set off along the motorway. It was empty. And I mean empty. There was no one on it but us. There were huge puddles of twig and earth everywhere, the remains of the obstructions, cleared that afternoon by the police.

At Fivemiletown, twenty-five miles from Enniskillen, the coach was flagged down by two policemen in flak jackets. They looked weary and infuriated.

'You can't go on,' said one of the policemen to the driver.

'There's barricades and bonfires all the way down the road to Enniskillen. You won't get through.'

The driver smiled. 'I did it last night,' he said. He sounded like an eager contestant in some cross-country game compèred by Anneka Rice.

'If you can get right round the roadblocks and come in beyond Tamlaght, the last turn-off before Enniskillen, you'll get home and dry, all right, but otherwise I wouldn't fancy your chances,' said the policeman.

The mourner from Derry went white. The mother and daughter squeezed each other's hands. I removed my Northern Ireland Prisons teacher's pass from my wallet and stuck it inside my sock. It was definitely not the sort of ID one would want an irate Loyalist at an impromptu roadblock to find in one's wallet. Then the coach snorted and hissed and we turned onto the tiniest of tiny country roads.

What followed was a vehicular nightmare as Buñuel might have offered it: twisting rural roads, no map, and total disorientation. The ordeal lasted for two hours and then, magically, I have no idea how this came about, we found ourselves steaming down the little side road with the stop sign at the end: *it was the turning that lay beyond Tamlaght*. All we had to do was go left, drive for three miles, and we would be in Enniskillen. We'd done it. We'd got past the barricades.

But now, two years later, reflecting on those events, I was quite clear that I did not want to repeat the experience; I did not want to find myself with Gina and Vassili, and probably my own children, frantically driving round the back roads of Antrim because the main road to the airport was blocked by a posse of lunatics.

I dialled the number of the emergency travel line that, according to the newscaster, the RUC had established to advise anxious drivers.

'Yes, sir,' said the bright, helpful, cheerful policeman at the other end.

'The Moira road to the airport, is it open?'

'At the moment it is, yes, sir.'

Something about that phrase 'at the moment' filled me with dread.

'When's your flight?' asked the policeman.

'Tonight, seven. Do you think the road will be open then?'

'It's open now,' he said blandly.

'What does that mean?'

'If you want to be sure of getting to the airport, leave now.'

'But it's nine o'clock in the morning.'

'I'm sorry, but we just don't know what'll happen.'

So that was it. Either we left immediately or we risked – well, the policeman didn't know what we'd be risking. It was a very Northern Ireland moment. Something awful was coming. It hadn't come yet but it probably would because that was what had always happened in the past.

Gina threw her tickets away. We rebooked from Dublin. At

three we left. We had a lovely journey through the winding, leafy lanes of south Fermanagh. This is the edge of Northern Ireland, far away from Drumcree. It would take time for the ripples caused up there to reach down here. Sinn Féin posters from the recent Assembly election were still much in evidence on the lamp posts.

I dropped Gina and Vassili at Dublin airport and turned round. I wanted to get home as quickly as possible. To my astonishment, as I retraced my journey through leafy south Fermanagh, I found that every (and I mean every) Sinn Féin poster had been torn down, thrown contemptuously in the ditch, and a Union flag put up in its place. Dozens, possibly hundreds of them. Somebody had been very busy on Sunday afternoon. I couldn't doubt it. Very bad juju was coming.

Thursday, 9 July 1998

Thursday was HMP Maghaberry day. I sashayed into the Braille room in the education block at ten. Several prisoners looked up from their work stations.

'Hello, you're early.'

It was true. I usually started at two and worked through to eight o'clock in the evening. However, I had been onto the police that very morning and had had the following conversation.

'Is the Maghaberry road open?'

'It's clear at the moment.'

'Has it been blocked, so far, this week?'

'Not so far, sir.'

'Will it be?'

'We don't know.'

'Have any roads nearby been blocked?'

'Yes, sir, Sprucefield, for two hours last night, from eight to ten.'

He had then told me, in a tone that was half jocular, half

exhausted, that (a) the Drumcree protesters were probably working their way down the motorway, which made it more than likely the Maghaberry road would be the next road targeted and (b) that the protesters' MO seemed to be, get home from work at six o'clock, have tea, get out, block selected road for a couple of hours, then go home at about ten in time to catch the climax of the evening's World Cup footie match.

That was all I needed to hear. I would go into the prison early and I would go home early and that way I would miss any brouhaha. I explained this now to the prisoners.

'Bad is it, like?' said Henry, a life-sentence prisoner who wrote challenging prose poems that denounced state capitalism, political correctness and welfare stateism.

'It's not wonderful.'

'We wouldn't know.' He grinned slightly sheepishly. It might all be happening, his look said, but inside, in the prison, events outside didn't have any reality until someone appeared, like me, all anxious and flustered.

Later I went on the wings. Although HMP Maghaberry is a Category A prison, I was allowed to move around without an escort, and to sit in the cells with the prisoners and go through their writing with them. As I wandered about, I noticed - surprise, surprise – that every prisoner in every cell had his television on, and most were following events at Drumcree. The mood was one I had never encountered before. All the prisoners I talked with seemed, for once, to be rather relieved (even pleased) that they were inside and not outside, in the midst of the mayhem.

Eventually I arrived at the cell of Ian, another lifer. He hadn't told me what he'd done and my policy is not to ask. Ian kept a diary. He handed me his week's work. His friend Frederick, or Big Boy, a Loyalist paramilitary, came across from his cell on the other side of the corridor and joined us.

'I don't see the point of fucking walking the Garvaghy Road,' said Big Boy. 'Just rubbing the noses of them fucking Fenians in the fucking shit, no fucking point, is there? The Orangemen should leave it out, so they should.'

'It makes you ashamed to be a Protestant, this Drumcree lark,' agreed Ian.

For the next ten minutes the two men talked a great deal of sense. The stand-off was ridiculous. It should be called off. In fact, all marching should be abolished, Republican and Loyalist.

I left the cell feeling cheerful. Prison sometimes lagged behind the outside world but here was the gratifying spectacle of prison well in advance of the outside world. If prisoners could be tolerant and pleasant and generous, why couldn't the rest of Northern Ireland manage that?

Then I bumped into a man in the corridor, and he said, 'Drumcree. I'd like to see some dead fucking policemen there tonight.'

There was nothing ghoulish or deeply heartfelt about the way he spoke. It was a simple statement of fact. This was what he wanted to see, and in that respect, prison and that prisoner were absolutely in line with a strand of opinion in the outside world.

When I got home that night I watched the news, and I learned that protesters at Drumcree were throwing blast bombs at the police, and the police were firing baton rounds (plastic bullets) back at the crowds. A girl had lost an eye. A man had been injured and was now in intensive care. The story since Sunday had been one of escalating bad temper, disobedience and hooliganism. The thing really was ratcheting up. I remembered the throwaway sentence in the prison. Perhaps the prisoner would get his wish and a policeman would be killed, I thought, and as this baleful idea occurred to me I felt something that I hadn't felt for a very long time: I felt afraid. I could not sleep. I read Karl Miller's *Dark Horses* until first light glimmered outside the window.

Friday, 10 July 1998

I did not watch the evening news. This was a wise decision. It would only upset me, wouldn't it? I went to bed. I was exhausted. But as soon as my head hit the pillow, my fatigue vanished. I sat up. I read more Karl Miller, but there came a point when I couldn't read any more. And what did I do then? Against my better judgement, and while my wife and children slept, I got up and turned on Ceefax. There were reports of more disturbances. The car of a woman going to hospital with her sick baby had been attacked by a pro-Drumcree picket because she wouldn't stop. And three men had been arrested in Newbuildings: they had attacked two policemen the night before, and the eleven-year-old son of one of the policemen, dragging them all from an unmarked car and beating them horribly.

I went back to bed. My son, Finn, was asleep on the other side. He had asked to sleep with me. He had anti-lice lotion in his hair and the room smelt of the stuff. I knew I wouldn't sleep now. I plumped up the pillows and lay back, thinking. Unless something was done immediately, all the Orangemen in Northern Ireland were going to converge on Drumcree on 13 July (when the 12 July marches would take place). That was the plan.

And when everyone converged on Drumcree, I thought, some stupendous ugliness would occur. It couldn't not - there was bound to be trouble with all those people bunched together. The most likely scenario was that the Orangemen would try to force their way down the Garvaghy Road. Then there would be bloodshed. There would be dead Orangemen. It would be Blair's 'Bloody Sunday', as an Orange leader had said. And once there were dead Orangemen, the Order would be able to characterise itself and its members as victims of the state. And when that happened, the Orangemen would at last have true parity of esteem with the Republicans, who had been sustained by their victimhood for the last thirty years.

And once that happened, my thoughts ran on, we would have a totally polarised society, with both communities feeling hard done by, oppressed and victimised. And that was a recipe for disaster, because if the last thirty years had shown anything, it was that a sense of victimisation was the concomitant of barbarity.

Then I remembered something from Ceefax. The pro-Drumcree pickets around the province were asking drivers for identification. I got up then, wrote a note to myself and left it on the kitchen table: 'Remove Prison Teacher's Pass from Wallet'.

First light was glimmering outside the window before I fell asleep.

Saturday, 11 July 1998

I got up and found the note. I went straight over to my study and removed the offending pass.

In the afternoon I went to teach at a summer school in a village in Republican south Armagh. (The district, to all intents and purposes, was Protestant-free so there were no travel problems). After the class, one of the students told me, quite categorically, that she believed sinister elements in the Home Counties in England were controlling events at Drumcree.

'Who?' I asked.

English Tory politicians, she said. They had instigated Drumcree and were keeping it going. It was the English way of holding onto Ireland, she explained.

But who? I asked again. And did she have any proof? She

said she couldn't name names. Not right now. She'd have to do some research.

What kind of research? I wondered, but I said nothing, of course. I let her talk on.

As far as proof went, she continued, a distinctive note of reproof in her voice, if I'd listened to the remarks of certain English Tory politicians, pre-Drumcree, as carefully as she had, I'd know what she meant.

I nodded, heart sinking. So the old Irish fantasy of Albion as ultra-perfidious and manipulative was alive and well. The Orangemen at Drumcree might be embarked on their biggest ever public-relations disaster, but if your politics were Republican, hardline and a tad paranoid, this was invisible. Drumcree, rather, was just another episode in the old story: big bad England, once again, was punishing poor suffering Ireland.

I went home and straight back to Ceefax. I gathered that the proximity talks in Armagh, designed to resolve the Drumcree stand-off, had broken down. No surprises there.

Furthermore, the Orange Order, at five o'clock that afternoon and while they were supposedly in the middle of the proximity talks, had requested permission from the Parades Commission to march down the Garvaghy Road the following Sunday afternoon.

Another night of insomnia.

Sunday, 12 July 1998

Woke up. Straight to Ceefax. I learned that three children had died as a result of an overnight arson attack in Ballymoney, County Antrim. On the news, a little later, I heard the grandfather of the dead boys being interviewed. He was called Patton. (Same surname as the 'Spirit of Drumcree' organiser and hardliner, Joel Patton). Patton, a Protestant name, surely. (One shouldn't think like this but one does). The dead children were from a mixed marriage, I guessed. My hunch (not an especially inspired one) was later confirmed. The mother of the children was a Catholic, her partner (but not the children's father) was a Protestant; they lived on a Loyalist estate together; this was why the house had been firebombed. The police had no doubt that Drumcree and the firebombing were connected. The dead boys had gone to a state, i.e. Protestant, school.

Although the day was wet we would have liked to go out, my wife and I and the children. But where could we go? The stand-off at Drumcree was continuing. Protesters were still out, the roads were probably still blocked. And there was a contentious march at Newtownbutler in the south of County Fermanagh.

In the light of everything, we decided the best thing to do was to stay home. We spent the day, improbably, doing a 500-piece jigsaw puzzle. In the evening we watched the World Cup final (Brazil v. France) and consumed vast quantities of popcorn. It was only a week since I had driven Gina and her son to the airport in Dublin. It seemed like a year.

Happy Christmas

I was driving slowly along a Fermanagh lane between high banks of hawthorn. Earlier in the summer the blossoms were snowy white but now they had a reddish tinge. Being a pretentious so-and-so I had recently waded through the full Proust and I remember I made the connection as I drove. He too had noticed the reddening of hawthorn as it aged. I felt gratified that my provincial life intersected, here at least, with that of the great metropolitan French novelist.

This reverie was cut short by a crash. It involved the two cars in front of me. And as it happened, just as everyone says, everything went slow like in a film. I saw the cars collide, shunt, judder, and finally come to rest on the forecourt of a VG shop. Miraculously, this just happened to be in the middle of that Irish nowhere. At this point the film ran out and I was returned to the normal-speed everyday world.

I braked, reversed, jumped out. Underfoot, broken glass everywhere, and the rattle of whirring fan belts from the smashed vehicles. In one car there were two women and in the other there was a man.

I went to the women first and turned off the engine. Though trapped by crumpled metal and twisted dashboard they were conscious. They asked for cigarettes. I asked what brand. The VG would oblige.

Then I ran to the man. As he fell sideways from his car, I turned his engine off. He was bleeding. His blood was vermilion shading to brown. I checked his pulse. How I found it, I will never know, as I can never find my own. But I found it all right between the bird bones on his wrist. Then I made him tell me his name and address and his date of birth. He was conscious. I was worried his neck was broken. I explained he must lie straight and still on the wet tarmac. Then I got the cigarettes for the women from the shop, and two coats with which I covered him.

I also made the obligatory call on my mobile. How and when I can't recall. In due course, as the women puffed on Embassy Regals and the man began to shake (I feared he was having an epileptic fit), sirens sounded in the distance, dim at first and gradually growing louder. One or two people had drifted up from nearby cottages and, as I waited for the emergency services to pull up, I distinctly remember one man whispering in my ear.

'Don't hang around,' he murmured nicely. 'They'll only want you as a witness and you don't know what kind of trouble that's going to bring you. Get in your car and go.'

'I was the one who rang 999,' I said. I waved my mobile.

'They've got my details already. They'd find me if I went now.

And, besides, isn't it against the law to leave the scene of an accident?'

'You know what?' he said. 'I feel sorry for you.'

I made a statement the next day in the police station and got a summons to appear at the preliminary inquiry.

It was six months before the date arrived. It was hard winter then. The hawthorn hedges were bare. The roads were icy. As I came into Omagh I met a knot of council workers stringing Christmas lights between lamp standards.

I entered the courthouse. In the foyer, arranged around the edges, occupying every bench and chair, were the numerous plaintiffs in the numerous cases that were going to be heard in the course of the coming day. Most were smoking and they were all trying to look hard. Their tormentors in the coming spectacle, the policemen and solicitors who were going to try to have them fined or sent to jail, were standing in the middle of the floor. None of them was smoking. They were just arranged in tidy knots, like in the Ferrero Rocher advertisement, talking and laughing. Whatever happened, they were going to have a good day.

A court official, dressed like an MCC umpire, checked my name off a manifest and explained procedure. 'There'll be a quick skate through the several dozen cases to be heard,' he said. 'When yours comes up – oh, God, it's a long way down – if it isn't contested it'll be settled immediately. But as it probably is going to be contested, it'll be deferred to later.'

'When will that be?'

'This afternoon probably.'

'So why did they call me here for ten?'

'I know, it's mad,' he said. Clearly he had come across this sort of bourgeois complaint before.

I sidled into the courtroom. I read my *Guardian*. An official asked everyone to stand. An unprepossessing figure in a suit glided in and sat down under a coat of arms. The magistrate, I guessed.

Next a clerk said something quietly. The prosecuting police inspector stood up and said something. A solicitor said something. There were microphones but tellingly they were switched off. Whatever was said was inaudible not just to me but also, more importantly, to the shaven-headed, much tattooed, gum-chewing, Tommy Hilfiger-dressed youth who had come in from outside and was now standing beside me. Amazingly, when the magistrate asked him if he understood, he nodded (which was surely perjury).

'I want a pre-sentence report,' said the magistrate.

The youth was ordered back to the foyer, with a probation officer in hot pursuit, brandishing a form on which she would take down his details.

In front of me I noticed a policeman with whom I was vaguely acquainted. 'What was that about?' I whispered.

'He was drunk, smashed a few windows, and then hit the peeler sent to arrest him.'

The next case and several more thereafter were all equally mystifying. The authority figures were barely audible and when one could hear them they spoke a kind of incomprehensible legal gobbledegook. It made no sense to me and I presume it made no sense to the sad parade of angry, frightened, inscrutable young hooligans who appeared one after another, got their medicine – hefty fines and/or short sentences – then disappeared. The law, at its most basic, is something the middle class do, and the working class and the even more lowly underclass have done to them.

After an hour of this extraordinary but melancholy process, I was relieved to see the plaintiff was a fifty-year-old farmer in a Sabbath suit. He not only knew how to dress (unlike all those who had preceded him) but he also asked if he could address the bench.

'Certainly,' said the magistrate.

'I don't dispute the offence. I was driving and I was over the limit.'

The magistrate nodded.

'But if I lose my licence I shan't be able to drive the lunch up to my mother on Christmas Day.'

The solicitor added some further words about the plaintiff's formidable sense of filial duty towards his aged mother. It was clearly planned and it was a lovely idea. Unfortunately it didn't do the business. The plaintiff had several previous convictions. He was fined and lost his licence.

After this small excitement the procedure reverted to what it had been before. The middle class superiors punished more young men who'd done dire things. The only difference was that now I was attuned to it. Now I was able to follow what was happening. This was good in theory but in practice ignorance was probably better. The trouble was, now I could see what had been invisible before. This was the absolute, even if understandable, contempt in which the defendants held the whole process.

For instance: case twenty-four was a young man charged with assaulting another young man. He got six months. He received the news with a smirk, winked at a line of cronies and gave the thumbs-up sign. I wondered why he was delighted with six. Was this less than he had expected? Or was he happy with six because it would enhance his reputation as a tough nut? I suspected the latter.

A few cases later the proceedings got darker still. Another

young man was brought in. He had been out of prison for three weeks. While he picked his teeth with a thumbnail, the clerk read the sheet (a process that lasted a good five minutes). There were twelve charges of taking and driving, six of breaking and entering. In the mix there were also a couple of affrays, a malicious damage and a handful of credit card frauds. How anyone could do so much in so short a time was beyond me.

The charges finished, the solicitor, a nice-looking woman with grey hair that matched her expensive grey woollen suit, made a moving speech about the defendant's appalling home circumstances, his years in care, his lack of authority figures, blah, blah, blah. It was fruitless. The appeal for bail was declined. He would be remanded to jail, said the magistrate. The solicitor looked pained. The defendant, unmoved by the court's decision – he'd heard it all before – nonchalantly sauntered from the dock.

Eventually my own case number was called. Now my chance had come to appear, albeit as a spear-carrier, in this horrible drama and I felt . . . Well, frankly, I felt excited. It is strange how courts compel one to want to be part of the proceedings. I straightened my tie. I moved to the front of my seat, ready to answer the call to step down and put my hand on the Bible. Meantime, I heard the prosecuting inspector speaking. What was he saying? My God, he was asking for an adjournment. The reason, apparently, was the long list of other cases that would surely be contested in the hours remaining. The one I was involved in was seemingly less important. The magistrate nodded and assented and that, I realised, was that. For the time being, this was over.

I went home. Time passed. Then one day, while I sat pounding the keyboard, a large car, very low on its axles (clearly an unmarked police car weighted down by armour-plating), pulled up outside my study window. I went out to greet my visitor. He was a large man in a shiny suit.

'Mr Gébler,' he said, in a tone that combined cordial with ever so slightly menacing. In my experience it's only policemen who speak like that.

'Yes.'

'You'll be wanting this.'

'What is it?'

'A summons,' he said.

'I'm not in trouble, am I?'

'I don't think so.' He scanned the sheet. 'No, you're a witness.'

'Oh, yes, I remember now.' I felt greatly relieved. 'I saw a crash.'

He handed me the papers. Like all official documents, they were stiff and white and frightening.

I spotted the date. 'Oh, good,' I said. 'So I can look forward to another day in court next year.'

He turned towards his Sierra, said, 'Oh,' and turned back again. 'Well, now you know what that's for,' he said, and pointed at the summons, 'you know it won't be a bad one. Happy Christmas.'

The Fight

Jack, my twelve-year-old son, rang from town. Would I collect him?

What a good boy, I thought, putting down the phone and looking at my watch. It was eleven-thirty, the time he'd said he would ring. He might sometimes seem like Harry Enfield's Kevin but he wasn't. Alas, I reflected, walking out to the car, I was all too like Kevin's dad.

The signifiers of middle age were as various as they were

surprising. In my own case I had a new and unexpected appetite
for crime fiction written by women. I liked their versions of
the world where good is good and bad is bad and where, after
trouble and strife, middle-aged, middle class order is always
restored at the end.

I listened to tapes of these novels in the car incessantly.
That evening was no exception. I started the engine and
pushed in Ruth Rendell's *Road Rage*; then I drove through
velvety darkness listening to an actor impersonating Inspector
Wexford. The policeman's rustic accent was appalling and the
conceit of the passage not much better.

The bloodied body of a young girl was found impregnated
with gravel. To all and sundry this was a mystery, but not to
Wexford: he alone twigged that the girl had died by falling thirty
feet onto a gravel drive. It was curious as well as convenient
how Wexford was always able to see what no one else could,
but it was comforting too. Even when it was a bit naff.

When I reached my son, I turned off the cassette player. He
jumped in. 'Oh, Dad, I've had the best time ever.'

'Really?'

'There was a fight at the fair.' His voice trilled with pleasure.

'Ah,' I said. This was one of those middle-aged exclamations
that are like the tip of the iceberg and that supposedly suggest
the greater bulk lurking beneath. In this case 'Ah' meant that I
had seen some pretty hairy funfair rows in my time.

I remembered one now, at a funfair on Clapham Common
when I was twelve. I decided to hear his version, rather than
offer mine. One of the worst features of middle age has to be
my desperate need to prove that I was once young too.

My son narrated the story. Three gangs had been involved.
The parties met in the middle of the funfair, he said, surrounded
by revellers. Metal bars, baseball bats and a gun were produced.
Two men were felled. The riot police appeared. An ambulance

was summoned. It was all over in seconds.

'My God, a gun!' I said. In comparison, my Clapham Common incident was decidedly small potatoes: just a ruck on the grass between a few spotty lads while gypsies selling heather watched with bored expressions. 'Are you sure there was a gun?'

'That's what Michael said.'

'Oh, so it was Michael who saw the gun, was it?'

'Yep.'

The situation was clarifying. 'So where were you when this fight was happening?'

He explained: he should have brought his wallet to the funfair but he hadn't so he'd lost all his money, of course. The man
who owned the site where the funfair was pitched had a daughter called Maggie, and when Jack had told her he'd lost all his money (how he came to tell her he didn't explain), she had given him a pass. My son was actually enjoying a free ride on the dodgems at the time of the rumble and it was only when it finished that he'd met Michael and was told what he'd missed.

'Dad, brilliant craic this evening,' he concluded.

'Do you think Michael could have exaggerated?' My voice was mild and reasonable.

'Dad!' he exclaimed, in the tone he reserved for my more preposterous suggestions (such as, sweets cause tooth decay).

'Course he didn't exaggerate. It was a class evening. You can listen to your tape now.'

When I was young I infinitely preferred concocted narratives to those of older people – a James Bond film rather than a grown-up droning on about old times any day. But now, in middle age, I find the equation reversed. No narrative – even a Ruth Rendell, balm to my frayed middle-aged soul – is as compelling as a real one. This was one of the certainties of middle age. Another was that it was impossible to understand this until one actually was middle-aged.

'No, it's all right,' I said. 'I don't want to listen.'

'Oh! But you're always listening to your tapes, Dad.'

How could I possibly explain that the safe world of Rendell was unappealing compared to his excited narrative, even if there was a tincture of exaggeration in the mix? Or maybe that was unjust. Maybe there had been a gun. It didn't matter. I had no doubt that when I was young I had been intoxicated by the same kind of heady blind exuberance as my son was now. Furthermore, for all I knew, I had told an equally outrageous tale about the Clapham Common fracas when I got home. Of all the experiences or sensations that come in middle age, here was the most essential, I thought. I was seeing what I once was but that I no longer am.

'Here, I'll turn on the tape for you, Dad,' my son insisted.

He pressed the button and the bad impersonation of Wexford came to me through the speakers.

A Scare

It was a dull Sunday evening. My two sons (Finn aged ten and Jack aged thirteen) went out to the garden for a bout of play rugby. This involved wedging the ball between their chests, locking arms and wrestling. They came in later, exhausted, happy and drained of testosterone.

'We're going out,' I said. I was going, with their mother, to hear the local choral society sing Mozart's *Requiem Mass*, and the younger children, Georgia and Euan, were asleep. 'Back in a bit. No fighting.'

They nodded. They hadn't the energy for scrapping.

The house was silent when we returned. Each boy was in bed. My wife went to say goodnight. A moment later she returned to the living room, dragging the younger boy with her. Finn looked as if he was going to cry.

'Look at that,' she said, pointing at his chin.

I pulled him under the hundred-watt bulb in the kitchen. His entire chin looked as if it had been dipped in blackberry juice, then viciously rubbed with a hairy nettle. The skin was bright purple with livid red spots. To the touch it was cold and smooth.

My wife got a glass, pressed it under his mouth and together we peered down. The purple skin and the spots did not vanish with the pressure of the glass but stayed stubbornly in view. We'd read about this in the meningitis leaflet.

'I'd better ring the emergency doctor,' my wife murmured, and dialled.

'Whoopee,' Finn exclaimed. By now he was peering at himself in the mirror in the hall off the kitchen. 'I've a purple chin. No school tomorrow.' Then he looked at his mother. 'Is this men-something?'

My wife waved at him to be quiet. The doctor had answered. She relayed the symptoms. Then there was silence as she listened.

'We'll be straight down,' she said, finally.

Finn dressed. They piled into the car. I heard the noise of the engine fading as they drove away. Twenty minutes later, I heard the rumble coming out of the Sunday-evening stillness as they returned. The car pulled up and my wife came in, pulling Finn behind her. He threw himself onto the sofa. 'I won't go,' he wailed.

'The doctor hopes it's viral,' my wife said, 'but just to be on the booked.'

'I'm not going," he cried, and buried his face in a cushion.

'I've said to Finn,' said my wife, raising her voice so he would hear, 'I'll settle him in, and then I'll come home and you'll go down and you'll spend the night in the hospital with him.'

'Of course,' I said.

'We'd better pack an overnight bag,' my wife suggested.

With tears scalding his cheeks, Finn put his tartan pyjamas, Bart Simpson toothbrush and three Harry Potter novels in a plastic bag. Then he ran into his brother's bedroom and I heard him shouting, tearfully but also proudly, 'I have to go to the hospital for the night.'

A minute later I sat and listened for the second time that evening to the car engine fading into the distance. Two hours passed and then, out of the silence, came the noise of the engine as the car returned. I stood up. I would have to pack a bag myself. I was surprised to hear Finn's voice outside. The front door opened. He filed in, swinging his overnight bag, followed by his mother.

'Couldn't I have just stayed anyhow?' Finn asked grumpily.

'The doctor didn't think it necessary,' my wife said.

He slumped on the sofa, his purple chin glowing. 'I wanted to stay,' he said. Then he added, 'And they didn't even do a blood test.'

'It turns out,' said my wife, 'it's a bruise from this evening, from the bout of play-rugby. Finn even remembered his brother yanking his chin.'

On cue, Finn stood up. 'It's all Jack's fault.' He rushed down the corridor and barged into his older brother's room.

'Look what you did,' I heard him shouting. 'The doctor says you must have really pulled my chin hard to do this.'

His brother's reply was inaudible. Probably because he was – or had been – asleep.

'You were ages,' I said to my wife. 'What took so long if it was just a bruise?'

'The interrogation,' she said. 'The doctor asked Finn if

anyone was bullying him. If anyone was, he said Finn was to be sure to tell. Then the doctor told Finn to avoid rough games. Then he said Finn's teacher would want to know how he got the bruise. The teacher might have to tell Social Services. It could be very serious. Did I understand? And so on. It wasn't meningitis, thank God, but I could have done without all that.'

Finn came back and sat down. 'I wish I was in hospital,' he said.

'No, you don't.'

'But since I nearly was," he said, with quick cunning, 'can I miss school tomorrow?'

'We'll see,' his mother said.

In the morning, I found him at the hall mirror. The huge bruise looked like Desperate Dan's midnight shadow except that it was purple. We agreed he couldn't go to school like that. He spent the day lying on the sofa while proclaiming to anyone who passed, 'I'm a victim. My brother's too rough. I nearly had meningitis.'

Working at Writing 4

In Dublin in the early 1950s, an American woman called Leatrice Gilbert was the girlfriend of my father's best friend, Desmond. My father stole Leatrice from Desmond (which caused friction) and married her. They had a son called Karl. Then Leatrice returned to the US with Karl and divorced my father by post. He married my mother and they had a son, me: I was called Karl too. Desmond, my father's sometime best friend, married someone else and went to England (though not necessarily in that order).

Dissolve to 1983. I was twenty-nine. My father, having

divorced from my mother, now lived in Ireland with my stepmother, Jane. I lived in London. At a party in West Hampstead, given by a friend who was a composer, I bumped into Desmond. He still lived in London, he had a grown-up family, and he and my father had long since made up, he said.

'If you want to know about your father,' said the best friend, 'come and talk to me.'

Of my father and his life before my mother I had only a few crumbs of information. Now I had the chance to find out more.

I wrote Desmond's details in my Filofax. Then I left the party. It was cold outside. The London paving stones glittered with frost. I found my car, an old Morris Oxford, and put my Filofax on the roof. I fished in my pocket for the tinny little car key, opened the door and hopped quickly inside. It was good to be out of the cold. Then I drove off. Somewhere on the Finchley Road, my Filofax flew off into the darkness. It was only when I got home that I realised what I had done. The next morning I went back to the Finchley Road and scoured the gutters. I didn't find my Filofax and I never did contact the best friend.

Time passed. In 1987 Jane, my stepmother, died (which I hadn't expected as she was younger than my father). I moved to Enniskillen in 1989 and we had only been there a few months when my father, bereaved, lonely, baffled and frail, fell in his house in Dalkey, near Dublin.

The accident accelerated his Alzheimer's. Social Services in Dublin, who didn't want him occupying a hospital bed, insisted that I made him a ward of the Irish courts, that I put him in a residential home and that I cleared his house in Dalkey so it could be sold in order to pay for the residential home. Of the three tasks, the last was the biggest. My father's house was filled with his letters and diaries going back to the thirties and I had to cart them away. Now, had my stepmother not pre-deceased my father this wouldn't have happened: she would never have allowed his papers to fall into the hands of someone who she and my father regarded as hostile, dangerous and antagonistic to them, i.e. me. But that hadn't happened: she'd died first and then Alzheimer's had overwhelmed him and now all his papers, which I'd never expected to see or read, by order of the Irish state, were mine – and what an interesting read they made.

Now we jump forward to 1994, when John Fountain, as my half-brother Karl Gébler Mark 1 was now known, discovered that his father wasn't his mother's fifth husband, a Mr Fountain, as his mother had led him to believe, but my father, Ernest Gébler. John came to Ireland to see his father, my father (and to make friends with him, which, of course, wasn't possible, owing to my father's Alzheimer's), and on the same trip we met. After this happened I saw I'd been given a new strand to add to the others from which I would, one day, make the book I had been waiting many years to write about my father.

My son Euan was born during the morning on 26 January 1998 and my father died that afternoon.

Desmond read the obituary and wrote to me. (He found me through the phone directory). I wrote back. The best friend told me much about my father that I hadn't known.

Now I was free to write the book I'd always wanted to write, the one that would present my father in his full three dimensional glory, with his anger, his left-wing politics and his sardonic misanthropy properly displayed. All I needed was to formulate some simple rules to guide me through composition: so I did and they were: one, in this book I'd only include what I remembered and I would never alter anything to make the story better; two, other than at the front, I'd tell the story in the order in which it had occurred, eschewing flash-forwards and authorial prescience; three, I'd restrict what I would allow myself to know to what I'd known at the time – thus, in writing about my 1963 self, I'd only allow into the narrative what I had known in 1963. With this approach, hopefully, the finished book would mature as I had. These rules decided, I set to work. It was easy to write, really easy. The only problem was I wrote far too much. I had to cut it. I had to cut it a lot. So, too, did the copy editor.

I called the book *Father & I*, and when it was finished, printed, bound and ready for the bookshops, I asked the publisher to send a copy to the best friend.

Desmond wrote back almost at once, chiding me gently for some infelicitous assumptions. In the book I had said my father was a Stalinist. Yes, later he was, but it was not always so, said the best friend. In the thirties he had contributed pro-Franco and pro-Salazarite pieces to right-wing Irish Catholic rags. My father's left-wing Dublin friends had been appalled. My father, who was poor, reminded them that he was paid a guinea for his efforts.

I composed a reply. I began by agreeing money had played a part, a significant part. My father's childhood had been poor, I said, and I could just see him reminding the better-off that he wrote what he wrote because he needed the money. However, I continued, he was also psychologically predisposed to do as he had done. And that was all to do with *his* father.

His father, my grandfather, Adolf, was a deracinated Jew (I guessed, I'd never been able to verify this) and a full-blooded militant socialist. Relations between Adolf and his son, my father, were terrible: what better way to infuriate Adolf than to cheer on the Catholic right, as my father apparently had done in the thirties?

However, the father I knew in the 1950s and later was on the left, and in the letter to the best friend I tried to explain that too. The Second World War, I wrote, had turned my father leftwards, and then personal experience, the failure of his marriage to Leatrice, had copper-fastened his political stance.

He and Leatrice had been married only a couple of years when Leatrice had returned to the US, taking their son Karl, and then without having warned him to expect something like this, she had cursorily divorced him by post from Reno, Arizona.

This experience, I was sure, I wrote, had hardened my father's political opinions, deepened his admiration of Josef Stalin (this was 1952: the Georgian was still alive and he had, after all, just won the Second World War and saved the world from Fascism) and turned him into a world-class Yankee-hater. In my childhood, I continued, nothing cheered my father like news of the US, aka the Great Satan, getting a bloody nose. The Cubans and the North Vietnamese Liberation Army, the Viet Cong, were his especial favourites in this respect on account of how they humiliated the United States. By hurting America, they indirectly hurt the woman who had hurt him, my letter concluded.

I posted it blithely to the best friend; then, driving home, I began to fret. My book hadn't even hit the shops yet and already I knew it was lacking something, this move my father had made from right to left.

Then I thought, Hang on. We were only talking a nuance here. These details of my father's right-wing salad days: had they been in the book, yes, they would have added to a reader's appreciation of his character, but the lack of them did not make the portrait I had painted untrue. That was the point.

Humph. I was able to remonstrate with myself as well as the next man; the difficulty I had was convincing myself. I didn't manage it that time. All I could think was that Graham Greene was right in *A Sort of Life* where he had written that every writer's life ended in failure. He didn't mean failure as commonly understood – poor sales or rotten reviews; he was speaking of aesthetic failure. He meant that no book was ever finished and no book was ever right, either; in other words, every book was provisional. The only consolation was that now and again a generous reader would be prompted to offer information to plug the odd gap and rectify the odd infelicity, as the best friend had done for me. That was a nice idea but I would far rather have had the book right in the first place. But it wasn't and that was that.

The Painting

After my father had gone into his residential home, and the Irish state had told me to clear his Dalkey house, I went one Saturday afternoon to empty the garage. It was lit by a twenty-watt light bulb. He had put these horrible things all over his house when he was in the early stages of Alzheimer's.

I opened the garage doors to let in the sunshine. That was when I noticed the frames, along the wall, containing reproductions of Monet and Van Gogh. There was also a hideous reproduction of the *Mona Lisa* I'd never seen before. I'd keep the frame, I decided, but the smiling one would have to go in the skip.

I took off the hardboard backing and discovered, to my surprise, when I got it out of the frame, that the hardboard had a painting on it. It was of three sailing boats and was executed in a wonderful primitive style.

I took my seascape home and hung it up. Visitors often asked if I knew who had painted it.

'No idea,' I would say, which was true.

For years that sufficed. Then I had a thought so stunningly

obvious I couldn't see why it had taken me so long to have it. The artist who had painted it, surely, was Alfred Wallis, the great English naïve painter of seascapes who often worked on hardboard. Both my parents were Wallis fans (indeed, the first art exhibition they ever brought me to was the Wallis retrospective at the Hayward on London's South Bank in the early sixties), and furthermore, when I was a child, we'd spent six months near St Ives in Cornwall where Wallis had lived and painted. In those days, before Wallis's prices went stratospheric, you could pick one up cheap and my father, I presumed, had done just that and I hadn't known about it. Well, why would I? I was only six years old at the time.

'You know what?' I said to my wife, pointing at the seascape. 'I'm sure that's a Wallis.' I summarised my argument.

'All right,' she replied. 'Then how do you explain why your father used a valuable Wallis to back a *Mona Lisa* reproduction?'

The answer came effortlessly: 'He knew it was a Wallis when he bought it. But when the Alzheimer's began, he forgot it was, and that was when he used it to back the Mona Lisa reproduction.'

It made perfect sense.

I fetched my dictionary of art and looked up Wallis. There were pages and pages on the talented Cornishman. I read the text greedily. Wallises were worth thousands. I spent the evening sipping whiskey and discussing with my wife the various ways we could spend the money the auction of the painting would net us.

Obviously, with the painting unsigned, the next thing was to confirm that it was a Wallis. I traced the curator of the exhibition I'd seen at the Hayward when I was a child and wrote to him. Could he tell if mine was a Wallis? Of course, he said.

I hired a photographer, who took a professional ten-by-eight. I bought the world's most expensive jiffy bag. Nothing but the best for my Wallis. I sent the photo off to the curator. Once he confirmed what I knew, I would be rich. Now I really would have to decide what to do with the money.

A. S. Byatt, someone told me at this time, had built a heated open-air swimming pool with her Booker Prize money and declared it was the best defence a writer could have against melancholy.

Well, I decided, with the proceeds from my Wallis, I'd build a pool and keep my blues away. I contacted contractors and solicited quotations. My daughter, Georgia, excited by the imminent arrival of what she called 'the hot swimming pool', began planning a Barbie party at the poolside. Oh, those were happy days, *chez* Gébler.

A fortnight passed and the curator returned my photograph, enclosing a friendly letter. Yes, it was a seascape, he wrote, but there any resemblance to Wallis's work ended. It definitely wasn't one of his.

I gave my wife the letter.

'For once in my life I thought I'd be rich, and now it seems I won't,' I said gloomily. 'And how am I going to break the news to Georgia there'll be no Barbie party?'

'But if it had been a Wallis,' said my wife, reasonably, 'you'd have had to insure it, then decide when to sell and where. This is better. We've a lovely picture and no worries.'

But I was beyond consolation. I felt like the couple who had lost their winning lottery ticket. I smarted with the injustice of it. My mood wouldn't lift for weeks.

One evening, masochistically thumbing through my dictionary of art, I came on a reference to the writer J.P. Donleavy, sometime close friend and neighbour of my father. Donleavy had painted, and the illustration accompanying the entry was uncannily similar to my seascape. My heart soared. I had a Donleavy. Granted it wasn't a Wallis but, still, it was something.

'I think we've a Donleavy,' I said, passing the book to my wife.

She scanned the entry and asked, 'What are you going to do?'

'Nothing.'

I'd learned my lesson. I'd get years of pleasure imagining it might be a Donleavy, even if wasn't. Why risk losing that happiness by doing something as ridiculous as looking for the truth?

Results Day

My elder daughter India sat the Transfer Test (for grammar school entrance, the equivalent of the Eleven-plus that I'd sat and failed as a child) and went to grammar school. My oldest son, Jack, sat the Transfer Test and went to grammar school. Then came the time when Jack's younger brother, Finn, had to decide whether or not to follow suit and sit the Transfer Test.

'You don't have to sit it,' I said. 'There are plenty of other good schools besides your elder brother's.' These non-grammar schools had held open days during the winter just gone, and his mother and I had been to them with Finn in tow. Why not dump the test, we suggested, and go to one of these? No, he said. He must go to the local grammar like his elder brother, whom he so admired. He must also go, he doubtless felt, because we were one of those middle class families whose children automatically went to grammar school. Not to go would represent failure.

'What happens if you don't get an A?' his mother asked.

He shrugged. He had to try. So he sat the papers and then we forgot all about the Transfer Test. Christmas came, January followed, and then it was February.

'Only a week till I get my results,' mumbled Finn, when I went to say goodnight to him. The moment of truth was approaching.

The next day I talked to our postman. I live in the country. Our post comes mid-afternoon. We couldn't wait until three o'clock on Saturday for the letter from the Western Education & Library Board (WE&LB) with the grade. The postman said he'd leave our mail in the sorting office on Saturday morning for collection.

On the Friday night before, I couldn't sleep for ages. It was the tightness in my stomach, of course; that and my wife sighing beside me. She, too, was anxious.

The next morning I woke early. My eldest son had a rugby match; I had to drive him to school. I was delighted. Here was a legitimate way to postpone my visit to the sorting office. I ran my eldest son in, then remembered I had a library book to collect. Whoopee. Now I had another excuse to defer. On the way out of the library I noticed several shelves with old books for sale. A compulsion to comb through them overwhelmed me. There must be a bargain hiding here. There wasn't but the search killed another fifteen minutes. But then that was done. I couldn't put it off any longer.

I drove slowly to the sorting office, a hideous light-industrial building in the middle of green fields. It was all too easy, alas, to find a parking space.

I went in. There was a man at the hatch in front of me. He was signing for a box from Amazon.com. For years I've dreamed of finding a fellow bibliophile in Enniskillen, and now, I thought, of all the mornings of the year, I'd found him at last. I wanted to ask him what he'd bought. If the gods were on my side, we might fall into conversation.

Yes, but what if his box was filled with schlock? Or, worse, taxation manuals? I asked myself. Good point, I had to concede.

The Amazon.com man departed without my speaking a word to him. I moved forward.

'Yes?' said the postman behind the hatch.

I pointed at my pile. It lay on the counter at his elbow.

'It's the top one,' said the postman, passing them out.

I saw the uppermost envelope was franked with huge red letters, WE&LB. So this was it. 'That's the one,' I said.

The postman behind the counter smiled ruefully. He could spot a parent on the morning of the Transfer Test results at a hundred yards.

I drove home, the bundle on the seat beside me, untouched.

In the kitchen I found my wife at the table. Finn was behind her, reaching down the cereal from the top of the fridge.

'Well?' my wife said.

I pointed at the red-franked one. It was addressed not to Finn but to Mr and Mrs Gébler.

'Oh, for us,' she said archly. 'I'd better see what it is.'

Finn, Alpen in hand, watched with a puzzled look. How could the letter (which he guessed she was talking about) be addressed to his mother and father and not to him?

While Finn wondered, his mother, in less time than it takes to blink, had the letter opened, read and put back in its envelope. 'For you,' she said, handing it on to Finn.

I caught my wife's eyes. She was flushed. Was this despondency? Speak to me, my expression said. She glanced down.

Wondering what this signified, I heard a wild whoop.

'What did you get?' my wife asked our son.

Finn whooped again and punched the air. I took the letter from him and read it. I saw he had the result he needed to go to his elder brother's school.

That evening, when I went to say goodnight to him, Finn

looked up smiling from the pillow.

'I feel so much more confident,' he said, in a grown-up way.

'Whatever grade you got, whatever school you went to, you know you'd still be the same clever boy,' I said, like the liberal pedant I am.

He disagreed. His brother and sister had passed, 'and, Dad,' he added, 'if I hadn't I'd have felt so stupid.'

For a moment I was delighted and relieved. Then I remembered there were still two more to put through this ordeal, his siblings, my younger children Georgia and Euan. When they did it they would compare themselves to him just as he had to his brother and sister before him. Parenting, or this part of it at any rate, seemed to be on a loop.

Working at Writing 5

I accepted a commission to write a narrative history of the siege of Derry. It was one of Ireland's seminal military events and came about as follows.

In 1688 William of Orange invaded Britain and toppled his father-in-law, James II, from the throne. James fled to France, arriving there on Christmas Day, and then, early the next year, 1689, he went to Ireland where his superb lord deputy, Richard Talbot, the Earl of Tyrconnell, a pugnacious, pro-Stuart Catholic, was more or less in control.

The plan was for James to go from Ireland to Scotland, pick up a Jacobite army, sweep down to London and push William off the throne. Only one obstacle stood between James and Scotland and this was Derry, where recalcitrant Protestants loyal to William were hunkered behind the walls. James, unwilling to go to Scotland while Derry remained at his rear, sent an army to make the rebels submit. The defenders withstood the enemy's depredations at enormous cost, subsisting latterly on dogs and rats.

The end of the siege came finally after 105 days. Major General Percy Kirke, the butcher of Sedgemoor, sometime Stuart loyalist but now William's man, had bobbed off the Irish coast for nearly two months with a large flotilla before, finally, ordering his ships to break the boom the Jacobites had strung across the River Foyle and relieve the city, which they then did.

With Derry secure, William came over with an army, drove James back to France, squashed the Irish and created the Anglo-Irish Ascendancy. But centuries later the events at Derry continued to rankle. It was no coincidence that the first major set piece riot of the Troubles, on 5 October 1968, arose because Catholics, seeking to protest about their lack of civil rights, and Protestants, wishing to commemorate the siege, wanted to march in Derry on the same day.

I began to read around the subject and pretty soon I noticed a pattern in the way that historians told their stories. They would usually start a chapter with an assertion, loop back into the past and describe events that justified their opening assertion, then end at the point where they had started. I also noticed different chapters in the same book often traversed the same chronological period but from different points of view (those of different historical personages), which required the reader, in order to fully understand what was happening, to continuously cross-reference between chapters. It occurred to me that if I was strictly chronological, and if I described the way events (though in different fields of action) happened simultaneously, readers would get a better sense of what had gone on.

To think this was easy; to do it (which was what I then embarked on) was not. First, I had to break down all my source material into discrete elements; then I had to reassemble my shards of fact piece by piece into a timely sequence. It was the work of years, partly because it was time-consuming and finicky, partly because I had to break off to do other things.

One of these was *My Father's Watch*. This was a memoir, begun in 2001 (and worked on for several years), which I co-wrote with Patrick Maguire, the youngest of the so-called Maguire Seven. Following the Guildford pub bombings by the IRA, Patrick (then aged thirteen) and his family were arrested in December 1974. Tried in Court 2 at the Old Bailey, he and his co-defendants were found guilty of handling the nitroglycerine used in Guildford by the IRA. He was sentenced to four years in jail, but it was nearly twenty years before Sir John May declared that the convictions of Patrick and his co-defendants should not stand. As I worked on this book, it did not escape my attention that my pretending to write in the voice of Patrick Maguire (a working-class Londoner) was another variant of the authorial self-effacement I'd practised all my life, although instead of inventing a character to tell this story, I was now passing myself off as a living person.

Caught on a Train was another interruption to *The Siege of Derry*. On 31 December 1899, three men travelling by train from Dublin to County Mayo compete to tell the best Irish ghost story (all their stories coming from W.B. Yeats's 1888 anthology *Fairy and Folk Tales of the Irish Peasantry*). They appoint Archie, the fourteen-year-old waiter from the dining car, as judge. Archie is the novel's overall narrator, but within his account each competitor tells his story in his own voice, as Archie and the others listen. This novel, in other words, was built mostly from reported speech. Egmont published *Caught on a Train* in 2001 and later that year it won a merit award in the Bisto Prize for children's fiction.

A third interruption to my work on *The Siege of Derry* came in the form of an invitation from Nicolas Kent to write a play for London's Tricycle Theatre about the Omagh bombing on 15 August 1998 when the Real IRA planted a 500-pound bomb in the town. As I pondered how to tackle this, I remembered what I was told in Maghaberry Prison by prisoners of all stripes immediately after the bomb: a maverick Provisional IRA man (they gave me his name), disgusted by the peace process, had quit the Provisional IRA, moved to an irredentist Republican faction and made for them the bomb used in Omagh. Furthermore, the prisoners were adamant, everyone knew about the maverick and the bomb he was making. What nobody knew precisely was when and where the bomb would explode.

After remembering this an idea came into my head: I'd take Arnold Schnitzler's play *La Ronde* (which I'd never seen or even read, though I did know it was about a succession of characters infecting one another with syphilis), and re-set it in contemporary post-ceasefire Belfast. Instead of venereal disease passing from one character to the next, it would be the knowledge that dissident Republicans were making a bomb.

Then I read Schnitzler's play, and saw that, though I would need to change the characters from nineteenth- to early twenty-first-century archetypes, I could retain Schnitzler's overarching structure with its ten scenes and ten couplings, and I'd need fresh dialogue too; in the final draft of my version, called *10 Rounds*, I retained only one line from Schnitzler's original. The rest was new. The first performance of *10 Rounds* was given at the Tricycle on 23 September 2002, and the play was subsequently shortlisted for the Ewart-Biggs Award.

Despite the interruptions, *The Siege of Derry* was eventually finished and published. It was a very odd experience to hold the finished hardback in my hand. About 300 pages long, it hardly looked like a book for which I'd read dozens of books and which had taken years to write.

Envy

It seemed like a good idea. Come to the Edinburgh International Book Festival, said the letter. Stay in a hotel. Read from *Father & I*. Collect cheque. Go home. Oh, yes. In the beginning it always seems like a good idea.

Afternoon, on the second Friday in August, saw me in Scotland's capital. Several lifetimes ago I'd lived in this city. I'd had a girlfriend. We'd cohabited in her parents' house during our university vacations. The house was in the New Town. It was tall and lovely.

Mooching towards the New Town, a bit later, slanting sunlight brightening the façade of every house I passed, I decided I'd no purpose except to reacquaint myself with this place where I'd once loved someone. Then, a bit further on, I felt the New Town cobbles under my feet and I knew there was no way I could not do this.

And so, a few minutes later, I found myself outside the house of the parents of my ancient love. I wrote her a note and popped it into the letter box. Her mother was still in residence, I believed. She'd pass it on. At that moment a great cloud of dandelion seeds wafted up the street. Yes, I thought, walking off, it had been a good idea to come.

The next morning it was raining. In Charlotte Square (site of the Book Festival) the smells were wet grass, canvas and book glue. I took myself to the opening event. Brian Aldiss and Helen Lederer performed a play specially written by Aldiss. The premise was this. He was Hitler. He lived in Leith. He was unrepentant. She was a ditzy hackette writing a musical about the Führer. Her 'research' interview was the equivalent in talk of a blow job. It was quite funny, or would have been, I thought sniffily, late at night at a sci-fi conference after the bar had closed. But on a cold Saturday morning in Edinburgh, it didn't look quite so good. Such was my conceited conclusion. My own set was less than an hour away so my judgement was completely impure. I was really thinking, I will be better. It was a foolish thought to have had because in my experience superior thoughts such as these were invariably followed by a knock or rebuke, the purpose of which was to teach that such arrogance was foolish and should never be tolerated.

My tent was pink and purple. Mounting the podium I thought, I'll start with a joke. Welcome to the Barbara Cartland Memorial Tent. Then I turned and saw my audience. It was a small crowd of old ladies. Nothing like the full house Mr Aldiss and Miss Lederer had enjoyed. Ah. I might excel here but there'd be no one to witness it. It was an awful truth. At home I wrote and I knew my place. I had no other ambition but to write as well as I was able. Really, I had none. But put me in a circus tent and at once I came over all stroppy and competitive. I couldn't stop measuring myself against others. I wanted to beat everyone else. It was bad for art and probably for my heart as well.

I began to read. I sweated as I did but I couldn't take off my jacket. Parts of the microphone were secreted beneath. Reading finished, I gave a forthright description of the book. At one minute to chucking-out time the chair asked for questions. Deafening silence. The audience was either sated or floored. I could not judge which from the quality of the silence. There was certainly none of the noisy brouhaha that had filled the Aldiss-Lederer tent after their event. Of course, I reminded myself, they had done a revue. I was in a different game. I was in art.

Envy has nothing going for it. And here we see why. First I measured myself against others. I found myself wanting. That was painful. Then I put myself on a podium. I told myself I was in art. That was asking for a fall.

In the evening I went to the Book Festival party in the Spiegeltent. It looked like a New Orleans brothel. Someone told me it was famous. It was used, for instance, for the Perrier Comedy Awards.

I gravitated to a publisher and began to orbit him like a moon. He knew me. He said he was putting together a collection of myths. Did myth interest me?

Actually, yes, I said. My last children's book, *Caught on a Train*, was a reworking of Irish myths.

The publisher showed no interest but continued to describe his own project. He was going to get big-name writers to tell old-time myths. Günter Grass and Michael Ondaatje were among the names mentioned. Obviously, he continued, he'd have to have something Irish.

Of course, I agreed, seeing here a glimmer of opportunity. I mentioned some of my personal favourites from the Irish canon. He pressed his card on me. Would I email the details? I agreed, thinking, Surely this is an invitation to tender.

'Heaney would be so good, wouldn't he?' said the publisher, deftly, and with that he flitted away, like a bird disturbed by the footfall of an approaching predator. He wasn't in the least bit interested, I thought, in my doing anything at all for him.

Walking back to my hotel, I passed some merry Edinburghians roistering in the street. As I passed, a jig burst at that moment from a pub.

'Ah, Irish,' they shouted. The women lifted their skirts and performed a drunken pastiche of *Riverdance*.

Yes, I thought, cutting across the road, it's only ever a good idea at first to come.

She's Leaving Home

It was strange to be back in London's King's Cross. Last time I was here, I went to a tattoo parlour opposite the old Scala, and a man inscribed a rose on my upper left arm.

This Monday, more than a quarter-century later, I was in a minicab with my wife, my elder daughter India, and several suitcases.

Dinwiddy House was sighted. This was the hall of residence where India would live for her first year at university. It was a khaki and glass cube. Like most university buildings, it was hideous.

We heaved the luggage out and hauled it inside. Now the fun started. Like a prison, Dinwiddy House had endless security doors but no signs. We asked at least half a dozen Chinese students the way before we finally got to her room.

Actually, 'room' is a misnomer. It was really a rather nasty pod. The mattress was grubby. The wardrobe doors were hanging off. The drawers were missing their knobs. The shower (the room was en suite) had shed several tiles.

I listed the room's defects on the form supplied and marched to the accommodation office. A slim Barbadian woman with gold hoop earrings stood behind the desk.

'I'm not impressed,' I said, handing her the list, 'especially after having paid what I paid for the room.'

A pair of brown eyes gazed sadly at me. 'Once everyone's settled we'll turn our minds to repairs," she drawled, sounding like Prunella Scales in *Fawlty Towers*.

'Couldn't the room have been fixed *before* term started?'

'We've been very busy,' she said, faking a smile. In other words, would I just be grateful and stop complaining?

It was time to change the subject. We'd not lugged duvets and so on from Enniskillen. Where did we go, I asked, to get the bedding kit?

'C Block stairwell at six o'clock with a hundred pounds,' she said, taking the complaints sheet from the student behind me.

I stomped off like a peeved old colonel.

An hour later we stood in a queue in Woolworth's, our shopping trolley laden with pots and pans. India was in self-catering accommodation.

The man in front of us presented the girl on the till with a bag stuffed with sweets from the pick 'n' mix stand.

'Two ninety-one,' she said.

'I've only eighty-three pence,' he said, holding out a fistful of coppers. 'Tell you what,' he continued, 'take out the red ones. I don't like them red ones.'

At six I presented myself at C Block stairwell where I hoped to buy India's bedding. There was no one around. I went to the porter's lodge to complain.

''Course there weren't no one selling bedding,' he said.

'They sold out two days ago.'

'Why didn't the woman in the office tell me?'

'This is a student hall of residence. What d'you expect? Efficiency?'

I was annoyed but also, frankly, I was delighted. If there was no bedding, India would have to come home with us to the house in West London where we were staying. We could postpone cutting the umbilical cord for one more night.

I returned to the room. 'You'll have to come back with us.'

She frowned. 'No way.' If she didn't stay how would she ever make friends? 'I'll sleep under my coat,' she said firmly.

The three of us went to the porter's lodge. I complained again.

'I think I can get the loan of a duvet for her,' said the porter.

'Go on then,' said India. 'I'll sort it out.'

Her life without us was about to start. 'Goodbye,' we said. Brief kisses were exchanged. We left.

Outside, rain was pouring. There were derelicts and junkie girls sheltering in doorways. We should have sheltered too but we felt too depressed to linger. We just wanted to escape to the far side of London, to our friend Gina and her warm house.

We schlepped through the wet down Pentonville Road, then stopped at the bottom to cross. My wife was so wet even her lipstick was running.

'It's amazing,' I said, in my best cheer-up voice. 'We met all those years ago, and now, nineteen years later, here we are, dropping our daughter off at university. We'd never have guessed then it would end like this. Would we?'

She bit her lip and shrugged as if to say, no, we wouldn't have guessed and, if you don't mind, I'd rather not talk about it.

The green man flickered. We hurried across.

'Don't you think it's amazing, how it's ended?' I said.

My wife was silent and stone-like. She would not be drawn. We hurried towards King's Cross Underground. As we stepped in, air gusted into our faces. It was hot, and smelt of diesel and burnt dust, and for an instant it brought tears to our eyes.

Kids

My eldest daughter India went off to university with two staples in her wardrobe: jeans and trainers. This was the uniform of youth in the town of Enniskillen where she'd grown up.

Fifteen weeks later, when I arrived at Belfast International to fetch her home for Christmas, all had changed. I found her wearing a red felt skirt, tights with geometric stripes, an Afghan headscarf, biker boots, and jewellery from four nations.

The other four children, Jack, Finn, Georgia and Euan, were waiting in the living room at home, their eyes riveted to the gate. As I nudged the car between the piers, they all rushed out. There was a short orgy of sibling hugging and kissing. All the children had missed their big sister. Yet on the faces of the two older boys I saw that something wasn't right.

A few minutes later, when I found myself alone with them, Jack asked quietly, 'What's London done to my sister?'

'The boots and tights, yuck,' chimed his younger brother Finn.

'And the thing on her head,' said Jack.

'And the earrings,' said the younger brother.

My sons sounded to me like two old generals fulminating about a violation of the mess dress code. Come on, lads, I wanted to say, does it really matter if your friends in town see you with your big sister looking like she does? I knew that was really at the bottom of their complaint. Their friends would survive, wouldn't they? Of course they would. But adult pieties, like these, don't cut any ice with children, so I said nothing.

A few hours later the elder son came and found me.

'Take me to town, Dad,' he said. He wore Vans trainers, Sonneti combats, Fila socks and a Gap jacket.

'Why? Your sister's only just home.'

'It's the school disco.' This was an alcohol-free event for young teens like himself.

I drove him into town. On the outskirts he said, in the abrupt manner of the cusp adolescent, 'Let me out here.'

'But this is an industrial estate,' I said, 'and the school's half a mile away. I'll drive you up.'

'No,' he said, 'my friends are there.' He pointed to a cluster of boys, each dressed more or less as he was, standing in the shadow of a furniture warehouse.

I stopped. He got out.

'Half eleven at the school gates,' I called, through the passenger window.

He flapped a hand in acknowledgement. I drove off.

At eleven twenty-nine, I stood at the gates, the school towering on the hill above me, all lights blazing, music throbbing inside. Behind me was a mob of boys who'd already left the disco. I was wearing a suit and anorak; this was unfortunate.

'Hey, it's a peeler,' one wag shouted at me from the crowd.

'It's CID,' screamed another.

'Going to bang us up, are you?' yelled a third, in the mockney accent favoured on *The Bill*.

I ignored the jests and gazed up the hill. Crowds of happy teenagers were slithering down the wet asphalt path and flowing out of the gate beside me. I scanned each boyish huddle that passed, hoping to see my son. It was hard work searching for him because every boy looked the same; every boy had the same hair, shoes, jacket and trousers.

Then, in the mêlée behind, I sensed something. Trainers were scuffing, hard and soft body parts colliding. I turned.

'Ye wanked on my granddad's chair and left a wet puddle, so you did,' a boy shouted at another. He then nutted the second on the chin and kicked him on the side of the leg.

The victim shrieked, 'I didn't go near your granddad,' and started sliding towards the wet ground.

Do I intervene? I wondered. It was an appalling thought. I was one and they were many. Perhaps I could pretend to be a doctor. Yes, I thought, that would be good. I drew myself up and began to say, 'Heads aren't generally made to be jumped on,' which was about to happen, when the victim struggled to his feet and sprinted off. He was, I couldn't help noticing, the only one in the crowd not wearing the trainers-and-combats uniform of the rest but red jeans and spats and a coloured shirt and a silk scarf.

What a difference a few hours make. In my kitchen, when my son and his brother had acted like old generals, I had been irritated. However, a few minutes in the company of their peers had changed all that.

Fashion conformity is big in a small town, and at a certain age it amounts to tyranny. But my son was in the uniform, I thought, and I heaved a sigh. His dress code wasn't sheep-like conformity but a sign of wisdom, a way to avoid trouble. He hadn't yet appeared but the music had just finished so he would show up at any moment now. A crowd sauntered towards me that surely included him and, as it did, I prepared my brightest smile to greet him, my paragon of sensible sartorial acquiescence.

The Circus

Everywhere in Ballyshannon there were posters for the Vegas Circus. Tickets were five pounds and car parking was free.

My last circus (ten years earlier in Letterkenny) had been a dismal evening of duff acts and toe-curling audience participation. I had vowed never again. Such rules were fine until you collided with the reality of a mobile home in Donegal on a rainy Sunday afternoon and two young children chanting, 'We're bored.'

When my wife said, 'Let's go to the circus,' I had to agree. We piled into the car and drove to Ballyshannon. Car parking was indeed free. I was free to park in any street in Ballyshannon I wanted.

We joined the queue of women in summer dresses, and their excited children. I was reminded of Pinter's descriptions of Irish provincial audiences queuing to see McMasters' productions. My spirits began to rise. Then we reached the kiosk. It transpired the five-pound tickets were Saturdays only.

'It's very hard for circus people to make a living,' my wife murmured. 'Think of the animals.' I passed across four crisp ten-pound notes.

Inside, we found the last free bench, hard and narrow like those in gospel halls. There was a rank smell of cat and grass. A dapper man in shiny shoes announced, 'Alexander and his big cats.' A dun-coloured lion, four lionesses and a pair of tigers bolted down a tunnel and into a cage centre stage.

Georgia and Euan shouted, 'Real lions and tigers.'

Alexander, hair wet with Brylcreem, swaggered into the cage.

For the next twenty minutes his animals growled on cue and hopped about obligingly. Then the amplified theme from *The Lion King* cut, and a single spot picked out the lion.

'No talking,' the MC warned. Alexander pulled open the lion's mouth and put his head between two rows of sharp teeth.

I turned to see the audience behind. There wasn't one face on the tiered benches that wasn't terrified and fascinated all at once.

The next act was the clown, the improbably named Claude Phipps. His bravura act – it took a full fifteen minutes – involved convincing the audience that his bucket was full of water. When finally tipped, of course, it was found to contain only blue cellophane. My children squealed with delight.

Next Beatrice Spingler and her black Spanish stallions were in the ring. The horses pawed the ground and reared on cue; it was dull. My children were more impressed with the next act, Miss Victoria, a large woman dressed unpretentiously in spangled nipple covers and a thong, who did amazing things with hoops, and the Loony Toonies, four tumblers, who fell over a vaulting horse a hundred ways to the theme from *The Mask*.

The above, with generous helpings of Claude, took more than an hour. The intermission, padded out with donkey rides and a raffle, took a further forty minutes.

The second half started with Elaine (wearing even less than Miss Victoria), who swung on a rope and did quite breathtaking things. She was followed by Kerri, who also did things on a rope but was slightly less extraordinary. Kerri popped up again a little later, in a skimpy maid's outfit, and helped Claude spin thirty-two plates simultaneously, and Beatrice Spingler danced a tango on horseback with Alexander, the lion tamer. No one could accuse these artists of indolence.

At last we reached the final lap. The safety net went up and the Loony Toonies, now dressed in spangled catsuits and renamed the Flying Souzas, emerged into the big top. They climbed the ladders and, to amplified salsa, began to fly through the air. I, who hate trapeze, watched through my fingers. My children couldn't take their eyes off the figures swooping near the roof.

'Boys and girls, you are asked to stay in your seats, please,' said the MC, 'as Renaldo will now attempt the triple somersault.'

He tried it twice and was dropped both times. To restore our confidence, Renaldo decided on a double somersault while blindfolded.

Everyone looked up except me: I looked down at the floor strewn with popcorn. There was an interminable silence broken, finally, by a savage cry. I looked up to see Renaldo, dressed in the face cowl of a medieval executioner, hanging from the arms of the catcher. Even though I hadn't watched it, I recognised a *coup de théâtre.*

We walked to the car in silence. It was only when we were moving that Georgia spoke: 'A man put his head in the mouth of a lion and he didn't die.' There was wonder in her voice.

To be sure, the circus cost too much and the animals might have been wretched, but this ancient entertainment reached places in my daughter's psyche that modern forms never reached. She watched *Pokémon* religiously yet she never commented on it ever, but weeks on from the circus she was still saying, with wonder in her voice, 'A man put his head in the mouth of a lion and he didn't die.'

Letter from Romania

As the taxi moved onto the highway connecting the airport to Bucharest, the very first thing I saw was a billboard. It showed a naked woman lolling, like Sophie Dahl in the infamous Opium promotion. Apparently I could see more of her in the Sexy Club. Immediately below, a work gang, fluorescent bars on their bulky clothes, swept the road with old-fashioned brooms. This, in essence, was to be Romania: the old and new everywhere in collision.

The next morning I was taken to the Writers' Union of Romania's (WUR) villa in the city centre. Inside the front hall a man with a Julius Caesar haircut stopped me.

'Neptun?' he said.

This was the Black Sea resort and location of the literary festival that I had come for as one of the Irish guests of the WUR. It was close to Tomis, the Roman poet Ovid's place of exile.

'Yes.'

He led me into a library where the shelves were lined with old editions of Victor Hugo and Voltaire.

'Please.' He pointed at a heap of suitcases. They looked like an installation in Saatchi's County Hall gallery. I guessed they belonged to my fellow delegates. I added mine.

'Please.'

He had lit a cigarette and showed me a key. I needn't worry. My possessions would be safe. We went out and he locked the door.

I loitered, on and off, for the rest of the day in the vast hall of the villa. It was all marble balustrades and gilded statues – if Luis Buñuel had made a porno, he would have shot the orgy here.

That evening, coaches appeared. About a hundred delegates boarded (they were mostly Eastern Europeans but there were Scandinavians, other Western Europeans and a smattering of South Americans and Africans) and we set off.

Outside Bucharest the country was ominously dark, while the towns, what I could see of them by the woeful street lighting, were decrepit and empty. Several Romanian poets across the aisle from me got drunk on plum brandy. After four or five hours, the coach stopped and soldiers with inscrutable expressions stared in at us through the windows.

'Please,' announced a Romanian, through the PA, 'we cross the Danube now. No cameras.'

As we rattled over the bridge, one of the drunken poets was muttering to himself. What was this? Ceauşescu back from the dead? Were we spies? No, we were poets. He mopped sweat from his shining brow and shook his head.

The next morning we gathered in the conference centre for the Days and Nights of Literature Festival. In the room there were long green-baize-covered tables, impressive lights and a booth for the translators.

'When Ceauşescu was on holiday,' the English delegate beside me explained, 'his entourage used this place for meetings. His summer villa was very close to here, you see, on the coast.'

This festival was to take the form of colloquium. Each speaker had fifteen minutes on the topic 'Me, the other'. The first went to the front. He put his hands on either side of the microphone and began reading in a monotone. (This was the Party-approved public-speaking mode, it was later explained to me). There was a space, he said, between the other and him. When ignorance filled this void there was war and misery. But poetry – he was a poet, of course – could bridge the gap.

The second speaker's paper (delivered, like the first, hands on either side of the microphone, in a monotone) was a variation on this theme. Ditto the third, the fourth and the fifth. Every paper, indeed, covered roughly the same terrain and was delivered with roughly the same lack of aplomb.

I was with a knot of English and Irish delegates. (In adversity old enemies make common cause). At first we rolled our eyes. It was funny. As the morning continued it became distinctly less funny. By midday we were so bored we were passing notes, writing dreadful poetry (we each wrote a line in turn) and running a competition to spot the delegate with the worst haircut. In a packed Eastern European field this was less than easy. By the close of the first morning session, my head felt numb and leaden.

I asked for directions to the sea and followed a path through a linden wood. After walking for a few minutes I saw, at the end of a long green tunnel running through the trees, fine sand and a delicate patch of light blue sea. But when I came out of the tunnel I found myself on a concrete path. In one direction I saw a barbed-wire fence guarded by a soldier in fatigues. That must be Ceauşescu's old villa, I guessed. (I checked later: it was).

In the other direction the concrete path ran for some miles round an enormous bay. On the deserted seaside, there were bathing huts, showers, fixed parasols, cafés, stone aprons, sporting grounds, toilets, and groynes made of concrete skittles ten-foot high. In a word, there was everything man-made that could give a holidaymaker pleasure.

On the other side of the path there stretched for as far as I could see, within yards of the sand, a low-rise housing block that curved in tandem with the line of the coast. This was topped every thousand yards or so with a high-rise hotel. In short, the entire coast was covered with concrete.

I began to walk. The sun beat softly on my face. Mussel shoals spread like shadows in the shallows and their shells lay heaped in banks on the sand. I only met a dead dog and a woman in a pink bikini, who waved at me.

In the afternoon I returned to the room with the green-baize tables.

'Welcome back to the Party Congress,' said one of the English delegates.

'And you know what's on tonight?' said another.

'What?'

'They're going to read their poetry.'

'Oh, Christ.'

'And then guess what?'

'Tell me.'

'We get to do it all over again tomorrow. Hooray!'

On the evening of the third day, we put on our party clothes: we had the climax, the prize-giving. The coaches carried us through an unrelieved landscape of seventies social housing interspersed with parks and copses, all of which, since construction, had been left to atrophy.

In Mangalia we parked in a square in front of a theatre with a mural on the front. An idealised couple floated with their Christ-like baby son over a Romania full of new factories, bustling ports and abundant fields.

Inside I found the stage was swathed in blue and white cloth, a silver rose sprouted out of the apron and the shadow of a lyre floated overhead. The poets who hadn't read on the previous two evenings now read. There were twenty-two of them. Each read in his or her language. Then the translation was read, sometimes in English or French and Romanian.

Then there was the award ceremony with lengthy citations, all translated into English and French. There were two prizes. The Ovidius prize (worth $10,000) for the author who'd contributed most, and I quote, 'to freedom of expression and inter-ethnic tolerance'. This went to the Portuguese novelist Antonio Lobo Antunes. The second, the Festival Prize, went to the author who'd most enlarged the frontiers of literature. The winner was the Albanian novelist Ismail Kadare, who bore an uncanny resemblance to Philip Larkin. His prize was an all-expenses-paid fortnight in Romania with a partner of his choice.

Three and a half hours later, I was back outside on the steps. 'They're shameless, these poets,' I moaned. My real thought, though, I kept to myself. It was: one could get to hate them.

A police car and two police motorcycles were parked in front of our coaches. We returned to Neptun under police escort. I realised I had just attended the Romanian equivalent of the Man Booker.

The next day was for sightseeing so it was back in the coaches. First stop Constanta: it had a shipyard and the typical penumbra of concrete cubes built during Ceauşescu's reign but the centre was filled with beautiful nineteenth-century houses that had stucco-decorated fronts and exquisite wrought- iron balconies. There was also a verdigris-coloured statue of Ovid. We all got out and laid a wreath at the foot of the plinth.

Then we headed north. These are some of the notes I scribbled as I stared at the world sliding past the window:

> Flat landscape with no boundaries. Shades of the steppe. A wooden cart with a coffin driven by a peasant in a waistcoat moves along a mud track.
>
> A hamlet of one-storey buildings built of mud and straw bricks. Missing roof tiles replaced with old tins cunningly beaten into the shape of roof

tiles. Shoeless children chase a warped wooden
hoop. A woman in a coloured skirt beats a blanket
throwing up clouds of dust. Vast heaps of maize
piled outside each house.

Flat landscape again: fields of maize interspersed
with scrub. Cannibalised factory in the distance.
Another hamlet with more patched-up houses
and muddy paths and children with shaven heads.
Chekhov's story 'Peasants' comes to mind.

Back in the country a spur of railway track shoots
between maize fields to another derelict factory.

These pictures were repeated for hours. Eventually we
passed through deep woods and emerged on the far side at
our goal: Soan Monastery. There were two churches, an old
wooden windmill, its weathered boards the colour of molasses,
vineyards, orchards and gardens, all tended by monks and nuns.

I got out and found myself beside one of the translators.

'These are stone flowers.' She pointed at a flowerbed. The
blossoms were a deep blood red. In the distance there rose a
line of half-built monastery dormitories.

'The Church is expanding?'

She nodded.

'Was it persecuted?'

'Not at first, but later.'

'So tell me the story,' I said.

'What – of the Church?'

'No, the last fifty or sixty years in Romania.'

She sighed. 'In 'forty-four we have Red Army, liberation,
thereafter terror, executions, collectivisation, nationalisation
of assets. In 1948 we get Gheorghe Gheorghiu-Dej, general
secretary of the Party's Central Committee. It's just common-
or-garden variety Bolshevik nightmare.

'In 1965 Gheorghiu-Dej dies and we get Nicolae Ceauşescu. At first not too bad but then the problems start. He wants bigger workforce for industrialisation programme, so no abortions, no contraception. Same time, he wants to repay all Western loans. The people work harder and harder for less and less. Then we have systemisation programme for rural development. The peasants" houses are destroyed and they're rehoused.

'By nineteen eighties, things very bad. The shops are empty. There's no food, no fuel, not even light bulbs. We're in darkness, literally. But Nicolae and his wife Elena are still building wildly. There's the Palace of the People in Bucharest, the Danube-Black Sea canal, and the village systemisation is still progressing.

'By late eighties food riots, strikes, problems. December twenty-first, 1989, a hundred thousand loyalists brought to square in Bucharest for presidential address. The crowd starts shouting against Ceauşescu. His face is on television and for the first time ever he looks terrified. He doesn't know what to do. Then across Romania the television screens go blank but we've seen the truth. The emperor and his empress are finished. They flee and the rest is history.'

'Who actually shot him and his wife?'

'Army firing squad. After court-martial.'

Two nuns in long black gowns and head-dresses coaxed a flock of geese across our path.

'You sound bitter.'

'It wasn't a fair trial and you don't start democracy by denying fair trial even if the accused were tyrants.'

Lunch was served on a narrow veranda that ran around the refectory. There were quail's eggs, followed by sour cabbage leaves with beef and pork mincemeat and sticky polenta. Nuns with beautiful faces served us.

'Why would such lovely girls want to be nuns?' asked a Westerner.

'Today many do,' a Romanian explained patiently. 'Here they have order. Here they are safe.'

The reply sounded measured, yet somehow (or did I imagine this?) it seemed freighted with deeper, darker meaning. At least while they were here there was no chance of them, unlike so many other girls from Romania, being shipped to a brothel in Milan or Bremen.

In the background a splendidly robed man with an impressive beard was speaking on a mobile phone while at the same time directing the nuns.

'The Romanian Orthodox Archbishop of Constanta,' a Romanian explained.

'Doesn't he have better things to do than supervise?'

'He wants to be Metropolitan Archbishop of Bucharest. That's why he's giving us lunch.'

'Giving writers lunch – this will help him?'

'Correction, please, he's giving delegates to Writers Union of Romania literary festival lunch and this will definitely not hurt him.'

'Ah.'

'It's like you say: there is no such thing in this life as free lunch.'

It was my last morning. I was back in Bucharest. I wandered through a suburb of lovely French villas and found the Museum of the Romanian Peasant. It was a beautiful and vast nineteenth-century building that had survived the regime's last frenzied years of rebuilding.

Inside I moved slowly through the galleries. There was a room of carved peasant chairs, a wall of staves of authority and a collection of peasant dresses, the patterns stitched in luminous blue and red thread. There were dressed church crosses, an entire Romanian Orthodox church (warped and buckled like all the buildings in the German expressionist film, *The Cabinet of Dr Caligari*), brought in pieces from Transylvania and reassembled here, and a hall of headstones.

In albums lying on tables everywhere there were hundreds of black-and-white photographs taken by Romanian amateurs in the second half of the twentieth century. These showed that everything on display had once been the norm.

The Romanian aesthetic was decorative, colourful and plangent. It was Greece strained through France. I didn't doubt the peasant life that had created this aesthetic, and what Ceauşescu had extirpated was squalid and unequal, but what he had put in its place was dreary, drab and ugly. Frankly, it was worse, much worse. Oh, yes, he had made Romania worse.

I left the museum. Outside, the street sweepers were everywhere, running their brooms over the paving and along gutters. By chance I bumped into a young Romanian I knew by sight.

'You've been in the Museum of the Romanian Peasant?'

'Yes.'

'And?'

'Beautiful, but melancholy to see what was stamped on.'

A brown-faced youth came up with a broom and we moved aside for him. We watched in silence as he made his heap of rubbish. It was mostly dry leaves, mottled like old skin, but there were other bits of detritus mixed in. There were plastic straws, cigarette butts, some with lipstick smudges, and Styrofoam McDonald's boxes. There was a sheet of Romanian newsprint with a smudged picture of a farmer and his cow, a used condom, and a Levi's label.

'"It is only by viewing the vanished wealth of the past,"' said my companion, '"that we can understand how truly poor we are today." I think this is even on the wall in the museum.'

In silence we walked back towards the hotel with the sound of the bristles of the brooms rasping in our ears.

Guns

We were on our mandatory Sunday constitutional, my father, my brother and myself. I was eight or nine, my brother six or seven. We were on Wimbledon Common. It was dreary. It was November. White smog hung in the air.

We came to the row of horse chestnut trees. My brother and I began to search through the leaves piled on the wet ground for glistening shiny conkers. We filled our pockets and then began to lob them at one another. We threw them overarm like soldiers threw grenades, because that was what these were to us, and we added sound effects: 'Bang! Kapow! Pouf!'

'Playing war games again,' said my father, sarcastically. 'Nothing better in your heads, of course.'

He was appalled at the weapons we improvised (which we had to do as plastic war toys were more or less forbidden) and the battles we re-staged. For my brother and me, it was always Dunkirk or Arnhem or Tobruk, battles of which we had read in the *War Picture Library* comics that circulated in the school playground. Sadly, for him, we had no interest in progressive conflicts (the only acceptable sort of wars), the struggle of the Red Army against the Whites, or the Viet Cong against the French and later the Americans. The pro-war propaganda Western capitalism produced had corrupted us.

'And if you end up in the Congo killing blacks,' he once warned us, 'don't say I didn't warn you that's where your war games would lead you.'

My first child, India, was a girl. From the outset she was a dolls-and-tea-sets child. Other children occasionally pressed guns on her when she went to play in their houses. Out of politeness she played with them. She had no choice, she felt. And she was always very diplomatic, always fitted in with other children. But she had no appetite for guns or indeed anything boyish. Her mother gave her a garage once to rectify this. Our daughter was appalled. She recognised, as children do, the ideological premise behind the gift. The garage went into the loft and she went on playing with her dolls.

Our next child was Jack, a boy. When he was two we got the toy garage down. He loved it. He loved guns as well. He should have them, I thought. Despite my childhood fixation with war toys, I hadn't joined the army when I grew up. Childhood games don't determine your course in life.

My wife, however, thought differently. She didn't want war toys in the house. And when our son wanted to play war, she would always suggest he do something constructive instead. Like making a Lego castle. But the more she tried to channel his energy away from death and into life, the more interested he became in weapons and war. Finally, during supper one evening, he chewed his slice of bread in to the shape of a revolver and shot at everyone with it. That was it. His mother knew she was beaten.

The next day she returned from the local toyshop. Not with a plastic Winchester repeater or a Browning automatic (for which I had yearned as a boy) but a flintlock revolver with an engraved barrel. Since it was more an aesthetic object than a gun, she explained, it was easier to square with her conscience.

Our son received his gift with delight. We'd started on the slippery slope. Within months, all maternal opposition had crumpled. Uzis and M3s as well as swords and bows and arrows flooded in. For a while, our son and his younger brother (when he came along) played war obsessively. Then they outgrew this pastime. The guns rarely came out except when the sons of other anti-gun liberals came to play. They loved our house. They could play fiendish games of war there, and while they did, their mothers would mutter, 'I don't know what's got into him. He's never like this at home.'

And, of course, as they did I would nod sympathetically, glowing inwardly with self-satisfaction. The liberal naysayers had turned their children into potential warmongers. My sons, on the other hand, whose aggression was tolerated, had eventually lost interest in war toys and games (except when their friends insisted) and now looked set to mature into gentle men. In my childhood all was forbidden and I was unhappy. But in my sons' childhood, tolerance, not prohibition, had proved the better path.

And so I believed until Jack appeared with a pamphlet from the Army Cadet Force. 'I want to join,' he said fiercely. 'All my friends are.' He'd get to go up in a helicopter, learn to march, and fire a gun, he said.

'No,' his mother replied flatly, and I agreed.

But his will was stronger than ours. The morning of the open day for potential cadets, I found myself dropping him at the Territorial Army centre. 'Ring when you want collecting,' I said. He disappeared into a room where an ex-serviceman was lecturing boys.

My son rang when it was nearly dark. When I collected him, his expression was doleful.

'Good day?' I asked, as he climbed into the car.

'Rotten. I've been in the TA centre since half-eight this morning and I've done *nothing*. I've wasted a whole day.'

'You got to fire a gun.'

'For a minute. The rest of the time was marching and regimental history.'

'Once we get home,' I said, 'Can I throw away the cadet consent form? You're not joining.'

'Aye.'

I was delighted with myself. He'd had his way but in the end everything had turned out right. Tolerant parenting meant he now saw things my way. As soon as we got inside the house I opened the stove and was about to lob in the form when he said, 'Actually, don't burn it. I might join after all, you know.'

'I thought it was a waste of a day and you weren't going back.'

'Yeah, but if my friends do, I'll join.'

I closed the stove door. So, it was a lack of mates that was really at the root of his chagrin. Now I saw that this wasn't going to be the victory for tolerant parenting I'd assumed. Or, expressed another way, whatever you do, whether you prohibit or tolerate, in the end the child will always follow his own sweet way.

Baby

The alarm went off at seven. The Christmas holidays were over. It was the first day of the new term. The children had been sleeping late for weeks. I anticipated complaints – 'Oh, Dad, five more minutes. I'm tired.' It couldn't have been more different. One after another the four younger ones, at the touch of my finger on their shoulder, sat up, rubbed their eyes and swung their feet to the floor. But the fifth, the eldest, India, I left sleeping. She was twenty. She had no school. She was about to have a baby and today was the day.

'You know why the children woke so easily?' my wife asked, at breakfast.

I didn't.

'They know India's going into hospital today. They've picked up on our anxiety.'

I went to my desk and tried to write. The words came but they had no lustre. In the afternoon I drove my daughter and her partner to hospital. After I'd dropped them, I found myself hankering for a drink while it was still daylight, which I hadn't for years.

It was later that evening, when we were home and the younger children were in bed, that India rang. The doctor, for whom she'd been waiting since I'd dropped her off, had finally visited. (It was only hours not days so I suppose we should have been grateful). The baby was breech. A Caesarean section would be performed the following day. My wife's face was drawn. And I could just hear, faintly, drifting from the receiver, that my daughter's words were mixed with sobs.

The next morning I overslept by an hour and a quarter.

'I know why,' said my wife at breakfast. 'You don't want this day to come.'

After the school run I went to the hospital. My daughter was in an antiseptic cube filled with humming machines – the recovery room. My wife was already with her. Surgery phobia had set in. My daughter was weeping.

'It'll be all right,' said my wife, mopping her face. 'The doctors are experts.'

We set off for the operating theatre along dark corridors with huge windows that overlooked other dark corridors. At the operating theatre double doors we said goodbye and our daughter, still crying, was whisked through. Only her partner was allowed inside with her.

While we waited, a friend appeared. Mary was in the hospital on another errand. Her eyes were green and wet. Her sister, explained Mary, had just got some news. She had incurable cancer: death was imminent.

The greater suffering of others is supposed to put one's own anxieties into perspective. But the truth is that, no matter how badly others fare, your own preoccupations persist. I nodded, I sympathised, but all my thoughts were for my child and her child, my grandchild, and the life they were likely to have together.

The doors swung open and a nurse barked at us, 'Boy, healthy,' then vanished.

Baby himself appeared in a blood-spotted blanket. He was small and sleepy. In the recovery room there was weighing and measuring. Then his mother was wheeled in, sutured, ready to feed.

My wife went to bed early that night. She was mangled, she said, by the day's events. I watched *Rumble in the Jungle*, the documentary about the Ali-Foreman fight in Zaire on 30 October 1974. As I watched I kept wondering how nobody had noticed at the time that President Sese Seko Mobutu was a monster. I decided, grumpily, that everybody was stupid, always was, always would be. Obviously, I was in the wrong mood, for this film, for anything.

When I got into bed my wife was already asleep. As my breathing fell in with hers I began to drift. Before my mind's eye, the familiar, pre-sleep scenario unrolled. I was walking in the suburban London street where I'd lived as a child, holding my mother's hand. Everything was going well until, reaching the kerb of Cherrywood Lane, my foot went out to the uprising tarmac and I jolted awake.

I got up, made a hot whiskey, then picked Roald Dahl's *Going Solo* off the shelves. I had never read this account of his service with the RAF in the Middle East during the Second World War but I assumed it would be like everything else of Dahl's. It would be astringent, economical and flawless, the only type of prose to which, at that moment, I could pay attention.

It worked for a while until, pausing between chapters, I flicked to the front in search of the potted biography with, I hoped, Dahl's date of birth. To my horror India, the new mother, had scrawled on the page – I had forgotten that this was once her book. In the big looping writing of a ten-year-old she had written, 'This book belongs to India Gébler. I don't think *Going Solo* is as good as *Boy* but it is still very enjoyable and exciting.' Well, that was that. The dam gates opened and all the memories and anxieties that filled the inner reservoir gushed out in an unceasing torrent.

The first light of dawn, when it finally showed, was the colour of woodsmoke.

The View from Enniskillen,

County Fermanagh: Sunday, 16 March, to Sunday, 23 March 2003

Sunday, 16 March 2003

After a walk on a Donegal beach with the children, I entered a pub for Coke and crisps. Twenty men with angry eyes were gazing at the television while their women and wee ones sat quietly behind. I glanced up at the screen and noticed in the top left-hand corner 'Celtic – 1 GERS – 2'. What was GERS?

'Who are Celtic playing?' I innocently enquired of a large man on a spindly stool.

'Rangers,' he said grumpily.

I wondered, in a vague way, what he thought the outcome of the match would be. I would ask him. Then I noticed the 'Made in '69' tattoo on Mr Grump's forearm, which suggested he was born at the beginning of the Troubles and might well be a Republican. I realised my simple question might annoy him and decided against asking it.

I retreated with my children to the women's quarters at the rear. The match continued. For a moment Celtic looked like scoring. The fans' mood rose. I could feel the mood change in the bar. It was palpable. Then Celtic failed to score and it fell again. The whistle went – Rangers had won – and the mood of the fans in the bar dropped to the floor. The television was immediately turned off as if it were in some way complicit with what had happened. One or two fans swore violently, though the majority sat in silence, nursing their grievance. Finally, someone called out for a pint and the talk haltingly restarted. Naturally there was no mention of the match.

I should explain that when I was being made, God forgot to add the sport gene to the rest of the chemicals in the tube, with the result that I have never been interested in sport. My sons have often said they wished I had the sport gene (because they have it), and I have always agreed until I collide with situations like this. The fans' desolation (thickened here, of course, with something sectarian) might only have lasted seconds but even seconds of such desolation didn't seem worth it. But I hadn't got the gene so I was bound to say that, wasn't I?

Monday, 17 March 2003

The day started at the local sub-post office. It is also a shop. The postmaster gets the *Guardian* in especially for smug old me. All the other papers for sale were of the nasty, icky variety that were more fiction than fact. Naturally I disapproved, yet I wasn't able to stop myself looking. I had to look. It was research. If I didn't, how could I call myself a modern novelist?

That morning, though, it wasn't the smutty ones that caught my attention. It was the *Irish News* headline VIOLENCE IN BELFAST AFTER OLD FIRM CLASH. After Sunday's Rangers versus Celtic CIS Insurance cup final, I read, rival fans had fought in Belfast and Lurgan.

Ah, I thought, and remembered the post-match atmosphere in the Donegal pub of the previous afternoon. Oh, yes, not to have the gene that made one care so passionately, it had to be an advantage, surely.

The evening news in Northern Ireland was full of Robin Cook's resignation from the Labour government because of his inability in all conscience to support the Allied attack on Iraq. The evening news on the BBC referred to the standing ovation Members had given the ethical Mr Cook. Cue long shot of Labour benches. Mr Cook, having just finished his speech, was seen to sit while, simultaneously, two MPs were seen to stand, before the camera zoomed in to show Chris Smith and Frank Dobson patting Mr Cook's shoulder.

Now, everyone knows the real thing when they see one and this definitely wasn't a standing ovation. Yet to say the broadcaster was lying won't do either. Theirs was an exaggeration, designed to make us want to watch, that was as close to without actually being a lie as the broadcaster could safely go.

Our news providers have endlessly argued that because governments and states dissemble, we need them because they alone provide us with the accurate information we have to have in order to exercise proper judgement.

Yes, the argument is sound: there is just one problem. Our news providers have failed to take on board that their sharp practice, of the kind just described, has dented their credibility. We don't trust them any more than we trust our masters.

Tuesday, 18 March 2003

For the last two years I had been writing a novel called *August '44*. The proofs arrived a few weeks back, since when I had spent many days going through them, making final changes.

When I woke I remembered that three o'clock was set as the time the publisher's copy editor was going to telephone and I'd give the last corrections down the line. In preparation for this I spent the morning combing through the book, checking every alteration. At three the call came and I gave my corrections. By four the job was done, and the book was finished. This should have been a great moment. But it wasn't. I felt deflated and melancholy.

Over the last twenty-four months I'd lived with this book it had become – gulp – a friend. But now I'd lost that friend: my friend was gone. George Eliot, famously, I remembered, on finishing one novel, always got a fresh piece of paper and started the next immediately because of precisely this problem. Why hadn't I done that? I got a piece of paper with the idea that I'd jot something down. But nothing came. I told myself that within a day or two I'd have to start something even if it wasn't much cop.

Wednesday, 19 March 2003

I was on a diet. Looking in the cupboard after supper and seeing that there was no tin of tuna for me to take to Maghaberry Prison for lunch the next day, my wife announced we would walk to the shop, along with the younger children, Georgia and Euan. The exercise would be slimming.

We set off. Each parent held a child's hand. The night was dry. A huge moon hung in the sky. The air smelt of wet grass. Dogs barked in the yards of the farms we passed.

We made the sub-post office and bought the tuna, then retraced our steps. At the top of the last hill, the lights of our house twinkling below, we heard an engine roaring and tyres squealing. Then, from out of the dusk, heading straight up the road towards us, hurtled a car with only one headlight on full beam, a smashed bonnet and no number plate.

'Shine the torch at him!' my wife shouted. I must throw the children over the fence and into the field, I thought as I did this, though even as I had the thought I recognised it was too late for that.

The driver saw us and wrenched his vehicle sideways. His car crossed to the opposite side of the road, hit the verge, bounced off and sped on, vanishing into the evening murk.

'Bloody joyrider,' my wife muttered.

We hurried down the hill, anxious to get home as quickly as we could. The grass scent was gone now and the night air smelt of petrol fumes and scorched rubber.

Later, after I got home, I began to tremble. It was shock and the delayed realisation that if we'd been a bit further down the hill, if the driver hadn't seen the torch or us, he might have ploughed into us and then . . . well, it didn't bear thinking about.

Friday, 21 March 2003

In order to support my numerous children I have always served several deities simultaneously. This Friday it was the silver goddess. I was writing a screenplay provisionally titled *The Cello Player*.

The director and I sat at the dining room table all day, talking and filling in little white cards, one for each scene. On each card we wrote a brief description of the scene and the key lines of dialogue.

By the end of the afternoon (the culmination not only of that day but of weeks of work) we filled in the last card. Then we laid them all out in lines on the table and read them. The disconcerting part, as the film played in my head as I read, was the absence of any sense of the toil expended in filling the cards in. This was one of the great curiosities of literary endeavour. Work never looked like the product of hard work. It looked like – well, in this case it looked like just a straightforward sequence of events scribbled on some cards and the labour of at most a day. Some of my paranoid writer friends have always believed that this was the real reason no one liked paying us, and at moments like this I was tempted to agree. Literary work rarely, if ever, reflected the labour taken to make it, and worse, the better something was, the less the effort to make it showed.

Sunday, 23 March 2003

The sun was shining so I took the children back to the Donegal beach where we had walked the previous Sunday. The tide was out and the wet sand flats, dotted with walkers, stretched to an inky blue horizon. It felt like a stage set or a painting, as beautiful landscapes often will.

We got home tired and happy and unencumbered with cares. It couldn't last. From out of cyberspace a message had come and there it sat on the computer screen.

Question: How do you know the world is mad?

Answer: When the world's greatest rapper is white, the greatest golfer is black, the Americans are accusing the French of arrogance and the Germans don't want to go to war.

It was a nasty piece of racial stereotyping, of course, but, as with those horrid tabloids that I saw every morning when I went to get my *Guardian*, I just couldn't stop myself looking. I wondered then if I might be able to get tablets on the National Health to control these terrible urges. Oh, how nice if there were something, the equivalent of an appetite suppressant for the psyche, that would just stop one looking.

A Walk

Great storm clouds hung in the sky that day. The dark grass in the fields rippled like water. In the valleys hawthorn blossom was heaped at the side of the road, like newly fallen snow, while higher up, gorse blossoms were scattered everywhere on the tarmac. The petals were surprisingly white; once they separate from the mother bush, they lose their characteristic deep yellow.

On the Coa Road, I saw a single black eye peering up at me

from the verge. I bent forward, like the boy in *The Borrowers* when he spots little Arrietty lying in the garden. I was halfway through rereading Mary Norton's classic and this scene was fresh in my mind.

The eye was set in the sleek feathered head of a cock pheasant. He was lying totally still. Passing cars had probably frightened him and he had bedded down. Then, not hearing very well, he had failed to detect my approach until too late and I was towering over him.

We spent a long time regarding each other. The eye was dark, like wet liquorice. The body was utterly still. The bird must have been terrified. I was so very close. It struck me that when my chilly shadow fell over him it was exactly like the moment when the shadow of the boy falls over Arrietty.

I had my stick – an old South African knobkerrie. I always take it when I walk because occasionally I meet unfriendly dogs. I was holding it by the stem. The heavy end, the killing end, was in front of me. If this had been a hundred years ago, I thought, I'd have had no qualms about swinging it. Even if, first time, I had failed to kill the pheasant, I'd certainly have broken his wings and prevented his cumbersome flight. With the next blow I'd have finished him off. Then I'd have had him for supper.

For a moment I entertained the thought of doing this now. I could carry the bird home and hang him in the shed. Tomorrow I could bring him to my local butcher. I remembered he cleaned and plucked game birds for a quid a go, or at least that had been the going rate the last time I had asked.

And then, as quickly as it had come, the killing thought vanished. It was unbelievably pointless, I decided, to deprive the world of something so beautiful. It was also probably illegal. This, incidentally, in the list of reasons not to act, carried the least weight.

I walked on, my face turned to the world. On the verge great ferns reared up, their leaves sticky with sap and rigid like cardboard. Pairs of cabbage whites were fluttering about. Further on there were vividly coloured bluebells – more purple than blue – and tiny white wood anemones, like the polka dots on the day dresses my grandmother had worn in my childhood. In the sky there were magpies, their wings moving jerkily as if powered by clockwork motors, and in the ring fort up on my right, wood pigeons were cooing.

Further on, in the drive of an abandoned house, I came on half a dozen quivering grey balls of tweed. These were rabbits. They watched me with their bulging glass eyes and twitched but did not move.

In the gully at the side of the drive, I spotted what appeared to be a ball made of moss. I turned it over with the end of my stick. It turned out to be half a sphere with a small egg-shaped indentation set into it. This was lined with wool and feathers and trapped in the lining were tiny crumbs of eggshell. I decided to take this perfectly made nest home to show my children. I picked it up and continued on my way.

I walk most days in the Fermanagh lanes around my house. I get fantastic pleasure from the hedgerows and spinneys, the abandoned houses and unproductive bits of land that I pass. I love these places where nature flourishes untrammelled.

What I fear in the Ireland of the future is that all this will go. The hedgerows and spinneys will be torn out to make better fields, and the old houses and unproductive bits of land will become dumps or the sites of hideous modern bungalows. I've only lived in Fermanagh for part of my life but even in the time I've been here (a short period in the history of the world) the natural world (the rabbits excepted) has declined and retreated while the human world has advanced.

I'm not saying that in the future we're going to make things extinct. To be sure, everything I describe above will still be around in the years ahead. It just won't be flourishing widely and ubiquitously as it should be. I'll have to drive to it and I'll probably have to pay to see it too. Now, driving and paying are a bore but my real objection is to the absence of happenstance – random, unplanned, everyday entanglement. And why does this matter? Well, if we're not interacting with nature, which we can't be if it isn't thriving in its natural habitat, we'll forget we're only one species among many. That way lies pride, which comes before a fall.

The Horseshoe

It was the week before Christmas. I was in the off-licence attached to Cleary's pub buying whiskey. While the barman was getting me a bottle of Power's, I looked into the public bar. I saw a little man talking loudly, oblivious to the hush that had fallen and that I, even at a distance, recognised as the harbinger of pub violence.

Next thing a woman appeared behind him. 'I told you, Seamus, not to be drinking our money,' she shouted. Then she punched the side of his head. 'And I warned you what would happen if you did.' Another blow. 'I may be your wife but I'm not a fucking eejit.' She went to make a third strike but was stopped.

'Easy, Molly,' said the peacemaker.

Talk resumed; my bottle came. The warring couple shuffled out of view. I paid and left Cleary's.

A minute or two later, not more, in the street outside, I saw the warring couple again. She was the bosomy wife and he the runty husband, I thought, from a seaside postcard, and then I got into my car and I drove home and I forgot all about them until one Sunday several months later. I was parked at the town dump, the trailer piled with clutter from my shed, which I'd spent the morning emptying. Where I live, there are people who survive by picking through what the rest of us throw away and, as usual, there were half a dozen of those who practised this business waiting for custom at the dump. One was Seamus, the battered husband from Cleary's.

I waved at him, which, according to dump protocol, gave him the right to forage first through my stuff, and he joined me at the side of the trailer.

'It's wild warm,' he said, and put his hand into a tin of doorknobs. He removed a horseshoe I'd found in my house when I'd bought it and which I'd always meant to put up but hadn't. Earlier that afternoon, I'd found it in the shed and decided to dump it. Into the Jacob's biscuit tin with the doorknobs it had gone, although I noticed a twinge of anxiety, accompanied by the unexpected idea that what I had just done was unlucky.

'You'll need this, surely,' said Seamus, hanging it over the side of the trailer, 'but I'll take the doorknobs.'

He made the rest of his selection and we dumped the rest. When the trailer was empty I saw he'd piled what he wanted by a bicycle.

'How'll you get all those things home on a bike?' I asked, for there was a lot of stuff.

'There's a man sometimes runs out here with his car,' he said. 'Maybe he'll give me a lift back.'

But Seamus didn't know for sure that the man would be out later and he had no mobile to call him to check. I offered to drive him home. Along with the bicycle, we put everything he'd scavenged that day into my trailer and tied it down. The horseshoe was still where he'd left it. He handed it to me.

'This is a good one,' he said. 'You keep it.'

Once again there came the unwanted and ridiculous idea that to throw it away was to court bad luck. As I knew from both personal testimony and folklore, Ireland's fairies were dark and malevolent beings but they didn't like iron. An iron horseshoe was just the thing to ward them off, like garlic kept away vampires. It was superstitious nonsense, of course it was, and if Seamus hadn't been there I could have overridden my qualms and thrown it away, but with him beside me, I couldn't. Worse, I felt there was no reason not to keep it and, in fact, I felt I *must* hold onto it. So I stowed it on the back seat.

Half an hour later I drove into Seamus's estate. Limp tricolours hung from lamp posts and Bobby Sands, with his puffy face and terrible hair, eyed me suspiciously from a gable end.

'There's the house,' said Seamus, and I pulled up.

We began unloading the trailer. The front door opened and Molly, the pugilistic wife, emerged in a Mickey Mouse nightdress, followed by an Alsatian she addressed as Killer. 'Is it more rubbish you're bringing home?' she said, as Seamus sidled through the gate with a box of scavenged scythes and hedge-clippers.

'Molly,' he said, and rolled his eyes towards me, an unmistakable signal to her that if they were going to argue, could it please not be in front of the stranger?

She disappeared back inside. Seamus and I finished unloading. I said goodbye. Then I drove away past green, white and gold kerbstones, the empty trailer twisting and clattering behind.

I got home and my daughter, Georgia, ten years old, rushed out as soon as I appeared and squinted into the back of the car in case there was a bag of sweets or ice creams on the seat.

'A horseshoe!' she said. There was delight in her voice. 'Did you find it in the dump?'

'No,' I said, as I got out of the car. 'I've always had it.'

I got the horseshoe out and stood it on its rounded bottom on one of the kitchen window sills. To put it the other way, the rounded bottom uppermost and the open mouth below, was to court ill luck, for that way all one's good luck was liable to fall out, as Seamus had told me on the way to his estate. Although I'd known this, I had thanked him for the information.

'You weren't throwing it away, were you?' said my daughter. 'That would be bad luck, you know.'

'No,' I said, 'of course I wasn't.' I explained I had accidentally brought it to the dump and that as soon as I could I would screw it to the wall over the front door.

'Good,' she said. 'Good.'

Once I'd thought I was rational, a sceptic. Now I was no longer certain.

Emokhai

I couldn't face the Tube from Heathrow into London, not four days before Christmas, and vomit puddles everywhere. So I rang Sunshine Kabs. Of course they could arrange a driver. On Monday he would be waiting for me at the meeting point in Terminal One, name of Emokhai.

He was Nigerian and he drove a Volvo filled with Bibles, and before we even hit the slip road for the M4 he had embarked on his story.

In the 1980s, Emokhai had been a Lagos businessman, import-export. Anxious to expand, he'd got a six-month visa and hit London, then promptly run out of money. Rather than go home he'd joined a Soho minicab company. One night a man in a leather jacket had made Emokhai an offer. His wife was seeing another man. The deal was this: Emokhai was to drive him to 24 Riddle Road, Burnt Oak, and park. Leather Jacket would do the business; Emokhai would drive him back to Soho; two hundred quid, one hundred in advance. Leather Jacket waved two crisp fifties. Emokhai agreed.

'Twenty-four,' repeated Leather Jacket, and he lay on the car floor so that no one would see him on the journey.

Forty minutes later, Emokhai pulled up outside a suburban house.

Leather Jacket, psyched up by now, let out a horrible snort and, clasping a length of steel tube, got out and rang the bell. A man answered; the piping went wallop, straight in his mouth; teeth flew like sugar cubes, blood sprayed. The man dropped to the ground.

Leather Jacket ran back, shouting, 'Move it!' and threw himself onto the floor in the back.

Emokhai sped away, fearful yet exhilarated. His euphoria lasted all of fifteen seconds. Then he came to the end of the road and saw the white lozenge with black letters and read 'Riddle Avenue'. It had been the wrong address and the wrong man, only Leather Jacket, who presumably had never met his rival, didn't know that. Emokhai drove in silence to Soho, took his second hundred and said goodbye.

That night, Emokhai couldn't sleep. As he lay in his Bayswater room, he saw the flying teeth and spraying blood. The nightmares wouldn't stop; in the end he went home to Nigeria.

In Lagos, Emokhai then attached himself to a pastor. He wished to atone by serving God, but he was assailed by doubts. Maybe he should work with lepers or join a political party.

A day of prayer arrived, and a huge crowd came to hear the pastor, and among them a man, dressed entirely in strips of used bloody bandage taken from the dump behind the General

Hospital. He was popularly known as Bandage Man and famed in Lagos for his abusive harangues, which could last hours.

As the pastor started preaching, Bandage Man began to swear and shout. The pastor, closely watched by Emokhai, began to talk directly to Bandage Man. He talked and talked and talked, and eventually Bandage Man fell asleep.

At the end of the day, Emokhai had helped to carry Bandage Man back to the parochial house and put him to bed. Bandage Man had slept for a week, and when he woke up he was no longer a raging, abusive lunatic, but the man he had been before his madness, a man with a name, a trade and an address.

Bandage Man was washed and shaved. His hair was cut, he was dressed, and then Emokhai took him back to his compound outside Lagos. As they walked through the gates, women ran out and greeted Emokhai's startled charge. Where had he been these last ten years? they shouted. They'd looked everywhere, but they'd never found him. That evening there was a feast to celebrate the man's return. Emokhai left early; Bandage Man's miraculous recovery was the sign he'd been waiting for.

Now, several years later, he was back in London, at theological college. He did evening classes only, which was handy as it left him free in the day to drive cabs.

And what about the man in Riddle Road? Ah. Emokhai smiled. His intention, he explained, when he returned to England to start training, had been to seek out the victim, and apologise. But when he had gone to college on the first day to enrol, there had been a man in the queue who looked suspiciously like the victim. As indeed he was. The unexpected attack by the jealous steel bar-wielding husband had led *him* to God, and not just God, but the same college as Emokhai.

'That can't be true,' I said.

'It is,' said Emokhai.

'Really?'

'Really, I swear.'

Despite my disbelief, there was no trace of bad temper in his voice, just a quiet, persuasive certainty.

We passed Osterley Park. Winter sun touched the tops of the trees. I was in the grip of the faintly tranced sensation that a story well told and brought to its right conclusion always generates, and for the next few seconds, as the engine purred and the tarmac unfurled beneath us, all was well with the world. Whether or not any of it was true was beside the point: the tale had done its job and tranquillised.

Working at Writing 6

After *The Siege of Derry* I was commissioned to write a novel for young adolescents based on the body of Jewish myth about Rabbi Loew, a rabbi at the Prague synagogue during the seventeenth century. According to legend, he had made a Golem from river mud to defend the ghetto against Christian mobs inflamed by stories that Jews used the blood of gentile children to make the unleavened bread eaten at Passover. This vile calumny was better known as 'the blood libel'.

The novel opens in a cave in the South of France, where (in 1944) a group of Jews are hiding. In order to pass the time as they wait for liberation, and also to engage the attention of a feral adolescent boy, they mount an oral retelling of the Golem cycle. They get to the end of the story but the Allied troops don't arrive in time to rescue them and they're all killed, with the exception of the feral youth. It was an unusually bleak conclusion to a children's novel but I thought the right one. *August '44* was published in 2004 and shortlisted for the Bisto Prize.

The moment I finished *August '44* I went back to my children's publishers with a new idea: a retelling of the ancient possibly Bronze Age Irish epic first written down in the seventh century, the *Táin Bó Cúailnge* or *The Cattle Raid of Cooley*, the story of the invasion of Ulster by Maeve, Queen of Connaught, and the single-handed fight against her army mounted by the semi-immortal warrior Cuchulainn. The book was commissioned.

One thing I knew for certain before I started was that I'd be writing in reaction to the earliest and most famous English language version, *Cuchulain of Muirthemne: The Story of the Men of the Red Branch of Ulster* by Lady Gregory. With its ornate prose, indigestible dialogue and high moral tone, this version had been part of a programme to raise the self-esteem of early-twentieth century Irish readers, but nothing, I felt, could justify Gregory's sanitising of the Irish equivalent of the *Iliad*. My version, therefore, as distinct to hers (and the value of writing against something can never be underestimated) would be in simple English with the humour and violence of the Irish original restored.

The Bull Raid was published in 2005, followed, at last, by the book I'd been writing with Patrick Maguire, *My Father's Watch*, then *Henry & Harriet*, a site-specific play for the Belfast theatre company Kabosh, and *A Good Day For a Dog*, a novel about a prison vendetta into which I had poured everything I'd gathered and learned while teaching in prison. I had a lot of help from one prisoner, Jason Thompson, who corrected my infelicities, suggested improvements and alterations and copy edited the material. Before publication I wondered how other prisoners I'd got to know would find it. I'd had help but did it work? Was it convincing?

I took in a couple of copies of the first print run and passed them round. Not much was said until one day a prisoner who was a keen reader stopped me on the wing.

'We read your novel *A Good Day for a Dog*,' he said. 'Yeah, you drove the spade down good and deep with that one.' This was endorsement of the highest order and I was happy.

The Ceauşescu Sex Hotel

Outside, above the entrance, dusty tricolours were hanging limply from flagpoles. I passed through the door below and entered the lobby. It had the proportions of an aircraft hangar. The colour scheme was brick red. There was a single sofa where a middle-aged couple in golfing clothes sat bickering.

I crossed the marble floor, my footsteps echoing. An enormous chandelier loomed overhead, trembling and pulsating on account of the Dublin traffic thundering by outside. I reached the front desk. Its marble counter top was smeared with palm prints. I caught the attention of a woman in an Alice band.

'Can you help me?'

'No,' she said firmly. Then, turning to a woman who was buffing her nails, she said, with infinite weariness, 'Can you do this one?'

The nail buffer turned and called back over her shoulder to a man in a pinstripe suit, 'George, will you do this man? I'm busy.'

George presented himself. His suit, now he was standing in front of me, looked several sizes too big for him. 'Name?' His accent was Cork with a streak of Graham Norton.

'Gébler. I'm part of the publishing . . . event,' I said.

'That'll be in the Collins Hall,' said George.

'And what Collins would that be?'

He shot me his don't-be-an-uppity-Northerner-and-what-the-fuck-if-it-is-Michael-Collins-is-that-a-problem? look and asked for my credit card.

'But my publishers are paying.'

'For your room, yes, but you still might run up a bill.'

'I won't,' I said firmly.

'Well, you can't register unless I have your card details.'

'You don't trust me, do you?'

'No, I don't,' said George. 'But I promise you can watch me tear your details up tomorrow.'

So that was that. We transacted.

'You're in room sixty-nine,' said George, when this was done.

'It hasn't been modernised yet,' he continued, 'but it's fair enough.'

With these encouraging words ringing in my ears, I got into the lift. It smelt of Bakelite and perfume. I pressed a grimy button. The metal box clanked upwards. It stopped. I alighted. I was now in a corridor on the sixth floor. There was a strong smell of shampoo and, more ominously, semen.

I found the door of 69 and let myself into my room. The wallpaper was green with a cream stripe. The bed cover was russet and hairy. There was a hideous painting screwed to the wall of Venice at sunset.

These were my initial impressions. Basically my room was from a 1970s motel. Then I started to look more closely. This room, I saw, hadn't been touched since the workmen had signed off at least thirty years ago. There were cracks in the walls. All the plug sockets had come loose. The window overlooking the street (which was actually a door) had no lock. To commit suicide, all that was necessary was to turn the handle and step forward. The drop to the pavement would have done the rest. The bath was shedding its plastic coating. The toilet was cracked and there was a slimy puddle on the floor nearby. The cold-water tap didn't work. But the *pièce de résistance* was the half-dozen envelopes for the disposal of sanitary towels nailed to the wall beside the cistern.

Using my own bottled water, I made myself a cup of tea and sat down on one of the hideous beech-veneer chairs. I told myself not to be depressed because the whole point of being a raffish Bohemian was that one got to stay in places like this and later to talk wittily about them. That was when I heard the sound of girlish chatter coming through the thin plasterboard wall from next door.

'Oh, you wouldn't – you wouldn't dare! Oh, you are naughty,' the speaker trilled.

I wondered if she was reading for a part in a remake of a *Carry On* film.

Then I heard a male voice saying, 'I'm not taking no for an answer,' and I knew then that I was gravely mistaken.

I hurried to my publishing event. The Collins Hall was a mock-up Victorian theatre, complete with wobbling proscenium and heavy drapes. After several other people had spoken, it was my turn. I said why I wrote for children in general and something about the novel I'd just completed. I said I did it, even though I sometimes felt it was preposterous to write books, because I still believed in the value of literary narrative.

Afterwards I had dinner in the dining room along with several other writers. I mistakenly ordered cod and fennel. The meal, when it arrived, had been steamed so relentlessly that the two components had merged into a half-fish, half-vegetable new form of food. Somehow, the conversation turned to the University of East Anglia's creative writing MA and the luminaries the course had produced. One successful graduate writer was singled out for obloquy, being described by a speaker as weird.

'Weird, in what way weird?' asked a second.

'About personal space,' came the reply. 'Doesn't like having his personal space invaded. Doesn't like getting too close. Can't bear intimacy. Won't do sex.'

'That cannot be true,' I said. 'He's got children.'

'Yes, but you don't have to have sex to have children,' said the first speaker. 'Surely you know that.'

'And you can work wonders with a turkey baster,' said another, who hadn't spoken until now.

I decided to say nothing more and gave thanks I wasn't a success. Then I tried to eat my cod and fennel. I couldn't. I gave up.

Midnight found me once again at the door of my room. As I was about to insert my key in the lock, I heard the unmistakable sounds of sexual congress. They came from the same room where I'd heard the talking coming from before. Oh, no, they wouldn't be, would they?

I let myself into my room. And, oh, yes, they were. The earth was moving next door and so was the furniture.

Well, they couldn't go on all night, I thought. It would have to end. I turned on the television to drown the sounds of orgasm and had another cup of tea.

When the television went off thirty minutes later, all seemed quiet next door. But as I pulled back the covers to get into my bed, I heard what sounded ominously like the soundtrack from an adult film. They were watching the adult channel. However, the sound was on low, which was very thoughtful of them.

But then, a few minutes later, as I lay in bed waiting for sleep, I heard, superimposed on the sounds of fiction, the sounds of fact. The couple was not only watching other people having sex, they were having it at the same time.

I found the earplugs without which, as a fully subscribing neurotic, I never travel. They're made of wax. I heated them by rubbing them in my palms. I moulded them. I put them in. I lay down again. I could no longer hear the lovers banging away, which was a blessing. On the other hand, what I could hear now, which I hadn't heard before, was the sound of my own breathing, and my own being. It may seem like a reasonable trade-off, but trying to get to sleep with the sound of your lungs thumping away is only slightly easier than trying to get to sleep with two people going at it like rabbits.

But I managed. I nodded off. Then some time in the middle of the night one of my ear plugs fell out. I woke. They were still at it. The plug went back in. I nodded off again. When I next awoke, the grey light of a Dublin dawn was slanting through the glass in the death door.

They must be done by now, I thought. Out came the earplugs. But, oh no, they were still going strong.

There was nothing else for it. I filled the peeling bathtub with steaming water and steeped myself until the tips of my fingers had gone wrinkly and prune-like.

Then I had a shave and got dressed. I was beginning to feel slightly more human. Next door they had the shower running and were in it together, judging by the sounds.

He was talking now. 'Go on, go on,' he was urging, while she was obligingly doing whatever she was doing.

Then he cried out, and she shouted joyously, 'Are you feeling better now?'

I went to the dining room. The man in the chef's hat in the servery had a glass eye. He prepared me a dish of watery scrambled egg and soggy mushrooms. Handing me the plate, he said, in a fake American accent, 'Have a nice day.'

'Well, the rest can't be any worse than the start,' I muttered, and skulked to a table where I found one of the writers I had met the night before.

'I have to say I've filled in the complaints sheet,' she said brightly, as I took my seat. 'Have you?'

I shook my head.

'In the comments box I wrote, "This reminds me of one of those hotels that Mr and Mrs Ceauşescu built. Romania was full of hideous dumps like this.'"

Well, that'll go straight in the bin, I thought.

I had a meeting after breakfast and I didn't get back to the sixth floor until nearly eleven. As I approached my room, the door of 68 began to swing open. Ah, now I would get to see the famed couple.

She came out first. She was plump, like a model in a Rubens painting. She had Nana Mouskouri black-rimmed glasses and lacklustre black hair. Her ankle-length denim dress reminded me of the long skirts I'd seen Mennonite women in Canada wearing.

He was next. He was thin and pale. He had very short hair and rimless glasses. He was like one of those ethereal young men in an early Chagall painting. He also looked a bit like a young Elvis Costello.

And they were the ones who'd made such a rumpus? That didn't make sense. I'd been expecting Christina Aguilera and Justin Timberlake lookalikes, not two real people like this pair. But they were the ones and of that there was no doubt: they had come out of room 68.

'Good morning,' she said, in a squeaky voice.

Her lover nodded.

'Good morning, I said.

I packed my suitcase and made my way wearily to the lift. It trundled me to the ground floor. The door opened. I exited. I began to make my way across the echoing marble floor towards the front door. I could see through the dirty glass to the street beyond.

'Hello, Mr Gébler.'

I turned and saw George gesticulating from behind the desk. 'Me?'

'Yes, Mr Gébler, you.'

I went over.

'Don't you want to see me tear up your card details?' he asked.

Ah, I remembered. 'Yes,' I said. Then I said, 'I didn't sleep very well.'

'Oh, really? Why not?'

'Who were the people next door to me?'

'I'm not certain I can tell you,' he said. 'Why do you need to know?'

He waved a slip in front of me that bore the imprint of my card. He tore it into several small pieces and threw them into an ashtray.

'So what was wrong? Why didn't you sleep, Mr Gébler? Traffic?

'No. It was that special thing people "do" in hotels.'

'Ah.' He smiled knowingly.

'Hammer and tongs, all night long in sixty-eight,' I said.

'Thank God for earplugs.'

George leaned forward. 'Can I tell you something in confidence?' he whispered. 'And if you say a word of this may you go blind.'

'You can trust me. I'm a writer.'

'Well, this place has a bit of a reputation as a Sex Hotel.'

'You don't say?'

He nodded, and beamed with delight.

I said goodbye and hurried off into the street.

The English Poet

It was early evening and I was in Rhodes Town with an English poet. At his suggestion we had left the conference on the Future of Literature in a Global Economy and come to the café where we now sat. Greek men played dominoes all around us, smashing the tiles on the tin tabletops with gusto. I could see the Mediterranean and there was a smell of drains and fish, wet cork and aniseed.

The poet started speaking: he told me that he was mad for Greece. He could be free in Greece in a way he never was when he was home in England. And he had never been a man for blondes. On the contrary, the olive-skinned, black-haired, brown-eyed Greek women were his preferred physical type. Of course, he continued ruefully, he hadn't had much success with the ladies recently.

The poet was small and compact, like a leprechaun, with dainty hands and tiny feet. He looked sixty. I knew he was eighty. He'd got his *Collected Poems* with him and the year of his birth was on the inside flap at the back. I'd had a look.

The poet came from Gravesend. He talked through his nose, like Ken Livingstone. He was old Labour, he boasted proudly. He had no time for Tony Blair, or George W. Bush, or the War on Terror, or the invasion of Iraq. He was, he said, pure 1970s, completely unreconstructed.

The poet wore a natty blue suit. 'A tailor in Athens made it,' he said. 'He got the design from a sixties pop magazine he had lying about his workshop. It's actually a copy of one worn by Dave Clark, of the Dave Clark Five.' This delighted the poet. 'The styles of yesteryear are back,' he said, chuckling.

The poet used the poeticism 'yesteryear' self-consciously, and then explained that this was a word he loved to use in speech but that he'd never use in his verses. When it came to his poetry he stuck to the rules laid down by George Orwell in *Politics and the English Language*. No foreign words, no jargon and no affectation: his poems were written in plain English for plain people.

After our third ouzo, the poet cleared his throat. He obviously had something to say. I wasn't surprised. I knew he had brought me here because he had something to say.

'You might perhaps have heard of my wife,' he said. He gave her name. 'She was at your children's primary school in Enniskillen. They were at one of her storytelling workshops.'

'Did I meet her?' I asked.

'No, I don't think so,' said the poet, 'and she never said anything to me about having met you. But she certainly registered your surname when she met your sons. After all, how many Géblers does one meet in a small Northern Ireland primary school? Not a lot. She mentioned the name to me when she came back from teaching and we were sitting in our flat in London. And now here I am in Rhodes with the father of the children with the unusual unIrish name that made such an impression on my wife.'

'Yes, I remember now, I remember your wife coming,' I said, and his eyes lit up.

'I knew it.' He was delighted.

'And where is she now?' I asked. 'Didn't she want to come to Rhodes?'

'At her home,' he said.

I had opened a door with my careless question, I realised, one I now heartily wished I hadn't.

'In Herefordshire,' he added.

But I shouldn't worry, I thought, because now it seemed he'd opened the door further and asked me to step into the room beyond.

'So, what happened?' I said quietly.

'It was literally the day she got home from Enniskillen,' he said. 'She was talking about the children with the unusual surname, your boys, and then she said, "Johnboy" – she called me Johnboy – "I'm unhappy, Johnboy. I don't love you any more." Just like that. Just like I'm talking to you. She didn't care, she said, if she got a divorce or not. She wasn't bothered. She wasn't going to marry again anyway. She was certain of that. She just didn't want to live with me anymore.

'We'd a little house in Herefordshire where we used to go weekends. She said she'd live there. She'd always loved the country, probably because she's Cornish, and I could stay in the flat in Kensal Green, she said, which I did. So with that coming right after talk of your surname, you can imagine yours is one name I've never forgotten.'

We ordered more ouzo and I asked if it might make a poem, his story and then us meeting in Rhodes?

'No,' he said, 'I don't think so, and to tell you the truth I haven't got any poetry out of the break-up. In fact, I haven't written a word of poetry since she left. Oh, I can manage reviews and journalism but the real stuff just isn't coming any more. Forty-five years married and I thought I knew her. It turns out I hadn't a bloody clue. If you're that dense, how can you write poetry anymore? Well, I can't.'

Later, he wanted my address. He wanted to send me his *Collected Poems*.

'No, don't send them,' I said. 'I'll buy them on Amazon, I promise.'

'But I want to inscribe the book,' he said.

To the one whose name I'll never forget, I imagined.

Looking for Des

I am kind and I care – at least I like to think so. Alas, as I've come to realise, my altruism has often more to do with what frightens me than with helping others.

In 1981, when I was twenty-seven, I was in the sumptuous

premises of the British Academy of Film and Television Arts (BAFTA) in Piccadilly. I had made a film for the English Arts Council about the culture of Irish emigrants in Britain called *Over Here*, and it was being shown. As I drank at the bar, a man who might have stepped straight from the pages of an Isaac Bashevis Singer story introduced himself to me.

He was big-boned and well-groomed and he spoke with the spectacular clarity of those who have overcome a lisp. He had a piercing gaze when silent but looked away into the distance whenever he spoke. Somehow he knew of my film. Later, when I knew him better, I saw this wasn't surprising because he was friendly with a lot of people and had a way of picking things up. In fact he picked everything up: he knew everything, he knew everyone.

He was from Ballinasloe, County Galway, had founded the Irish Writers' Co-operative with Neil Jordan and was now living in London. He was the author of the novel *The Ikon Maker* and the collection of short stories *The Diamonds at the Bottom of the Sea*, both of which I had read. His prose was studded with extraordinary images but these were narratives with strong stories, not poems masquerading as fiction. His name was Des Hogan.

We became friends and I visited Des in a succession of rooms that he rented. His lodgings were always on London's outskirts, near travellers' sites and scrap-metal yards, and in all of them the rural was still palpable; those areas had only been very recently incorporated into the city.

The last of the outposts, the one where Des lived the longest, was in Catford. I made my first trip there on a Sunday in the summer or autumn of 1982. I got lost, ended up at the dog track and had to call Des's landlady, Barbara Smoker, from a public phone that smelt of pee.

His home, in Stanstead Grove, was a suburban villa.

Barbara Smoker occupied the top two floors and Des had the basement. I approached through a garden teeming with flowers. The entrance was a set of French windows. Inside were two minuscule rooms: one where Des slept and wrote on a manual typewriter and where his cat, Eamon, was lying asleep, the other a kitchen-cum-sitting room with a vast table and an eclectic mix of chairs.

I took a seat; it was now impossible to move because the room was so tiny and the furniture so large. The other guests included Kazuo Ishiguro and his partner, Lorna. Des had decorated the walls with postcards and coloured fabrics from Berwick Street Market. He had a talent for turning unpromising interiors into beguiling spaces for next to nothing. His interiors also left me in no doubt that he was an artist in everything he did, not just his writing.

There was an oven somewhere, and once several bottles of wine had been opened and consumed, Des produced a vegetable stew, scones, and aubergines baked with cheese. The meal, improvised rather than created by following recipes, was delicious and, as with everything Des did, unique.

The conversation was only partly serious: I remember a long debate about the value of working as an artist as opposed to working for social services (like Ishiguro's partner), and Des recited some of Mandelstam and Akhmatova's poetry. There was a lot of gossip, too, but it was genial: Des didn't do nasty or bitchy. He loved to know everything about everyone but his curiosity was tempered by tenderness. He also had an aura of probity. I felt he was a man I could trust and I felt certain he would never use whatever I relayed to hurt or undermine others.

For the rest of the decade we remained friends. He would come to my flat in Maida Vale. Or I would go out to Catford. Or we would meet in Patisserie Valerie in Soho. He always claimed not to know anybody but whenever I was with him in central London he seemed to know almost everybody.

Then in 1989 I went with my wife and our two children India and Jack to live in Enniskillen. We rented a flat in a house on lower Lough Erne where, it transpired, Des had lived at some point during his peripatetic career. On 11 July 1990, the night before the Twelfth, we did a reading together in the Robin's Nest, a pub in Lisburn, near Belfast. We were in a function room at the top of the building, and throughout the evening inebriated Orangemen kept peering round the door to see what was happening. Loyalists on Eleventh Night can be volatile, especially when softly-spoken southerners appear on their radar. I was quaking. Des, however, seemed completely unfazed. After that I saw him a few more times when I was over in London.

Our last proper conversation in London was in 1992 or early 1993. I was staying in a flat in Portobello Road and he rang the bell. 'I just guessed you might be here,' he explained. Did he guess or had he picked up from a third party that I was staying there? I never found out.

He was carrying a satchel. It looked bulky, heavy. Would he like to hang it on the hook on the back of the door? No, he said. He wouldn't put it down. He never put it down. It was filled with his manuscripts, he said, and when he was not at home he never let it out of his grasp.

This Des was not the Des I remembered. That man was expansive and humorous, happy and light. This man was diffident and withdrawn, troubled and heavy. I offered him a seat. He declined. He went to the window and looked out into the street, as if he was expecting to see someone. He did this more than once. Something was wrong. He knew I knew it, and he began to explain the reasons for the change in his character.

The first was an altercation, some months before, with a

West Indian employee in Tesco's supermarket in Catford, following which he had come to believe, he said, that the West Indian population of Catford was now intent on hurting him. He believed the threat was serious.

The second was an unpleasant legal problem. For several years he had bought an annual ticket to the Ladywell swimming baths in Catford; he had swum and used the sauna, assuming the ticket gave him access to both facilities. It didn't. He wasn't entitled to use the sauna, and this had recently come to the attention of the management at Ladywell. A possible fraud charge loomed; this would be followed, if it happened, by an appearance in court, a hefty fine, his picture and the story in the paper along with his address, a criminal record, and God alone knew what else.

Due to these troubles, he said, plus other cares he didn't wish to go into, he was no longer the man I had known. Maybe with time he would go back to what he had been, and it was certainly his intention to resume his old open-handed, friendly ways. He had plans that would make him happy again, oh, yes, but what these were, he wouldn't say, only that he had them.

I went back to Enniskillen and the following Christmas I sent a card to Catford. It came back stamped NOT KNOWN AT THIS ADDRESS. Perhaps, I thought, Des had got on his bike (he was a dedicated cyclist) and headed somewhere out of London. That surprised me. He'd loved Stanstead Grove; he'd said he'd never leave it. But apparently he had.

Over the years that followed, when in London, I would ask mutual friends about Des. But no one could tell me precisely where he was. All I got were vague rumours. He was in Berlin. He had a German friend, Sammy, and Sammy was dying and Des was nursing him. Then Sammy was dead and Des was gripped by incapacitating grief. He was in Prague, where he haunted the old Jewish quarter. He was in Amsterdam. He had given up fiction in favour of travel writing. He was in America, at the University of Alabama. He was in Galway. Then I heard he was in east Clare, living in a caravan or a mobile home, and local yahoos were tormenting him. Then he vanished again.

More time passed and then, one day, I opened the *Irish Times* to see a new story by Des. The blurb mentioned that he was now living in a resort town in the south-west of Ireland and had recently given a reading in Galway. Brilliant, I thought. I wrote to him care of a third party but heard nothing. Then I realised that, in connection with a literary competition I was judging, I would be in a town close to where he was living. I would try to find him, I decided.

On a damp June day, with another writer who had offered to drive me, I found myself heading for the resort where Des was. I had no address so when I arrived I went to the police station. It was unmanned but I depressed a verdigris-covered lever in the middle of the front door, and the voice of a guard in a distant barracks came out through the speaker above.

'How can I help you?'

'I'm looking for Des Hogan.'

'What class of a fellow would he be?'

'He's a writer.'

'I don't know of any writers of that or any other name,' said the gnomic guard. 'Why don't you go and ask at the post office?'

I followed his advice. The postmaster knew exactly where Des lived and told me how to find him: then he added, 'Of course, you won't find him there. Up at the crack of dawn and off on his bicycle and away to the sea to swim so he is.'

'Oh.'

'Every day, all three hundred and sixty-five of them,' said the postmaster.

I thanked him but said I thought I'd try knocking on Des's door anyhow.

A few minutes later I found myself in a dusty lane at the back of a row of old houses. I saw a woman in her kitchen topping a boiled egg and rapped on her window.

'I'm looking for Des Hogan.'

'Who is he?'

'The writer.'

She looked blank.

'He has a bicycle.'

'Funny,' she said, 'he's been living beside me a brave few years but I never got his name until you said it just now.'

She marched back along the dusty lane and halted in front of a solid metal gate. A garage with a flat roof loomed behind it and there was a workshop nearby with old cars littered around it.

She banged on the gate with a strong red hand, making a booming sound. A dog appeared. He stuck his snout through a gap and began barking and whining.

Ten minutes passed. No one was at home. I wrote a note and tucked it in at the side of the gate. The woman went back to her egg and I retraced my steps to the post office. I had one of my books for Des and I left it with the postmaster. Caught on a Train is about Victorian travellers in Ireland who retell old Gaelic folk stories competitively, like the pilgrims do in Chaucer's *Canterbury Tales*. Des had always loved old stories – especially those told by Irish travellers – and of all my books I believed this was the one closest to what he liked.

I left the post office but I was not quite ready to abandon my quest. With my companion I went down to the strand where the postmaster had said I might find Des swimming. The sea was black. The clouds were grey. The sand was the colour of brass; here and there it was studded with what looked like great lumps of black jelly. On closer inspection these turned out to be slippery black rocks. I spotted several men in woollen hats. None turned out to be Des.

After a fruitless hour we got back into the car. My companion had a reading to give in the town where we were staying. As we nosed back the way we had come, I scrutinised every cyclist we passed. None turned out to be Des – but that should hardly have come to me as a surprise. In life, narratives have a nasty habit of going their own way and refusing to be resolved, which is one reason why we need fiction. Stories compensate for the disappointments of experience.

Our car emerged into the countryside and we found ourselves on a long road that went up and down like a roller-coaster. A car overtook us while, at the same instant, a cat appeared ahead. A road kill looked inevitable but the animal sprang miraculously out of the path of the idiot overtaking us and made it to the safety of the hedgerow.

I settled back and thought about Des, who loved cats. I felt disappointed and thwarted. I had wanted to find him so that I could discover where he had been, what he had done, what he had written and what he was going to write. I also felt guilty. I should have made more effort to keep in touch. Behind those predictable feelings, though, was something more troubling. Des, a great writer who had been cheerful and effective in London, had been driven by calamities to the Atlantic edge of Europe. Now he led an energetic but largely solitary existence. Yes, he was reading in public again and I understood the Irish publisher, Lilliput, were going to bring out his backlist and his new stories. But that was not how I had imagined him when I'd known him in the eighties in London. In those days, when he lived a pure, simple, almost priest-like life and devoted himself to writing, I'd imagined a very different trajectory for him. He wasn't accident-prone, and he didn't do drugs or have disastrous relationships. He was destined, or so I'd thought, for some sort of glory.

I thought that was the end of my ruminations but, like

a Russian doll, there was one final thought, which I now unpacked. I had believed my trip was an act of friendship but now I saw it wasn't. I have fantastic control over my life yet what I fear more than anything is losing that control and being made to go where I don't wish to go and to do what I don't want to do. I had no idea if this was Des's story, but I had come, I realise now, not for his sake but because I needed to be reassured that his story was not what I most feared for myself. That's the trouble with us human beings. We try to do good, but any good we might do is always mixed up with so much else.

Oedipal Envy

In 1964 I was ten. My parents were separated. My mother lived in a small terrace house in Putney. My father lived in what had been the family home, a pebble-dash mock-Tudor semi in Morden. My brother and I still attended our Morden primary school but we spent alternate nights with each parent. We spent a lot of time on the 93, the bus that ran between Putney and Morden Underground stations.

My father was a writer with odd working habits. He liked to work at night and sleep by day. The clatter of the Remington keys as I drifted to sleep was a perennial childhood memory. Even when Phyllis (who became his last wife) moved into the Morden house, his schedule remained unchanged. He was, he said, a night owl.

My father entered the world of letters via the Gate Theatre in Dublin in the thirties. He wrote plays. Later he switched to novels and made a lot of money. By the sixties he was back at drama again. He wrote a television play, a two-hander. The working title was *Shall I Eat You Now?* but eventually he settled for *Call Me Daddy*. The play concerned an unhappy elderly man called Hoffman and the entry into his life of a young woman called Janet. Who seduces whom – the cunning male or the conniving female – lay at the heart of the drama. It was, of course, a reconfiguration of his autobiography. The play's heroine was obviously my stepmother Phyllis, as became abundantly clear when my father decreed that henceforth she would answer to the name of Jane. It was, incidentally, an edict with which she was happy.

Call Me Daddy was directed for television by Alvin Rakoff and was transmitted in the Armchair Theatre slot. In 1968 it received an American Academy of Arts and Sciences Award, the Emmy, for the best entertainment programme. My father rewrote the television play as a novel, called *Hoffman*, which was transformed into a feature film (he scripted it for the fabulous sum of £40,000) that starred Peter Sellers in the lead role. From one fifty-minute play he had made a fortune. He bought a large house in Dalkey, Dublin, and he moved there with Jane.

Fifteen years later my stepmother died and my father got Alzheimer's. An official from the Irish Chancery Courts entered the Dalkey house, collected every manuscript he could find and took them away in a trunk to the Four Courts for safekeeping. I made my father a ward of the court. The Dalkey house was cleared and sold. My father went into a home. Ten years later he died. The Chancery Court returned the trunk of manuscripts to me. It was bound with white tape to show it had never been opened since it had been sealed. It went straight into my loft with the tapes uncut, and after that I forgot all about it.

Then I got an email. It came from the director of the Armchair Theatre version, Alvin Rakoff. From the internet, he informed me, he had learned I was the executor of my father's estate, and among the works listed as being available was a stage version of the original television play he had directed. This was all news to me.

He had just seen a video copy of the Armchair Theatre production, Alvin Rakoff continued, and it was wonderful. If the stage version was as well written as the television version he would put it on at a small theatre he had at his disposal. Did I have it?

I went to my loft with my son, Finn. We undid the white tapes and lifted the lid back to reveal a mound of yellowing papers. While Finn held the torch I sorted through the contents and found six bulging files with *Call Me Daddy* written in my father's ragged hand on the flaps.

I carried the files to the living room and the phone rang. It was Mr Rakoff. As we talked I pinned the receiver between head and shoulder, and sorted through the dusty papers. First I found the original Armchair Theatre rehearsal script, with its covering sheet giving the names of all the personnel, including the director, and then I found the stage version, quite different from the television version. My father had even made a plan of the stage set, which he had attached. Eureka!

The next day I took the play to HMP Maghaberry where I taught and where I had the use of a photocopier. As I stood by the machine in the Education Department, watching the copied pages shooting out, I felt a most unexpected sensation. It was a mixture of envy and resentment. *Call Me Daddy* had been on television and in the cinema and between hard covers. It had had its time in the sun. Now, surely, it was the son's turn. I wrote plays. Why wasn't it one of mine that I was copying to send away for consideration? It just wasn't fair.

For the rest of the day these evil thoughts pursued me up and down the prison wings and hovered on the edge of my consciousness in the conversations I had in one cell after another with the various prisoners I was helping to write.

The next morning, as I wrote the address on the envelope in which the photocopy I'd made of the play would go to Alvin Rakoff, the evil feelings persisted. Maybe I should put one of my own plays in the envelope too, I thought, along with a coy covering letter. Perhaps he might like to consider some of the son's work. I might mention that, unlike my father, who was dead, I was very much alive and had a family to support.

I fetched one of my own plays from the shelves. I opened the unsealed envelope ready to drop it in. An image flashed in my imagination. I saw the envelope open and my play along with my father's slithering out. My stomach curdled. Alvin Rakoff would be appalled, wouldn't he? Had I been in his position, I would have been disgusted at the horrible mix of neediness and Oedipal resentment implicit in the action I was contemplating. He'd asked for my father's work, not mine. For me to try to muscle in like that – well, frankly, it was shameful.

Shame anticipated can be a marvellous corrective. I put my own play back on the shelf and sealed the envelope. As I drove to the post office, with the envelope on the passenger seat beside me, two lovely thoughts came in quick succession. Not only had I done the right thing and not made a fool of myself, which was a relief, but also I had acquired an incident that I might profitably turn into prose. Here was a little seam to mine.

The Launch Party

The floor tiles were black-and-white, like a chessboard, and I moved slantwise across them, like a bishop. This was in the entrance hall of the Lanyon Building, Queen's University, in

Belfast, and I was going to a party. It was a book launch.

I turned from the echoing hall and entered a short corridor. It was panelled with wood the colour of tarnished brass, and it smelt of baked radiator paint, floor polish and the musty odour made by wet wool when it dries indoors. In the Irish climate, with its endless rain, such smells are ubiquitous.

The party room was at the corridor's end, and coming through the door towards me was the chatter of the guests who'd already arrived. Their acoustic sounded familiar. Well, of course it would.

It was partly that these were the same people who were at the last book launch here and the one before, book events invariably attracting the same crowd, and it was partly that the speech susurrus generated at book events is universal. Every book event I've ever attended, even ones abroad that weren't in English, have had the same sound. Scribblers and hacks talk the same wherever you are. The only variant is volume, which is in direct ratio to alcohol consumed.

Tonight's event, judging by the small trickle of noise flowing along the corridor towards me, was a sober one. I wasn't fussed. No, let me be more precise. I wasn't in the mood for licence. I was in the mood for sobriety. It was partly the time of year. It was early in December. I had done ten weeks of teaching at the university (I was the Royal Literary Fund fellow at Queen's, my job, essentially, to help students improve their essay writing) and I was heartily sick of talking about essay structure and paragraph indentations, the difference between the past and present tense and how to use the comma. I couldn't wait for the remaining two weeks to be over and for the holiday: after the holiday came January, and January was empty, there was no teaching in January, and in January I was hoping to write.

Unfortunately, once term finished and before I got to January, there was Christmas. I was not a fan and my secret fantasy was to opt out. However, this was never going to be anything more than a fantasy because my family (one wife, five children, two grandchildren) was not going to wear my derogating. They were all Christmas aficionados. They were mad for it.

Then on top of teaching and Christmas there was the much bigger and more problematic business of making a living. The wider economy was in terrible shape and O'Grub Street, where the Hibernian scribbler scratched a living, was looking even less hospitable than usual. Was I going to be able to survive? I was worried.

And, as if that weren't enough, I was also snarled up by what had been called, when I was a student, existential anxieties.

Old Mother Earth was definitely unwell. Now I can't say I was lying in bed at night fretting about the melting ice caps and the polar bears (indeed, I was heartily sick of the fucking polar bears) but I knew something was up: the climate was out of joint. Our leaders denied anything was awry, of course, but that was a lie. We were in trouble, big trouble. But what could be done? I had no idea and this uncertainty was yet another reason why I didn't feel so good as I went down the corridor towards the party.

Then I entered the party room and my mood sank further. What was I doing here? I could have been at home, reading Tony Chekhov, whose tender-hearted, clear-eyed stories always improved my mood, or my current new passion, Jonathan Swift, whose disgust and anger, and whose precise descriptions of human vanity and folly, I was finding surprisingly comforting. (Here, at least, was a voice that wasn't in denial. Here, at least, was a voice that told it like it was – human beings were weasels).

So why was I there? Why did I go to such parties? The answer came quickly. Given the difficult economic times, it was more important than ever that, as a writer, one attended such events. It might lead to something.

The speed with which the hackneyed response came out of whatever part of the brain it was made in was alarming enough. The only thing that was more frightening was my willingness to endorse it.

I sniffed the air. There was a strong sweet wine smell. No doubt about it, this was a publishing party with publishing-party wine. I glanced at the hospitality table. There was red, there was white (judging by the labels they were generics but, hey, what did I expect?), plus Fanta, and Ballygowan, the still and sparkling varieties.

I ought not to imbibe, I thought, but Fanta or Ballygowan was not a choice. I would have the wine.

I got a glass of white in some Health and Safety-sanctioned non-glass transparent beaker and took my first sip. I thought it was a shame Health and Safety didn't worry more about what we were given to drink and less about what the drink was given to us in. (I also realised for the nth time that as the years have rolled on my thinking has steadily become less *Guardian* and more *Daily Mail*. There really was absolutely nothing to recommend about the ageing process.)

I found I was standing near an academic I was friendly with. A couple of weeks earlier I had been reading stories by William Carleton, nineteenth-century Ireland's answer to Charles Dickens, and I knew he was an admirer. He'd written an essay on Carleton. I'd read it, too, and liked it, and I told him this now (yes, that's what people at book parties do – they talk to one another about what each other has written) and this in turn led to a conversation about the description of the fight in Carleton's great story of Irish violence, 'The Battle of the Factions', which Carleton begins, 'For the first twenty minutes the general harmony of this fine row might be set to music, according to a scale something like this: Whick whack-crick crack-whick whack-crick crack-&c., &c., &c.' Carleton continues in this onomatopoeic vein for two or three more pages.

The passage, said my academic friend, was like something out of *Finnegans Wake*, consisting as it did of the most extraordinary literary notation of the acoustic of violence. I nodded in agreement and inwardly I decided, yes, I was pleased I had come. I had learned something: Joyce might be great but he wasn't necessarily always first.

Sadly, from my point of view, the proceedings now got under way. Publishers made speeches. Poets read their poems. (The book being launched was an anthology and most, though not all, of the contributors were poets). An academic and his wife played some Irish airs.

As I stood listening, I made a mental note: if ever again I had occasion to launch one of my books, there would be no speeches, and there would be no reading from the text. There would just be drink and talk, talk and drink, and nothing else.

The official part of the evening concluded, I began to prowl the room, talking to people I knew. With the first I discussed Christmas. We agreed it was a massive capitalist swindle, but we were both grumpy bookish types so we were bound to think the same.

With the second person I found myself discussing the inability of any student, even the most brilliant, to write grammatical, properly punctuated English – at least, I said, that was what I had decided was the norm.

This was a conversation I'd had dozens of times, and even as I was talking and listening, in some other part of my personality (the part that criticises and dreams up exquisite punishments), I was imagining an eternity in Hell for the O'Grub Street dead where only one subject of conversation would be permitted by the little devils policing the writers' circle, and that subject would be students and their woeful grammar.

I saw this would be a particularly exquisite torment because such talk would excite us (we O'Grub Street types, we care hugely about the language) and such endless talk without the opportunity to do something about it (like correct a script with red ink) would depress us. It would be the equivalent of masturbation without ejaculation, forever, and that would be some punishment.

I can't remember what I talked to the third person about but with the fourth, insanely, I returned to the subject of student grammar. It was too much and Mr Inner Monitor who keeps an eye on everything I say became impatient with me.

'Why are you having this conversation yet again?' he demanded, as I wittered on about 'would' and 'could' and 'can' and 'might', and why no one can use these properly because schoolteachers weren't doing their job any more. 'This is pointless,' said Mr Inner Monitor. 'They're students, they've scrambled their brains with too much drink and too much Ecstasy, so of course they can't use "would" and "could" and "can" and "might" Get over it.'

Four or five glasses of warm white wine later, I found myself standing outside in the cold with my friend who loved Carleton, a thin cold rain falling from the black sky above. I was talking about money, complaining that nobody ever paid me enough for what I did, when I heard shouts and jeers. I glanced over my shoulder. There they were, three drunk young men, weaving their way along the pavement on the far side of the low wall right behind us, the wall that separated town and gown, the city of Belfast and the campus of Queen's University.

I rambled on about money, the parsimony of my numerous employers and the strange expectation of so many in the world that as a writer one is happy to write for free. 'Would you ask a plumber to plumb for nothing, a coffin maker to make a coffin for nothing? No, but writers are endlessly expected to put out for nothing.'

Meanwhile, the three youths climbed (with difficulty) the little wall, staggered up and came to a halt behind us, forming a little quarter-circle.

We turned to face them. They were in their late teens, and the one in the middle carried a half-empty bottle of Buckfast wine.

'Have you been at the Buckfast?' I heard myself saying.

'Yes,' replied the Keeper of the Bottle, waving it and making the wine inside slosh and bubble evilly. 'Buckfast, best drink in the world,' he shouted.

'We're drunk,' explained the one on his right. He was beefy and big, the muscles of the group.

'Yeah,' agreed the third, from the other end of the line.

'We've been drinking. We've been going hell for leather.' He smiled benignly. He didn't seem quite as drunk as the other two. He was tall, quite thin and had sandy hair. He was the intellectual, I decided. So now I had them pegged, running from left to right: Muscles, the Keeper of the Bottle, and Brains.

'And we've left a pile of empty Buckfast bottles behind,' continued Brains, 'where we started drinking.'

'Would you have each had a bottle of Buckfast?' I asked (an appalling concept).

'Yeah, yeah, lovely lovely Buckfast,' they roared, and cheered in unison.

'Settle,' said Brains, after the cheering finished. The trio straightened up and focused their unsteady gazes on us.

'Are you at Queen's?' asked Brains.

'Yes."

'You teachers?'

'Yes.'

The trio guffawed with a mix of mockery, sympathy and admiration.

'Isn't it boring talking shite to students all day?' asked Muscles.

'Of course not.

'Are there lots of fit girl students?' said Brains.

'Yes,' we agreed carefully.

'Do you get to ride them?' said the Keeper of the Bottle.

'Of course not.'

They cheered in derision, clearly disbelieving us, after which the talk of students and how it was to teach flowed on. As the conversation went back and forth (us, smiling, genial, a bit wary; them, smiling, genial, drunkenly enthusiastic), Mr Inner Monitor was trying to guess where they were from.

Now, I know one shouldn't, and as a fully paid-up liberal I would love to deny it, but I did. Of course I did. I have always done this when there's a remote possibility of violence. You just do if you live in Northern Ireland.

These ones, I decided, from their account of the route they'd taken through Belfast, which, after a couple of innocent questions, they had told me without knowing they were being pumped, were inner-city Prods from Sandy Row. In which case, just as long as they didn't get the whiff of popery from us, or imagine they'd got it, my friend and I, who were both in our fifties and knew how the city worked, would be fine.

The drunks moved closer. They were so happy. They embraced one another and protested their undying love for each other 'though not in a gay way, you understand,' said Brains), then insisted on shaking hands with us, throwing their arms around our shoulders and declaring we were all new best friends.

Mr Inner Monitor didn't like this. It wasn't their touch that worried him but the power of the emotion. They might love us but we did not reciprocate their feelings. We didn't love them back. How could we? We weren't drunk or young. We would soon have to extricate ourselves from their embrace and they might not like that. They might feel hurt, spurned, and no one likes to feel hurt or spurned.

But, as Mr Inner Monitor also knew from past experience, in this situation, the sooner it was made explicit that feelings were not reciprocated the better. A signal had to be sent that we wouldn't be staying to drink Buckfast and talk shite.

'I've got to get my bicycle,' I said. My bicycle (which actually belonged to the friend in whose flat I stayed when I was in Belfast) was chained to a bicycle stand a few yards off. I walked over, unlocked it, put on my helmet, and came back, wheeling the bike.

'You've got a bicycle,' said the Keeper of the Bottle, incredulously. He was clearly disgusted. 'Don't you have a car?'

'It's easier to get around Belfast on a bicycle,' I said.

'Shite,' he said.

'Shite,' they said.

'The only man's your car,' said the Keeper of the Bottle.

At this moment a van with 'Queen's Security' written on the back stopped a few yards away. Two burly blokes in reflective jackets, one carrying a brick-sized walkie-talkie, climbed out and strolled over.

'Well, lads,' said Walkie-talkie. His handset buzzed.

'Where are you?' a voice demanded, from some distant control room.

Walkie-talkie lifted the brick to his ear. 'At the location,' he said.

'How many?' said the voice.

'Three,' he said.

'Do you need back-up?'

At that moment a second van drove up and two more big men got out.

'No,' said Walkie-talkie. 'Peter and Paul's here.'

Peter and Paul sauntered over, the one known as Paul, though he was white, sporting an Afro. It was dusted with fine rain and the droplets glistened in the light that came from the street lamps. It was, without doubt, some of the most impressive hair

I had seen since the 1970s.

'Well, what's up?' said Peter and Paul.

Walkie-talkie looked at the drunks, then gestured at the pavement beyond the low wall. 'Lads,' he said, 'on your way, please.'

'But we're talking,' said the Keeper of the Bottle. He waved the bottle at us as if that would somehow prove we were together.

'We're all friends,' said Muscles, meaning us and them, and hoping, I think, that we'd speak up for them. There was no chance of that, of course.

'No, you've got to go,' said Walkie-talkie.

'Yeah, come on,' said Paul, 'don't make it difficult.

'Can I touch your Afro?' said Brains, slyly.

Paul smiled and shook his head emphatically. 'No.'

'Just a little touch, *pleeease*? It looks so lovely and soft.'

'Don't touch my hair,' said Paul, in a way that left the youths in no doubt that they had met their match.

'Come on, lads,' said Walkie-talkie. He and the other three surrounded them and started to nudge them away. The trio didn't want to leave but they weren't staying unless they resorted to violence and that was out of the question. They were outnumbered. They were outmanoeuvred. They were going, and that was the end of it.

They let Security slide them to the wall and push them out into the street beyond. From there they hollered goodbyes to us, their new-found friends, and then, proclaiming that they were off to get more drink, they stumbled away, watched by the four men from Security.

It was time, I thought, that I, too, went home. I shook my friend's hand. Then I wheeled the bicycle past the security men (still watching the Sandy Row Three as they lurched off) and out to the road.

Then, having turned the lights on, I started to pedal away. I went slowly, carefully. This was partly because the tarmac, on account of the fine rain, felt treacherous under the bicycle's wheels, but mostly because I was preoccupied, as I always was after attending anything to do with publishing, by anxious thoughts.

I had published two books in the spring since when, other than the odd review in the *Irish Times*, a column in the *Belfast Telegraph* and a few stories, I'd written little and published less.

Since the spring I had thought about the books I wanted to write but I had got no further. I hadn't written anything, mainly because of all the teaching I'd been doing. This lack of progress was destabilising and depressing but for most of the time I managed to park these anxieties on the edge of my consciousness where, though I knew they were there, I was able to avoid engaging with them. Most of the time this strategy worked but now I couldn't stop them moving from the edge to the centre of my thoughts.

I called myself a writer but unless I got more words written, and sold those words for money, I wouldn't be able to call myself a writer any more, and if I persisted in calling myself a writer while publishing so little, it wouldn't be very long before the art police arrested me.

As these thoughts came I felt hot. Within seconds my heart was racing. The way anxiety took a physical form was always a surprise. So also was the speed with which it came on. I felt dizzy and the scarf around my neck was now too tight. I should stop and loosen it, I thought. Then I heard the shouts.

'Hey, it's our university friend. Hey, stop.'

Embroiled in thought as I had been, I had passed the Sandy Row Three without noticing them – but they had seen me, and now I saw Brains had broken from the other two, slipped between parked cars and was running after me.

'Hey, mate, wait up,' he shouted. 'My mates are pissed, and

they're going too slow. I need a lift, mate. Give us a lift to the Ormeau Road, mate.'

I had a fleeting vision of Brains catching up, grabbing my sleeve, the bicycle skidding and me falling off. This was not how I'd seen my evening ending. Oh, no. I pushed down hard on the pedals but Brains was determined. He was running very fast and narrowing the distance between us. I could tell that from the volume of his calls.

I changed gear and pedalled still more ferociously. He wouldn't catch me now, I hoped. A few moments later I heard him shouting again and, given the acoustic, I judged the length of tarmac between us had grown again.

I reached the bottom of University Square, the T-junction with College Park. I had to stop. I braked. I looked back. Muscles and the Keeper of the Bottle were still on the pavement, mooching drunkenly along, but Brains was in the middle of the road, gesticulating widely and blocking a car that was trying to come down the road; the driver was gamely waiting for him to move and I could hear the engine ticking. Brains was backlit by the car's headlamps, a wild dark figure at the end of a play.

'Goodnight,' I shouted (horribly disingenuously), and then I pedalled on along College Park and down Rugby Road, passing Palestine, Jerusalem, Damascus and Cairo Streets. My anxiety about not writing was gone. The spurt of effort had driven it out of my system. I felt calm and ruminative and I began one of those compare-and-contrast exercises.

Were the Sandy Row Three, I wondered, ever anxious? I decided (unjustly, I'm sure) that, no, they lived very much in the present, they lived for pleasure, so no, they weren't anxious. I, in contrast, was always worried about the future, especially my future as a writer, so I hardly lived in the present and hadn't much pleasure either.

There was no value in these speculations (there couldn't be:

they were heavily freighted with self-pity). What came next in the sequence was the illuminating part.

It was the throb of envy, solid and real, absolutely concrete and irrefutable, that I felt for the unencumbered life that I fancifully and probably erroneously believed they were living. I wanted not to be anxious, always fretting about money and always angry about Christmas and wishing that I could escape it. I wanted to be like them, and when I was younger, I imagined next, before I'd got onto O'Grub Street, I had been. Then I'd lost all that and now here I was, pedalling towards the Ormeau Road on a wet December night, heavy with concerns, rather than light and insouciant, as I once was. Now, there was something to ponder.

The End of the Novel

When I started writing professionally, that is, for money, in the 1980s, fiction was king (and queen). 'Write a novel,' my agent always said, on those occasions when he deigned to speak to me. Later, he sang from a different hymn sheet. 'Fiction is finished,' he said. 'The future is non-fiction.'

He was right. In these islands, at least, publishers had stopped publishing fiction like they used to, other than that of a few stars, such as Ian McEwan, Martin Amis, J. K. Rowling or that of good-looking recent graduates of the creative writing MA at the University of East Anglia. They wanted to publish non-fiction. Why had they switched? I think it was like this.

Once upon a time, if you were, say, a Victorian housewife living in Bath, contented, relatively prosperous and literate, the only way you could find out about the world beyond Bath was to read, and among the books that you would read, novels would have featured hugely. Through your reading you'd have found out about what you didn't know, and the information would have come into your head via your imagination. You would have taken long, complicated books (by the likes of Scott, Dickens and Thackeray) and turned the words on the page into lively flickering images inside your skull.

In the twentieth century everything changed. First came the cinema, which did surprisingly little damage to the imagination, and then television. That was when the rot set in. Television in the West, and in particular the British Isles, gave people access to what they used to get from books, especially novels.

Now, if you were a housewife in Bath (assuming she existed, this wife of Bath), you didn't have to go to the bother of reading (which required effort) if you wanted to find out about the world: now you could find out everything you could possibly want to know first from television and later (quite a bit later) from the internet.

There was a lot of good television (and a lot of rubbish, a lot more rubbish, actually), but as far as providing information went, it did a reputable and commendable job. However, television had two deleterious effects. One, it provided the pictures that the imagination used to provide so our imaginations grew flabby and lazy, ineffective and defective. This in turn meant that it became much harder for us to extract images and narrative sustenance from a book than it was for our ancestors. They were able to roar through a hundred thousand words in a few hours and get a stream of marvellous images as a reward. For us, generally, it was hard work steaming through a book. How much easier to turn on the box.

The other deleterious effect of television was that it has made us suspicious, especially of fiction. Television and then the internet showed us just about everything that anyone on this planet had done, or had thought about doing or would like to do. Fiction, in comparison, started to look pale and sad, paltry and inadequate. Fiction, we discovered, was never as rich and surprising as real life: real life, on the contrary, was always, always richer than fiction, and anything anyone could make up. That melancholy discovery undermined our collective respect for fiction writers. We had always thought that novelists were telling us the most extreme things about human experience. We discovered that this wasn't true. Television and later the internet showed us that things were much more extreme than novelists had ever told us.

And from that, in turn, sprang the new appetite for true stories, stories that were authentic and had behind them real people and real experiences. Readers wanted that and publishers were delighted to supply it. There was no better way to sell a book, they knew, than to wheel out the writer and have them say, on television, 'Everything in my book is true. It happened to me. It happened to my wife. It happened to whomever.'

The great problem, of course, with the wave of non-fiction that overwhelmed us was how bogus so much of it was. So much of it was fiction, or quasi-fiction masquerading as non- fiction. I believe non-fiction writers have a duty to try to tell the truth. Sadly, in case after case, they have lied, conflated, suppressed, omitted and invented. And this brings me to perhaps the strangest part of this whole story. Novels, which were lies, and which everyone knew were *invented*, went into decline, while non-fiction, which, as often as not, was as invented as the fiction it had usurped, triumphed. And once that had happened then it really was true: the world really was mad.

Empire of Light

When I was twelve or thirteen, I was taken on holiday to Venice. Besides St Mark's Square and several churches (all now forgotten), I was also taken to see the Peggy Guggenheim Collection. The works were housed, as far as I remember, in a great crumbling palace. I recall wandering through several small rooms (the building made a huge impression) and the moment when I stepped into a room with a canvas by René Magritte hanging on the wall.

The painting was called *Empire of Light* (*L'Empire des Lumières*). The bottom half showed a house (a Parisian villa, perhaps?) at night, surrounded by trees. The top half showed lots of Magritte's signature clouds bobbing around in an azure sky on a summer's day.

Empire of Light stopped me in my tracks. I remember staring at it for several seconds and not being able to work out what it was, whether it was a night scene or a day scene because what I was seeing was a night and a day scene in the same frame.

Eventually, my brain recalibrated itself and I saw that *Empire of Light* was a cunning blend of night and day. After that came a great rush of excitement. It was the combination – putting night and day together in the way Magritte had – that was brilliant. Then there was the way the conceit had been executed, the way the two had been blended so that it had seemed the painting was a representation of two things that were never naturally together. Finally, *Empire of Light* gave me the feeling that a house seen in the dark gave me and that a summer sky gave me, but at the same time. The result was that my reaction was infinitely more powerful than if I'd seen either a night or a day scene on its own.

More than forty years later I still remember the moment I saw *Empire of Light*, which must say something about Magritte's powers. I often find myself thinking about the painting as an emblem of what, as an artist, copying Magritte's technique, I might do. We can all put one idea across but how much better if we can put two contradictory ones into the viewer's (or the reader's) mind at the same time. Now there's an achievement worth aspiring to.

Endpiece

After many (I thought) happy years, both my hardback publisher, Little, Brown, and my children's books' publisher, Egmont (following the death of my editor, the great Miriam Hodgson), said that they didn't want to publish me anymore. They both gave me the same spiel: they said I should go to a smaller publisher because that would be better for me. However, the truth was that I was just an author, like many others, who didn't sell enough copies and that was why I had to go. I tried others but soon discovered that most UK publishers had an enunciated if not formally stated policy of not taking on middle-aged literary authors.

Inevitably, with age, I feel increasingly that the world has 'gone to the dogs' and, in particular, that little bit of the world I care about most, which is the Kingdom of Literature. On top of the abolition of the Net Book Agreement (and partly as a consequence of it as well), all sorts of other deleterious developments have worsened the lot of writers over the last fifteen years, among which, and in no particular order, are the following: the rise of branding; the enslavement of publishers to media endorsement by celebrity presenters, like Oprah Winfrey, to the extent that this has become a principal measure of success among publishers; the obsession with physical appearance, which in turn has meant that publishers demand ever younger, ever more photogenic authors; the decline of the editor in publishing houses in order to save money; the rise of storytelling gurus (the best known is probably Robert McKee), whose courses give non-practitioners the false belief that they understand 'the secret of narrative' and, therefore, are right to insist that writers do exactly what they say (which writers then have to do if they want to get commissioned); the abandonment by publishers of the idea that writers have lifelong careers and that, given the right support over a lengthy period, they can develop; the failure of payment for literary endeavour either to keep pace with inflation or to reflect the actual amount of labour involved in literary production; the atrophy of community (writers, whatever is said to the contrary, have never been more marginal and their enterprise more quixotic and ridiculous); and, finally, the eclipse of literary forms that once helped writers to survive, such as the short story.

All the above and more (this list is far from exhaustive) have changed the work experience of writers. However, I also know everything is cyclical: these circumstances and the conditions they have produced can't last forever. The trick, therefore, is to survive until things change back, in which case my best option, I believe, is to follow the strategy for successful living proposed by Camus in *The Myth of Sisyphus*. I must endure cheerfully. In other words, I just have to outlive the fuckers. And I have. I published another novel *The Dead Eight* in 2011 and I shall go on.

ABOUT CARLO GÉBLER

Carlo Gébler was born in Dublin in 1954. He was educated at Bedales School, the University of York, where he studied English, and the National Film & Television School. He has a PhD from Queen's University, Belfast.

He started his career in television and made a number of documentary films for Channel 4 and others including *Over Here* (a film about traditional Irish culture in England which he made for the Arts Council of England), *Two Lives: A Portrait of Francis Stuart, George Barker* (a film about the English lyric poet that he made for the South Bank Show), *Plain Tales from Northern Ireland* (a series for BBC network), *Put to the Test* (winner Royal Television Society award 1999 for the best regional documentary), *Student Life* (a six part series about life at Queen's made for BBC NI), and *The Suspecting Glance – Conor Cruise-O'Brien*. His most recent work for television was *The Siege*, a film for BBC NI about the 1689 siege of Derry, which he wrote and presented. *The Siege* was transmitted in 2013.

He is also the author of several novels including *The Eleventh Summer, August in July, Work & Play, Malachy and his Family, Life of a Drum, The Cure, How To Murder a Man, A Good Day for a Dog* and, most recently, *The Dead Eight* (shortlisted for the Kerry Group Irish Fiction Award in 2012), the short story collection *W9 & Other Lives*, as well as several works of non-fiction including the memoir *Father & I*, the narrative history, *The Siege of Derry*, two travel books, *Driving Through Cuba* and *The Glass Curtain*, and *My Father's Watch* (which he wrote in collaboration with Patrick Maguire who was the youngest member of the Maguire Seven). He has also written several novels for children including *Caught on a Train* (merit award Bisto since 1997 he has been writer-in-residence in HMP Maghaberry. In addition he has taught creative writing at prize), and *August '44* (which was shortlisted for the Bisto), as well as several plays for both radio and the stage, including *Dance of Death* (an adaptation of Strindberg's play cycle produced at the Tricycle Theatre, London), *December Bride* (based on the Sam Hanna Bell novel and which was a Classic Serial broadcast on BBC Radio 4), *10 Rounds* (which was short listed for the Ewart-Biggs Prize), *Henry & Harriet*, (a site specific drama commissioned by Kabosh Theatre for the Belfast Cathedral Arts Festival), and, most recently, *Charles & Mary* (a play for BBC Radio 3 about the lives of the brother and sister who wrote the classic children's introduction to Shakespeare, *Tales from Shakespeare* and was shortlisted for the Irish Playwrights Award).

Carlo Gébler's other literary work includes the librettos for *Adolf Gébler, Clarinettist* and *The Room in the Tower*, (both written for Roger Doyle), and *Number Seven*, (written for Sean Doherty), and journalism. As well as working for publications including *Critical Quarterly, Departures, Dublin Review, Fiction Magazine, Financial Times, Guardian, Harper's & Queen, Independent Magazine, Irish Independent, Irish Press, Journal of Music in Ireland, Literary Review, Los Angeles Times, Mail-on-Sunday, Observer, Omnibus, Prospect Magazine, Spark, Daily Telegraph, Sunday Telegraph, Times, Times Saturday Review, Sunday Times, Times Literary Supplement, U-Magazine, Travel Magazine, Sunday Tribune* and *Vacuum*, he was a television critic for the *London Times*, and he has at various times also worked as regular columnist or critic for *Fortnight Magazine, Jazzwise Magazine and the Belfast Telegraph*. He also reviews regularly for the *Irish Times*.

As well as his film-making and literary work, Carlo Gébler has also worked as a teacher and academic. In the early nineties he was a creative writing tutor in HMP Maze and since 1997 he has been writer-in-residence in HMP Maghaberry. In addition he has taught creative writing at Trinity College, Dublin, where he has been a visiting fellow four times, and at Queen's University, Belfast. He was also the Royal Literary Fund Fellow at Queen's for two years. Carlo Gébler was elected to Aosdána in 1990. He is a past chairman of the Irish Writers' Centre. He has judged the Irish Times International Fiction Prize, the Glen- Dimplex Award and the Rooney Prize among others. He is married. He has five children. He currently lives outside Enniskillen, Co. Fermanagh, Northern Ireland.